DAYBREAK
Practicing *the* Presence *of* God

ADRIAN ROGERS

MINISTRIES

with ADRIAN ROGERS

Daybreak: Practicing the Presence of God
Copyright © 2007 by Love Worth Finding Ministries.

Published by: Love Worth Finding Ministries
2941 Kate Bond Road
Memphis, Tennessee 38133

10-digit ISBN: 0-9702099-5-9
13-digit ISBN: 978-0-9702099-5-5

Design by Eternity Communications.

Printed in Belgium.

PREFACE

When we began planning this devotional journal, we were excited about it because although Adrian Rogers graduated to glory in November 2005, you will see he is the main contributor in every aspect of this book—from the title, and content, to ideas on how to use it.

You may not be aware of this, but when Dr. Rogers began his preaching ministry over 50 years ago, long before Love Worth Finding, he had a radio program called "Daybreak." Here's how he described that early broadcast, "I used to do a radio program many years ago—back in the 50s. It was called, "Daybreak." I would go many times to the station at 6:45 in the morning and preach for 15 minutes, or sometimes I would even do it by tape. But every so often I would find myself doing that radio program live. Then at 7:00, I'd meet with fellows at the church and we'd have prayer."

What a way to start your day—in God's Word, then followed by prayer. That's what we hope you will do. Spend time each day reading and meditating on God's Word. And then take these nuggets from the messages of Adrian Rogers and let God apply them to your heart.

We also wanted to include something that you could actively use in your daily walk with the Lord. Several years ago, Dr. Rogers mentioned an idea that he wanted to incorporate in a daily devotional. The section of your journal that reads: "Spiritual Concerns and Prayer requests" and "Today I will" are his inspiration, and we hope you will find them helpful as you record your prayers, praises and plans.

So as you open the pages of this devotional journal, practice the presence of God by having your Bible ready with pen in hand and heart open to hear what God has for you. For it is so plainly stated in 1 Chronicles 16:27, "Glory and honour are in His presence; strength and gladness are in His place." Isn't that something we all want?

We hope this book will become a favorite of yours and that *Daybreak: Practicing the Presence of God* will provide encouragement and inspiration each day and in each circumstance.

And finally, please let us know how God is using this book to enrich your life or that of a dear family member or friend. We always enjoy hearing from you!

THOU WILT SHEW ME THE PATH OF LIFE: IN THY PRESENCE IS FULNESS OF JOY; AT THY RIGHT HAND THERE ARE PLEASURES FOR EVERMORE. Psalm 16:11

JANUARY 1

"BLESSED BE THE LORD GOD OF ISRAEL; FOR HE HATH VISITED AND REDEEMED HIS PEOPLE." Luke 1:68

Fanny Crosby wrote, "Redeemed, how I love to proclaim it! Redeemed by the blood of the Lamb; Redeemed through His infinite mercy, His child and forever I am." Do you love to proclaim it? Oh, how I pray you do.

Isaac Watts wrote, "Were the whole realm of nature mine, That were a present far too small: Love so amazing, so divine, Demands my soul, my life, my all." Have you given your soul, your life, and your all to this Amazing Love?

Jesus did not bathe this planet with His blood to have you serve the world, the flesh, and the devil. He died to make you holy. You are not your own. First Corinthians 6:20 says, "For ye are bought with a price: therefore glorify God in your body, and in your spirit, which are God's."

What do you think Isaac Watts meant when he said that the amazing love of God demands your soul, your life, your all? How does that kind of commitment play out in your daily life? Take a moment to write out some goals for that kind of commitment.

Spiritual concerns and prayer requests ....

....

....

....

....

....

....

Today I will... ....

....

"For I am the LORD your God: ye shall therefore sanctify yourselves, and ye shall be holy; for I am holy: neither shall ye defile yourselves with any manner of creeping thing that creepeth upon the earth." Leviticus 11:44

Some people think that to be holy means to be odd. No, we're to be different. We have too many Christians doing unbiblical things who claim to be holy when in reality they are just odd!

Holiness is not achieved by what we have on, where we sleep and eat, or how many spiritual things we do. It is not primarily a matter of dress or style of hair. And we don't become holy if we live in a commune, monastery, or convent. There is no holiness in a hole.

God makes us holy by the blood of His Son. And in return of this great love, we endeavor to live holy lives because we love Him. Holiness is a state of *being*, not *doing*. It is a God-induced, God-developed character trait that grows in us as we grow in our love relationship with God.

❀❀❀

Take a snapshot inventory of your life. Where do you need to start making changes to live a more holy lifestyle? Do you know of any area in your life where you are not living in obedience to the call of holy living?

Spiritual concerns and prayer requests...

....

....

....

....

....

....

Today I will..

....

JANUARY 3

"THEREFORE, MY BELOVED BRETHREN, BE YE STEADFAST,
UNMOVABLE, ALWAYS ABOUNDING IN THE WORK OF THE LORD,
FORASMUCH AS YE KNOW THAT YOUR LABOR IS NOT IN VAIN IN
THE LORD." 1 Corinthians 15:58

Where are the courageous children of God who will speak on their Father's behalf—speak of His Truth, His mercy, His love? Psalm 119:46 says, "I will speak of Thy testimonies also before kings, and will not be ashamed."

There is an old saying: "What's down in the well, comes up in the bucket." What happens when you are up against a wall? Do you back down and deny your faith? Or do you stand firm despite the verbal assault on your beliefs?

✦⊰❈⊱✦

When was the last time you entered into an in-depth conversation with someone about God? What is keeping you from having that conversation this week? Perhaps you think you don't know anyone. Then ask God to lead someone to you who needs to know Him.

Spiritual concerns and prayer requests...

....

....

....

....

....

....

Today I will... ....

....

JANUARY 4

"Not forsaking the assembling of ourselves together, as the manner of some is; but exhorting one another: and so much the more, as ye see the day approaching." Hebrews 10:25

To exhort is to comfort and encourage. We need each other. We ought to be exhorting one another by saying, "Isn't God wonderful? Where would we be if we didn't have the Holy Spirit? Don't you just wish we were more like Jesus? Let's be true to Christ!"

We live in a climate that keeps our hearts tender. If we stray away from that climate by skipping worship services and fellowship opportunities, we will get away from the people of God and our hearts will grow hard. When we exhort one another, we are sharing Christ.

There's something that happens in our hearts when we tell others about Jesus. It keeps our heart tender.

Read Proverbs 27:17. Are you this kind of friend? Do you have these kinds of friends? If not, then ask God to help you be this kind of friend and bring you this kind of friend today!

Spiritual concerns and prayer requests...

....

....

....

....

....

....

Today I will..

....

JANUARY 5

"FOR BY GRACE ARE YE SAVED THROUGH FAITH; AND THAT NOT OF YOURSELVES: IT IS THE GIFT OF GOD: NOT OF WORKS, LEST ANY MAN SHOULD BOAST." Ephesians 2:8-9

The devil is very clever when it comes to our faith. Let me tell you what he did once to me because he may do the same thing to you.

He will start agreeing with you so he can trip you. He'll say, "Sure, you're saved by faith in Christ. But how do you know that your faith is good enough or strong enough to save you? What if your faith is too weak? What if you don't make it?"

He tried to cause me to put my faith in my faith, rather than put my faith in Christ. Have you ever heard someone mention the phrase "saving faith"? Although we may say it, in retrospect, there's no such thing. You are saved because God the Father loved you so much He sent His Son to suffer the pain of His wrath on your behalf.

You are saved because God did it all—He called you (read 2 Thessalonians 2:13-14). He bought you (read 1 Corinthians 6:20). He will keep you (read Ephesians 4:30).

Spiritual concerns and prayer requests...
....
....
....
....
....
....

Today I will... ....
....

"JUDGE NOT, AND YE SHALL NOT BE JUDGED: CONDEMN NOT, AND YE SHALL NOT BE CONDEMNED: FORGIVE, AND YE SHALL BE FORGIVEN." Luke 6:37

Sometimes Christians look at people who have committed adultery or murder and compare themselves to them. They may even say, "They're dead in their trespasses and sin."

I want to tell you something. They are no more dead in their trespasses and sin than your sweet daughter or precious parent who has not received Jesus Christ's gift of salvation. There may be some degree of corruption, but there are no degrees of deadness.

All lost people are dead people in need of the Savior Jesus Christ. You may think you don't have a testimony to share because you didn't get a Ph.D. in sin before you were saved. Perhaps you were saved as a little child. Well, it took as much of the grace of God to save you, as it did to save a murderer on death row. Never forget that, precious friend.

Dead people need to stop comparing themselves with other dead people. The ground is level at the foot of the cross.

❦

Has Satan ever tempted you to play the comparison game? What if he were to start today? Practice what you are going to say to him, right now, to defeat him at his own game before it begins.

Spiritual concerns and prayer requests...

....

....

....

....

....

Today I will…...

....

JANUARY 7

"FOR THIS IS THE LOVE OF GOD, THAT WE KEEP HIS COMMANDMENTS: AND HIS COMMANDMENTS ARE NOT GRIEVOUS." 1 John 5:3

Real love costs. That's right—it's not free like it was referred to in the sixties. Love is a verb. It is a great and grand commitment.

Sometimes a young man will casually say to a young lady, "I love you." Oh, he loves her all right. He loves her like a man who loves oranges. He takes an orange, cuts a plug out of it, squeezes the sweet juice from it, throws it on the ground like a piece of garbage, wipes his mouth and says, "Man, I love oranges!"

Let me tell you, real love is not that way. Real love lives to give. Lust lives to get.

❧

Are you dating someone and wondering if it is true love? True love says that God is holy and therefore you are to be holy. Read 1 Peter 1:15-16. If you are struggling in any area in your relationship, it's time to have a heart-to-heart talk with God and get things right with Him *and* then share what God has shown you.

Spiritual concerns and prayer requests ....
....
....
....
....
....
....

Today I will... ....
....

JANUARY 8

"Henceforth I call you not servants; for the servant knoweth not what his Lord doeth: but I have called you friends; for all things that I have heard of My Father I have made known unto you." John 15:15

What is the blessing of obedience? Intimacy with God. You will come to know things that you could never know any other way when you become intimate with God.

And yet people are still asking, "How do I understand the Bible?" Friend, you will have a knowledge that surpasses anything you could gain from a school of learning when you serve the Lord in obedience. Jesus said we become His friends when we become His servants. And a friend knows all things.

Amos 3:7 says, "Surely the Lord GOD will do nothing, but He revealeth His secret unto His servants the prophets." Have you stopped growing? Perhaps it is because you have stopped obeying. The way to have insight into the heart of God is through obedience.

❧❦❧

Talk to God about your relationship with Him. Do you feel like His servant? Do you feel like His child? Do you feel like His friend? All of these things are facets of a relationship with God. Ask God to teach you how to strengthen your relationship with Him today.

Spiritual concerns and prayer requests...

....

....

....

....

....

....

Today I will…...

....

JANUARY 9

"THOU BLIND PHARISEE, CLEANSE FIRST THAT WHICH IS WITHIN THE CUP AND PLATTER, THAT THE OUTSIDE OF THEM MAY BE CLEAN ALSO." Matthew 23:26

What happens when we try to help others? We almost always start on the outside. We think if we can change the environment of a man (his home, clothes, food, education), then we can create a new man.

It cannot be done. It was in the Garden of Eden that man got into trouble in the first place. Cleaning up the outside is just reformation. When you clean up the inside, you are regenerated.

Jesus is telling the Pharisees they don't need another bath, they need a new birth. Now, I'm not saying we shouldn't help others. We ought to do these things.

But men need more than soap and soup; they need salvation. They need a birth from above not merely a boost from below.

Do you have a list of people who are lost? Pray over that list today—asking God to use you in the process of leading them to Him and that He would regenerate each one to be born again.

Spiritual concerns and prayer requests ....
....
....
....
....
....
....

Today I will... ....
....

JANUARY 10

"TRUST IN THE **LORD** WITH ALL THINE HEART; AND LEAN NOT UNTO THINE OWN UNDERSTANDING. IN ALL THY WAYS ACKNOWLEDGE HIM, AND HE SHALL DIRECT THY PATHS."
Proverbs 3:5-6

If Jesus Christ is Lord of your life, you are going to give Him the first consideration in every decision you make. You will ask, "What is the will of God? What is the purpose of Jesus? What will glorify my Father?"

Have you ever worked for a company and they decided to transfer you? So many people, because of their financial obligations, discuss it a little with family and friends, and then make plans for the move.

Sometimes the transfer happens so quickly, prayer is forgotten. Friend, if God wants you to go, then go. If God doesn't want you to go, then you need to stay. But, you'll never know until you get alone with God and let Him tell you what He wants.

❧

What decision do you need to make today? This week? This month? This year? Have you prayed about it? Take time today to ask God what He wants you to do, and then wait on His answer. Be patient and don't light your own fire (read Isaiah 50:10-11).

Spiritual concerns and prayer requests...
....
....
....
....
....
....

Today I will... ....
....

JANUARY 11

It was terrible at Simon Peter's funeral. Jesus was there and He said, "It's a shame that Peter had to die so young. He was just getting the hang of walking on the water. I shouldn't have told him to get out of the boat." It was one of the saddest funerals.

Now, I hope you're saying, "Wait a minute!" because we all know that Peter didn't drown when Jesus called him out of the boat (see Matthew 14:22-33). And you will not drown either when Jesus calls you to do something humanly impossible.

Peter may not have walked very far on water, but I would say he walked farther than anyone else has ever walked on water! Don't worry about getting out of the boat if that is what God calls you to do. It is safer on the waves with Jesus than in the boat without Him.

※❖❖❖❖

Has God called you to do something and you have not done it because you didn't think you could? Maybe He's called you to trust Him in a situation that appears hopeless or perhaps He's called you to speak up for your faith, when you know it will result in great loss or shame. Ask God to give you strength to trust Him to provide all that you need for what He has asked you to do (Proverbs 3:5-6).

Spiritual concerns and prayer requests ....
....
....
....
....

Today I will... ....
....

"THE LIGHT OF THE BODY IS THE EYE: THEREFORE WHEN THINE
EYE IS SINGLE, THY WHOLE BODY ALSO IS FULL OF LIGHT; BUT
WHEN THINE EYE IS EVIL, THY BODY ALSO IS FULL OF DARKNESS."
Luke 11:34

There have been times when I have sensed myself growing cold
spiritually. I felt the power seeping out of my life and felt that
Jesus Christ wasn't as real to me as He used to be.

In times like this, I would get alone in my study and begin to give
things back to God that I have subtly taken off the altar. I gave Him
my physical body and my right to life. I gave Him my health, my
strength, and my ability to preach. I gave Him my reputation and my
children. I gave Him my cars, my clothes, my house. And when I
honestly, earnestly, and sincerely gave all to Him, the joy returns to
my heart and I sense my relationship with God restored.

❖❖❖

Ask yourself: Do I love God more today than I did yesterday?
Am I as thirsty for His righteousness as a man who is dying of
thirst? Am I willing to go and to do whatever He asks me to do? If
you cannot answer yes to these questions, you need to pray for faith to
do what Jesus calls you to do in Matthew 16:24-25.

Spiritual concerns and prayer requests...

....

....

....

....

....

....

Today I will…...

....

JANUARY 13

"Watch therefore, for ye know neither the day nor the hour wherein the Son of man cometh." Matthew 25:13

When I was in college I remember cramming for my final exams. Now, I know that wasn't always the best way, but sometimes it was all I could do with the busy schedule I carried.

If I didn't stay up, it was almost impossible to keep up, so I had to cram. Have you ever done that? Jesus tells us to be ready for His return because it may happen at any time. Are you ready?

If you read the writings of the Apostle Paul, you will learn that he wanted to always be ready for Christ's return. Paul was not a citizen of earth trying to get to heaven. He was a citizen of heaven only sojourning here on earth. And he was ready to go whenever God called.

❧❦❧

Prayerfully read Matthew 10:37-39, 1 Corinthians 7:29-31 and 2 Timothy 2:15. Are you willing (and ready) to go anywhere, to do anything God asks of you? God may not call you to go anywhere or He may even call you home, but if He did, would you go? Are you ready to go?

Spiritual concerns and prayer requests..

....

....

....

....

....

....

Today I will... ....

....

"Thou therefore endure hardness, as a good soldier of Jesus Christ." 2 Timothy 2:3

Many of us talk a good religion. We're like the young man who called his girlfriend and said, "Sweetheart, you are so precious to me. I love you so much I'd fight wild beasts to be by your side. I'd tread on broken glass to hold your hand…and if it doesn't rain, I'm going to come over and see you tomorrow night."

Many believers are high on sentiment and low on sacrifice. We don't know what it is to fight for the Lord Jesus Christ. If you're looking for an easy way to serve the Lord, you can forget it. We're called upon to endure hardness as a good soldier of the cross. How much hardness would you endure?

Here's a little test: When was the last time you fasted through a meal? When was the last time you spent an hour in prayer? When was the last time you spent your vacation on a short-term mission trip? When was the last time you were persecuted for your faith? When was the last time you spent a night in jail because you shared your faith?

Spiritual concerns and prayer requests..

....

....

....

....

....

....

Today I will…..

....

JANUARY 15

"BEHOLD, I GIVE UNTO YOU POWER TO TREAD ON SERPENTS AND SCORPIONS, AND OVER ALL THE POWER OF THE ENEMY: AND NOTHING SHALL BY ANY MEANS HURT YOU." Luke 10:19

Have you ever thought about the Great Commission being a mission impossible? But it isn't because of the basis in which Jesus gave it.

You see, Jesus said that all power, authority, and dominion is given unto Him in heaven and earth (see Matthew 28:18-20). Dominion was first given to man, but man gave it over to the devil in the Garden of Eden.

Jesus received it back from the Father and gave that authority to each of us. Does Jesus have authority over the devil? Yes! Then, so do you. Does Jesus have the victory? Yes! Then, you have the victory. Is Jesus Christ enthroned? Yes! Then, you are enthroned. The victory is yours through Jesus Christ.

Ask the Holy Spirit to show you what your fears are, then confess them as sin. Repent, then reach up and take hold of His right hand that is outstretched to sustain you and give you the victory!

Spiritual concerns and prayer requests ....

....

....

....

....

....

....

Today I will... ....

....

JANUARY 16

"O KEEP MY SOUL, AND DELIVER ME: LET ME NOT BE ASHAMED; FOR I PUT MY TRUST IN THEE." Psalm 25:20

You may be saved today, and yet you are feeling incredibly lonely. Let me give you a practical pointer. Quit dwelling on it. Reach out to help someone else who is lonely.

Luke 6:38 promises that when we give, it shall be given to us. There is a locked-in likeness to what we give. It is the law of the harvest.

If you want friendship, you must show yourself friendly (see Proverbs 18:24). Keep a stack of cards handy to send a note of encouragement to a friend or get a prayer list and intercede for others.

You can literally travel around the world by means of prayer. Jack Hyles, a great preacher, said, "There is no life so empty as a self-centered life and there is no life so centered as a self-emptied life."

As you pour out yourself to others, the Holy Spirit will pour Himself into you.

❦

This week do one of these things each day: (1) Write someone an encouraging note; (2) Do something nice for one of your neighbors or coworkers; (3) Pray for five people who are lost that God would save them; (4) Send an ecard to a loved one; (5) Call a new friend and ask how you can pray for him or her; (6) Give a friend a hug; (7) Tell a stranger that you hope he or she has a blessed day.

Spiritual concerns and prayer requests ....

....

....

....

....

Today I will… ....

....

JANUARY 17

"THE LAW OF THE LORD IS PERFECT, CONVERTING THE SOUL:
THE TESTIMONY OF THE LORD IS SURE, MAKING WISE THE
SIMPLE." Psalm 19:7

I once read of a saint who said, "I have no greater pleasure than
to be in a nook with the Book." Do you think that way? The
Bible is the book that the martyrs held to their bosoms as the
flames crept closer and closer.

This is the book that the saints put their head upon as they went
from this world into the next. This is the book that gives bread to the
hungry, water to the thirsty, life to the wayfarer, strength to the weak,
and a weapon to the warrior.

God's Book rejoices the heart. It is completely trustworthy.
There are over 6,000 promises in the Bible and not one has ever been
broken.

❦

Find seven promises in the Word of God. Write them down and
try to memorize one each day this week.

Spiritual concerns and prayer requests ....

....

....

....

....

....

....

Today I will... ....

....

"RECOMPENSE TO NO MAN EVIL FOR EVIL. PROVIDE THINGS
HONEST IN THE SIGHT OF ALL MEN. IF IT BE POSSIBLE, AS MUCH AS
LIETH IN YOU, LIVE PEACEABLY WITH ALL MEN." Romans 12:17-18

A certain minister served a church for many years; then one day the church asked him to leave. He was talking to another preacher friend and he said, "What they did to me was dirty. After all I did for them and they have treated me this way."

The friend who was sharing this conversation said, "It's a shame he didn't do it for God." Whatever area you are serving in, don't do it for people. Serve the Lord.

If you do right, people may mistreat you, but what difference does it make if you are serving the Lord? God will prove Himself faithful and will reward you for your obedience. Don't bow to bitterness. Tell God what has happened. Let Him deal with it in His time. He'll take care of it.

❦❦❦

Do something extraordinary for a stranger this week. Do it as a fragrant offering of love to God.

Spiritual concerns and prayer requests...
....
....
....
....
....
....

Today I will… ....
....

JANUARY 19

"For I will be merciful to their unrighteousness, and their sins and their iniquities will I remember no more."
Hebrews 8:12

Have you ever felt like you have used up God's reservoir of forgiveness? Perhaps you've thought, *I don't have a right to come and ask Him to forgive me again.*

Friend, it doesn't matter how many times we have sinned. Suppose you came back to God for the 5,000th time with the same sin. Will He forgive you? Yes, indeed He will. As far as He is concerned, it is the first time you have come to Him. Why? *Because He has forgotten all the other times.*

God punishes sin, but He doesn't hold grudges. The God of Jonah, David, Mark, Peter, and Jacob, is *your* God and *my* God. I have come to Him so many times and asked Him for a second chance. And guess what? He has given it. And I know that if He can give me a second chance, He will certainly give you another chance. Failure is not final.

Have you been hesitant to go to God this week to ask His forgiveness about something? Run to Him right now.

Spiritual concerns and prayer requests..

....

....

....

....

....

....

Today I will… ....

....

JANUARY 20

"NOW THEREFORE THUS SAITH THE LORD OF HOSTS; CONSIDER YOUR WAYS." Haggai 1:5

What does the "Lord of hosts" mean? It literally means the Lord Almighty, and it speaks of the greatness of God.

Martin Luther in his hymn, "A Mighty Fortress Is Our God" uses the Greek word for the "Lord of hosts" when he writes, "Christ Jesus, it is He; Lord Sabaoth, His Name, from age to age the same, And He must win the battle."

When David faced Goliath, he used the same name for God, "Thou comest to me with a sword, and with a spear, and with a shield: but I come to thee in the name of the LORD of hosts" (1 Samuel 17:45). Though Goliath was a huge man, David said he wasn't too big to hit if God was on his side.

❧❧❧

There are over 230 references to the "Lord of hosts" in the King James Version of the Bible. Two Psalms resplendent with this description of God are Psalm 46 and 84. Worship God by reading these today.

Spiritual concerns and prayer requests...
....
....
....
....
....
....

Today I will... ....
....

JANUARY 21

"AND THAT EVERY TONGUE SHOULD CONFESS THAT JESUS CHRIST IS LORD, TO THE GLORY OF GOD THE FATHER." Philippians 2:11

The fourth and fifth chapters of Mark give us marvelous illustrations of all the things that God has placed under the authority of our Lord Jesus.

You'll find Jesus stilling the storm (vv. 4:35-41), which tells us He is the Master over disaster. You'll find Him healing a demon-possessed man (vv. 5:1-20). That means He has authority over demons. Next, Jesus healed a woman who had been bleeding for twelve years, so even disease is under His domain (vv. 5:24-34). The final illustration of Jesus' authority in these chapters is exhibited when He raised Jairus' daughter from the dead (vv. 5:38-43). Whatever befall—be it disaster, demons, disease, or even death—Jesus Christ is Lord!

Are you or someone in your family suffering? Proclaim Jesus Christ as Lord over that problem. Ask what He would have you do. Trust that He will provide. Step out in faith believing that He will take care of all your needs.

Spiritual concerns and prayer requests ....

....

....

....

....

....

....

Today I will... ....

....

"THERE IS NO FEAR IN LOVE; BUT PERFECT LOVE CASTETH OUT
FEAR: BECAUSE FEAR HATH TORMENT. HE THAT FEARETH IS NOT
MADE PERFECT IN LOVE." 1 John 4:18

Are you gripped with fear about something? Let me give you
some hope. Love is the answer to overcoming your fear
because love is the Christian's security blanket.

When you were a child, did you have a teddy bear or a blanket
that gave you a sense of security—something you wanted to hold close
to you and get wrapped up in? Well friend, the Holy Spirit of God
is the believer's warm, loving security blanket.

I read the verse, "Perfect love casteth out fear," but it never rang
true to me because I had never done anything perfectly except sin.
Then, I read the verse in the Living Bible. It says, "We have no
fear of someone who loves us perfectly."

God's perfect love can eliminate all dread. It is not our love for
Him, but His perfect love for us that will cast out our fears. The
question isn't: Am I brave enough? The question is: Do I trust His
love enough?

Memorize 2 Timothy 1:7-9 this week.

Spiritual concerns and prayer requests ....

....

....

....

....

....

....

....

Today I will… ....

....

JANUARY 23

"AND BEING FOUND IN FASHION AS A MAN, HE HUMBLED
HIMSELF, AND BECAME OBEDIENT UNTO DEATH, EVEN THE DEATH
OF THE CROSS. WHEREFORE GOD ALSO HATH HIGHLY EXALTED
HIM, AND GIVEN HIM A NAME WHICH IS ABOVE EVERY NAME."
Philippians 2:8-9

Sometimes we overcompensate Jesus' humanity to prove that
Jesus is God.

But, if you think of Jesus masquerading as a man instead
of truly being a man, then you've missed out on a blessing. You see, it
is the humanity of Jesus Christ that teaches us how we are to live as
Christians in this world.

And how did He live? He said, "He that sent Me is with
Me: the Father hath not left Me alone; for I do always those things
that please Him" (John 8:29). He lived in subjection to His Father.

And because He chose to submit, God gave Him authority.
Here is the principle for you and I to live by: We will never be over,
until we are willing to be under. Authority does not develop on its
own. It always comes from a higher source of power.

❦

Search your dictionary and concordance, then write out your own
definition of the word "humble." Would that be descriptive of
you? Ask God to cause you to have the attitude of His Son.

Spiritual concerns and prayer requests..

....

....

....

....

Today I will…..

....

JANUARY 24

"Now the Lord is that Spirit: and where the Spirit of the Lord is, there is liberty." 2 Corinthians 3:17

Formalism and worship are two separate things. When you are worshiping the Lord, there needs to be freedom *and* order.

Worship is not real quiet music and everyone sitting still and not smiling. That's not worship. Some people say, "Well that's a dignified service." And I've said this before, "They don't know the difference between reverence and rigor mortis."

If you study worship in the Bible, you'll find out that worship was marked with brightness, spontaneity, and joy. The early Christians had something that fire could not burn, swords could not kill, water could not drown, and jails could not hold.

They knew the holiness, loveliness, and glory of God in a life-changing way.

Read Psalm 5:7 and 29:2 and take some time today to worship God in joy and truth.

Spiritual concerns and prayer requests..

....

....

....

....

....

....

Today I will..

....

JANUARY 25

"JESUS ANSWERED AND SAID UNTO HER, WHOSOEVER DRINKETH OF THIS WATER SHALL THIRST AGAIN: BUT WHOSOEVER DRINKETH OF THE WATER THAT I SHALL GIVE HIM SHALL NEVER THIRST; BUT THE WATER THAT I SHALL GIVE HIM SHALL BE IN HIM A WELL OF WATER SPRINGING UP INTO EVERLASTING LIFE." John 4:13-14

Have you ever been outside working in your garden or bicycling or playing football and become thirsty? You go inside and grab a soda, and boy, it seems to hit the spot.

You return to your activity, get thirsty and go for another soda. It is satisfying at first, but it doesn't seem to keep you quenched.

Finally, you fill a big tall glass with water and you're satisfied. Why? If you look at the ingredients on the soda container, it says it is artificially colored and/or artificially flavored and/or artificially sweetened. It doesn't have that touch of authenticity.

There are a lot of us who are trying to satisfy our thirst with things that are artificial and what we need is the water of life. When was the last time you quenched your spiritual thirst with the sparkling refreshment of time spent with God?

Are you married or dating? Do you remember your first date and your excitement? Make a date with God for one hour (and church doesn't count!). Mark your calendar and make it your FIRST priority.

Spiritual concerns and prayer requests..
....
....
....
....
Today I will... ....
....

JANUARY 26

"THY WAY IS IN THE SEA, AND THY PATH IN THE GREAT WATERS, AND THY FOOTSTEPS ARE NOT KNOWN." Psalm 77:19

I have seen the Sea of Galilee on which the Lord Jesus walked, but you cannot see His footsteps. When a boat goes through the ocean, it doesn't leave a trail does it? When a wagon goes across land, it leaves a trail, but a boat doesn't.

In today's passage in Psalms, God is saying that we will never know Him by studying history—by simply studying what He has done. His ways are mysterious. You can try to make sense of God with all your ingenuity, creativity, and intelligence, but God says we will never know Him that way.

We have to lay our intellect in the dust and say to God, *Show me the way. Cause me to fall in love with You all over again.*

❧❀❧

When was the last time you wrote a love letter? When was the last time you received one? Spend some time today and write a love letter to the Lord.

Spiritual concerns and prayer requests..
....
....
....
....
....
....

Today I will…..
....

JANUARY 27

"AND [JESUS SAID] UNTO THEE, THAT THOU ART PETER, AND UPON THIS ROCK I WILL BUILD MY CHURCH; AND THE GATES OF HELL SHALL NOT PREVAIL AGAINST IT." Matthew 16:18

There are many people who say, "I believe in Jesus, but I just don't believe in the church." That is like saying, "I believe in football, but I just don't believe in stadiums, the grid iron, goal posts, and shoulder pads."

Jesus loves the church. He gave His life for the church. If you are ever going to be victorious in the spiritual battles of life, you must realize that Christianity is not a "lone ranger" religion.

The church is there to bind together and win the battle together. Sabine Baring-Gould wrote the famous hymn "Onward Christian Soldiers." One stanza really stands out in this regard: "Crowns and thrones may perish, kingdoms rise and wane, But the church of Jesus constant will remain. Gates of hell can never against that church prevail; We have Christ's own promise, and that cannot fail."

If you are currently not involved in a church, you can go to the Southern Baptist Convention's web site [www.sbc.net] and perform a "church search" using your zip code or zip codes in the area if yours does not bring back any results. Ask God to help you begin to find a church today.

Spiritual concerns and prayer requests ....

....

....

....

....

....

Today I will… ....

....

JANUARY 28

"REMEMBER THEREFORE FROM WHENCE THOU ART FALLEN, AND REPENT." Revelation 2:5a

When Joyce and I were on our honeymoon, we were driving south of Daytona Beach back to West Palm Beach. I was so in love that I had two eyes on her, and no eyes on the road.

A policeman hailed me over and told me I had broken the speed limit of 35 mph. I was surprised because I hadn't seen a sign that changed the limit from 55 to 35. He said, "All right young man, here's what I want you to do. Turn around and drive back about three blocks. Look at the sign and go on."

That was my punishment. The officer made me go back before I could go on. That's exactly what our Lord is saying to us when He tells us to return to our first love.

❧❦❧

Read the books of First, Second, and Third John this week—one chapter a day.

Spiritual concerns and prayer requests ....

....

....

....

....

....

....

....

Today I will… ....

....

JANUARY 29

"Behold, I set before you this day a blessing and a curse; a blessing, if ye obey the commandments of the LORD your God, which I command you this day." Deuteronomy 11:26-27

God is setting before you this day a blessing and a curse. What determines whether you receive the blessing? If you obey. What determines whether or not you are going to receive the curse? If you disobey.

There are six blessings God wants to give you today in exchange for your obedience: plenty (Isaiah 1:19-20), peace (Jeremiah 26:13), protection (Exodus 23:22), power (Acts 5:32), purity (1 Peter 1:22), and perception (Psalm 119:100).

Do you want Jesus to be real to you so that He's not just someone that you know or read about? Maybe you want to do more than "pray" to Him, you want to talk to Him, and you want to relate to Him.

❖❖❖

Read John 14:23. What does Jesus say is a result of your love for Him? And what does God promise He will do as a result of your action?

Spiritual concerns and prayer requests...

....

....

....

....

....

Today I will...

....

JANUARY 30

"ALL THINGS ARE LAWFUL UNTO ME, BUT ALL THINGS ARE NOT EXPEDIENT: ALL THINGS ARE LAWFUL FOR ME, BUT I WILL NOT BE BROUGHT UNDER THE POWER OF ANY." 1 Corinthians 6:12

There are certain weights that an athlete chooses to lay aside. They are not bad for other people, but they are bad for the athlete.

In the spiritual realm, it is the same for Christians. Paul tells us, "all things are not expedient." The word "expedient" is similar to the word "expedition." You see, Christians are going somewhere. If something doesn't speed us along the way, then it is excess baggage and we need to get rid of it.

❧❧❧

Ask God, "Do I own any legitimate, lawful things that can be put to better use and are keeping me from running the best race for You? If so, show me, that I may live a life that is completely surrendered to the cause of Christ." It might be a boat, a condo, a ring, an oil painting, or an antique collection. These things are not inherently bad. Maybe He wants you to sell whatever it is or maybe not. Just talk to Him about it.

Spiritual concerns and prayer requests...

....

....

....

....

....

....

Today I will…..

....

JANUARY 31

"BUT THE GOD OF ALL GRACE, WHO HATH CALLED US UNTO HIS ETERNAL GLORY BY CHRIST JESUS, AFTER THAT YE HAVE SUFFERED A WHILE, MAKE YOU PERFECT, STABLISH, STRENGTHEN, SETTLE YOU." 1 Peter 5:10

Isn't it wonderful to know that the works of God are perfect? That God's ways are perfect? And that His will is perfect? Now, I know that someone reading this may think, *But I don't know about God's will. I don't want to give myself completely to Him or He might send me to a remote desert as a missionary.*

Let me set the record straight. God's will is not so much something that you surrender to as it is something that you get in on. God will choose for you what you would choose for yourself if you had enough sense to choose it.

❦

Ask yourself if you have completely surrendered everything to God. Is there anything you are holding back? Is there any activity that you are still doing that does not please God? Is there anything you possess that dishonors God? It's time to clean house both literally and figuratively.

Spiritual concerns and prayer requests ....

....

....

....

....

....

....

Today I will… ....

....

"BUT HE ANSWERED AND SAID, IT IS WRITTEN, MAN SHALL NOT
LIVE BY BREAD ALONE, BUT BY EVERY WORD THAT PROCEEDETH
OUT OF THE MOUTH OF GOD." Matthew 4:4

I believe many churches are suffering a famine because their pulpits are not feeding heavenly bread to their flocks. If you are not feeding on the Bible daily, you are either not saved, or you are dying of spiritual malnutrition. *The only strength we have is found when we feed upon the Word of God.*

Job said, "I have esteemed the words of His mouth *more than* my necessary food" (Job 23:12). In other words, Job was saying that if he had to choose between eating physical bread or spiritual bread, he would rather have the Word of God.

How I pray that people reading this would commit to a daily routine of exercising on their knees in prayer and feeding with the nutritious bread of God's Word.

Have you ever thought about reading the Bible in a year? Visit www.crosswalk.com and go to Bible Study tools to begin today.

Spiritual concerns and prayer requests..

....

....

....

....

....

....

Today I will… ....

....

FEBRUARY 2

"FOR THE WEAPONS OF OUR WARFARE ARE NOT CARNAL, BUT
MIGHTY THROUGH GOD TO THE PULLING DOWN OF
STRONGHOLDS." 2 Corinthians 10:4

I believe that many of us are experiencing limited or no victory
because we have not learned to press through the battle on to
victory. You may be thinking, *But wait a minute, Dr. Rogers,
I want the victory.* Do you really?

Then, you need to know this: First, God wants you to have the
victory. Second, the measuring cup of your victory is in the palm of
your hands. That is, you are as victorious as you want to be.

The devil does not have a stronghold that we cannot pull down if
we will use God's weapons. The problem is that we may be using
spiritual weapons, but we are trying to wield those weapons in our own
strength.

❦

Read Ephesians 6:17. What is your sword? Whose sword is it?
Can you think of a battle that awaits you? How are you going
to use this sword?

Spiritual concerns and prayer requests...

....

....

....

....

....

....

Today I will... ....

....

FEBRUARY 3

"HE THAT LOVETH HIS LIFE SHALL LOSE IT; AND HE THAT HATETH
HIS LIFE IN THIS WORLD SHALL KEEP IT UNTO LIFE ETERNAL."
John 12:25

I heard the story of a man who was discussing with another the issue of tithing. He asked him, "How do you figure your tithe? Before taxes or after taxes?" He said, "Oh, I figure my tithe before taxes."

His friend asked him, "Why do you figure it that way?" He responded, "Because the Lord gets more that way." That's the kind of man who is going to get a blessing from the Lord.

Jesus said the Pharisees tithed from the mint plants (see Matthew 23:23). They would have an herb in their hand and count out each leaf one by one to give their exact tithe to the Lord—just enough and yet not too much. How precise they were!

❦

Oh God, give us men and women who pray: "God, I'm going for You with all that I am. I'm getting out of the boat with both feet. If You tell me to hit the ground, I'm going to hit it until You tell me to stop." Will you make that your prayer today?

Spiritual concerns and prayer requests ....

....

....

....

....

....

....

....

Today I will... ....

....

FEBRUARY 4

"AND LEAD US NOT INTO TEMPTATION, BUT DELIVER US FROM
EVIL: FOR THINE IS THE KINGDOM, AND THE POWER, AND THE
GLORY, FOR EVER. AMEN." Matthew 6:13

Why do you think we return to God time and time again to forgive us? I think it is partly because we fail to pray the other part of the Lord's Prayer: "And lead us not into temptation, but deliver us from evil."

We wake up in the morning and come to the end of the day and we say, "God, forgive me. I blew it." And He forgives.

Do you know why we fail? We've learned how to pray, "Lord, forgive me." But, we're not praying, "Lord, protect me." You wouldn't come to the end of the day and say, "Lord, give me this day my daily bread." The day is over.

This is not a prayer for the end of the day; this is the prayer to begin your day. *Lord, protect me.*

❧❦❧

Make it a habit by starting this day to pray Matthew 6:13.

Spiritual concerns and prayer requests...
....
....
....
....
....
....
....

Today I will...
....

FEBRUARY 5

"NOW THANKS BE UNTO GOD, WHICH ALWAYS CAUSETH US TO TRIUMPH IN CHRIST, AND MAKETH MANIFEST THE SAVOUR OF HIS KNOWLEDGE BY US IN EVERY PLACE. FOR WE ARE UNTO GOD A SWEET SAVOUR OF CHRIST, IN THEM THAT ARE SAVED, AND IN THEM THAT PERISH." 2 Corinthians 2:14-15

Thanks be to God who always causes us to triumph in Christ! And when we are enjoying this victory, we will be sending off a sweet, pervasive perfume of His glory.

Do you know how incense is made? It is made by cutting or breaking herbs, then crushing them into a fine powder. Then water is added to this powder to create a clay to form into sticks or cones.

What is the purpose of incense? To burn and create a fragrant aroma. When we are praising God in the midst of trials, singing songs of glory in the midst of persecution, claiming His victory when a problem arises, then we are emitting a sweet aroma that is unmistakable to the nostrils of God. This is the sweet smell of victory!

❦

Whatever it is that looks like a trial today in your life…thank God! Thank Him every time the thought enters your mind to grumble or complain.

Spiritual concerns and prayer requests ....
....
....
....
....
....
....
....

Today I will… ....
....

FEBRUARY 6

"THEREFORE WE ARE BURIED WITH HIM BY BAPTISM INTO DEATH: THAT LIKE AS CHRIST WAS RAISED UP FROM THE DEAD BY THE GLORY OF THE FATHER, EVEN SO WE ALSO SHOULD WALK IN NEWNESS OF LIFE." Romans 6:4

When Jesus Christ died, not only did He die for us, but also we died with Him. You may say, *Well what difference does it make whether He died for me or I died with Him? It's just a play on words.*

Oh no, it's not, my friend. When you're dead, then death has no dominion over you. You can't kill a man who is already dead. Let's suppose a man is put to death for a capital crime he has committed, and yet somehow he is raised back to life. Do you think he can be arrested again for his crime? Absolutely not. That would be double jeopardy. He paid the penalty of his crime.

It is necessary you understand that when Jesus died, you died, and the law has no more hold on you! Your sin debt has been paid in full because He died for you. You died with Him.

Find someone today and tell him or her the greatest news that has ever been told. Jesus took on the wrath of God. He died that they may live. Go! Tell!

Spiritual concerns and prayer requests ....

....

....

....

....

....

Today I will... ....

....

"BUT LET US, WHO ARE OF THE DAY, BE SOBER, PUTTING ON THE BREASTPLATE OF FAITH AND LOVE; AND FOR AN HELMET, THE HOPE OF SALVATION." 1 Thessalonians 5:8

A preacher friend was walking away from another friend, when his friend called out to him, "Well, so long! Love God. Hate sin. And watch out for trucks!"

Did he say, "Watch out for trucks?" Yes! And you know what? That's good advice! You will get hurt if a truck hits you—it doesn't matter whether you're saved or lost.

Now, why is this important? Because like the man said—we all need to love God and we all need to hate sin, but we are also human and we need to watch out for the things in life that may hurt us. God has given us the mind of Christ and we need to use that mind.

❧❦❧

R ead 1 Corinthians 2:16. Is your head in the clouds today? Are you alert to the things of this world that can harm you? Be sober. Be alert. And watch out for trucks!

Spiritual concerns and prayer requests..

....

....

....

....

....

....

Today I will...

....

FEBRUARY 8

"FOR, BRETHREN, YE HAVE BEEN CALLED UNTO LIBERTY; ONLY USE NOT LIBERTY FOR AN OCCASION TO THE FLESH, BUT BY LOVE SERVE ONE ANOTHER." Galatians 5:13

One of the signs you can tell you have stopped trusting God is that you cease to function. You simply drop out of life's activities. You start fretting over this and that; you get distressed over a loss; you get oppressed by the devil.

And what do you do? Close shop, draw the drapes, go to sleep, get up late. Have you ever been that way? Worry will do that to you. When you worry, it is because you are not trusting God.

You may say, *I lost my job.* Well, what are you doing? *I'm sitting around the house.* Well, quit it! You have more opportunity to serve God. Do good because you're trusting in the Lord.

Are you out of work today? Do what you need to do to find a job and when you're done...do good! Go to your church and ask them to put you to work. Go to your local mission and volunteer. Mow a neighbor's yard. Take a meal to a shut-in. Write a letter to a prisoner.

Spiritual concerns and prayer requests...

....

....

....

....

....

Today I will..

....

FEBRUARY 9

"THEREFORE WE CONCLUDE THAT A MAN IS JUSTIFIED BY FAITH
WITHOUT THE DEEDS OF THE LAW." Romans 3:28

If God the Father chose us and the Holy Spirit set us aside for
His holy purposes, then what part do you and I have?

There is divine sovereignty and human responsibility. You
have been sanctified unto obedience. Salvation is free, but you must obey.

God's divine sovereignty in choosing us does not nullify our
response to His call. *You have been saved out of this world, sent back
into this world to witness to the world, and that is the only business
you have in this world.*

Now, you do not work to be saved. You work because you are
saved. Someone has said and I agree: "I will not work my soul to
save, that work my Lord has done. But I will work like any slave for
the love of God's dear Son."

Twenty-four hours stand between you and this time tomorrow.
Right now, make a commitment to use one of those hours in
prayer for others. Ask God to save those who are lost in your family,
your neighborhood, your student body, or your workplace. Pray by
country or by continent—asking Him to send missionaries and equip
them to disciple those He saves.

Spiritual concerns and prayer requests..

....

....

....

....

....

....

Today I will... ....

....

FEBRUARY 10

"WHEREBY ARE GIVEN UNTO US EXCEEDING GREAT AND PRECIOUS PROMISES: THAT BY THESE YE MIGHT BE PARTAKERS OF THE DIVINE NATURE, HAVING ESCAPED THE CORRUPTION THAT IS IN THE WORLD THROUGH LUST." 2 Peter 1:4

Some people distort the doctrine that when a man is saved he is always saved. They get the idea if that is true, then they will sin all they want to.

If the only thing that keeps you from sinning is fear of losing your salvation, I wonder if you have really surrendered yourself to God and asked Him to save you.

Peter tells us that we have become "partakers of the divine nature." *Does that mean you don't sin any more?* No.

Before I was saved, I was running *to* sin. But afterward, I ran *from* it. You may slip, but you are saved.

Have a desire to live pure and clean to the glory of God.

※❈❈❈❈❈

Do you have a desire to be holy? Or do you treat the doctrine of assurance as a license to live a sinful life?

Spiritual concerns and prayer requests..
....
....
....
....
....
....

Today I will...
....

FEBRUARY 11

"AND HE SAID UNTO ME, MY GRACE IS SUFFICIENT FOR THEE: FOR MY STRENGTH IS MADE PERFECT IN WEAKNESS. MOST GLADLY THEREFORE WILL I RATHER GLORY IN MY INFIRMITIES, THAT THE POWER OF CHRIST MAY REST UPON ME." 2 Corinthians 12:9

There are three possible ways to pray when you are hurting: First, you can pray that God will give you an *escape* from the pain. That's normal—in fact, that's how drug stores stay in business!

Second, you can pray for God to give you the strength to *endure* the pain. And that, too, is a natural response. If we can't escape the pain, we can pray to endure the pain.

Third, the way we can pray is to ask God to *enlist* the pain in our lives for our good and His glory.

If we pray to escape our pain, then we see pain as our enemy. If we pray to endure our pain, then pain is seen as a master. But, if we pray to enlist our pain, we see it as our servant.

We are able to find God's grace to glory in our infirmities, that the power of God may be manifest in our lives.

❈❈❈

Are you hurting over something that has happened in your life? Ask God to give you strength to choose to enlist that pain for your good and His glory.

Spiritual concerns and prayer requests..

....

....

....

....

....

Today I will…...

....

FEBRUARY 12

"AND HE IS BEFORE ALL THINGS, AND BY HIM ALL THINGS
CONSIST." Colossians 1:17

There are critics of Christianity who say Jesus wasn't really the Messiah. All He did was arrange His life to fulfill the prophecies. And they're right! He really did. The only thing is that *He arranged it centuries before He was born!*

He arranged to be born in Bethlehem (see Micah 5:2). He arranged His peasant background and the humiliation He would suffer (see Isaiah 53:3). He arranged He would be betrayed and sold for thirty pieces of silver (see Zechariah 11:12-13). He arranged His crucifixion with the piercing of His hands and feet (see Psalm 22:16). He arranged to be buried in a rich man's tomb (see Isaiah 53:9). Jesus arranged to be followed by millions who would set out to tell others of Him with no hope of material gain or cost of their own lives. Oh yes! He arranged it all! Glory to God!

Praise God that He has created all things, He has arranged all things, and He is consummating all things for His glory!

Spiritual concerns and prayer requests...

....

....

....

....

....

Today I will... ....

....

FEBRUARY 13

"NOW HE WHICH STABLISHETH US WITH YOU IN CHRIST, AND HATH ANOINTED US, IS GOD." 2 Corinthians 1:21

What will God do for you if you will allow Him? He will establish you. In other words, He will make you stable, steadfast, dependable, and unmovable so that you will not be blown about by every wind of doctrine. This verb is in the present participle, which means it is with continuing action. It doesn't mean that this is once and for all.

God is in the process of establishing you. Now, where is He establishing you? In Christ. He is moving you closer and closer to Christ the Rock of your salvation. When you are saved, God puts you into Christ and then day-by-day He moves you closer to Him.

Examine your walk with God. What specific things do you see in your life that indicate you are closer to God than you were a year ago, a month ago, a week ago, a day ago?

Spiritual concerns and prayer requests...

....

....

....

....

....

....

Today I will... ....

....

FEBRUARY 14

"FOR IN THAT HE HIMSELF HATH SUFFERED BEING TEMPTED, HE
IS ABLE TO SUCCOUR THEM THAT ARE TEMPTED." Hebrews 2:18

After Jesus was baptized by John the Baptist, He was "led up of the Spirit into the wilderness to be tempted of the devil" (Matthew 4:1).

He did not overcome Satan as God, but as man anointed by the power of God. He could have said, "Satan, I want you to know that because I am God, I will obliterate you this moment."

Had He asserted His power as God, then when He asks us to overcome the devil, we could respond, "Sure, it's easy for you to say it. You're God. Don't expect me to do what You did."

Jesus didn't pull rank on us. But instead, God anointed Jesus as a man to do what we, as humans, can also do by His anointing. You and I have what we need to face any temptation. For, we are in Christ, and He is in us.

❈❖❈

Find out more about the humanity of Jesus Christ by reading Hebrews 2:10-18 and 4:14-5:10.

Spiritual concerns and prayer requests ....

....

....

....

....

....

....

Today I will... ....

....

"FOR WHAT MAN KNOWETH THE THINGS OF A MAN, SAVE THE SPIRIT OF MAN WHICH IS IN HIM? EVEN SO THE THINGS OF GOD KNOWETH NO MAN, BUT THE SPIRIT OF GOD." 1 Corinthians 2:11

Sidlow Baxter once said, "Your emotions are the shallowest part of your nature. Salvation is the deepest work of God. And He is not going to do His work in the shallowest part."

You may think you know me because you've heard my voice or read my words, but you cannot look deep down into my spirit. From the time I gave my heart to Jesus Christ, there has been a stamp of authenticity upon my heart saying, *Adrian, you belong to Me.*

It was not an emotional feeling, because emotions have nothing to do with my salvation. It was also not an intellectual thing because salvation cannot be rationalized. Salvation is a God thing.

Your salvation was made secure by the atoning blood of Jesus Christ. Praise God this Truth stands no matter how you may feel. Read Colossians 2:13-14 and thank God for His Spirit that made you alive in Christ!

Spiritual concerns and prayer requests ....

....

....

....

....

....

....

Today I will... ....

....

FEBRUARY 16

"FOR AFTER THAT IN THE WISDOM OF GOD THE WORLD BY
WISDOM KNEW NOT GOD, IT PLEASED GOD BY THE FOOLISHNESS
OF PREACHING TO SAVE THEM THAT BELIEVE." 1 Corinthians 1:21

The Word of God is indispensable for *salvation*. We are conceived by it. First Peter 1:23 says, that we are "born again, not of corruptible seed, but of incorruptible, by the Word of God, which liveth and abideth for ever."

The Word of God is also indispensable for *sanctification*. We are cleansed by it. First Peter 1:22 says, "Seeing ye have purified your souls in obeying the truth through the Spirit unto unfeigned love of the brethren."

Finally, the Word of God is indispensable for *sustenance*. We are completed by it. "And Jesus said unto them, I am the bread of life: he that cometh to Me shall never hunger; and he that believeth on Me shall never thirst" (John 6:35). Do you want to grow? Then, you better get into the Word of God.

How much time did you spend watching television, sending emails, or on the Internet this past week? How much time did you spend working on your appearance, your home, or your yard? How much time did you spend reading God's Word? Is there anything out of balance which needs correcting?

Spiritual concerns and prayer requests ....

....

....

....

....

....

Today I will... ....

....

FEBRUARY 17

"REJOICE IN THE LORD, YE RIGHTEOUS; AND GIVE THANKS AT THE REMEMBRANCE OF HIS HOLINESS." Psalm 97:12

Years ago, *Reader's Digest* published an article, which said that in order for a person to be happy and have fulfillment, three things were necessary.

First, they needed something to believe.

Second, they needed someone to love.

Third, they needed something worthwhile to do.

That's true, but not because *Reader's Digest* said it, but because God's Word affirms it. There must be more to life than your next breath and your next step.

And His name is Jesus Christ. He is indeed the fulfillment of all three of those needs. Jesus is the One to believe in, He is the Someone to love, and His cause is the something worthwhile for you to do.

Do you yearn for happiness? Every need in your life can be met through Jesus Christ.

❦

Where have you been spending your energies this past week to make yourself happy? The shopping mall, ballpark, or lake? There's nothing wrong with these if they are balanced by a life spent in prayer, in God's Word, in serving or in evangelizing the lost. Make a commitment today to dedicate your life to God.

Spiritual concerns and prayer requests ....

....

....

....

....

Today I will… ....

....

FEBRUARY 18

Jesus is not only the Cornerstone of the church; He is also the individual building blocks through every believer.

Have you ever heard of someone being a "chip off the old block"? That means he shares the nature of his father. In a sense, every child of God is a chip off that Block.

By ourselves...we are not all that much. How many one-brick buildings have you seen? One stone can be easily tossed around, but if you take a lot of them and put them together, there is strength.

Our Lord is building us together to gain strength from one another. It is amazing what can happen when the body of Christ is unified.

Step outside your comfort zone in sacrifice to the work of the Lord. Reach across cultural, socioeconomic, or racial lines to bring unity in the body of Christ. How will you do that? Pray and God will show you.

Spiritual concerns and prayer requests..

....

....

....

....

....

....

Today I will...

....

"HAVING THEREFORE, BRETHREN, BOLDNESS TO ENTER INTO THE HOLIEST BY THE BLOOD OF JESUS." Hebrews 10:19

Someone once asked me, "Dr. Rogers, the Roman Catholics and Episcopalians have priests. Why don't the Baptists?" And I responded, "We do! You're looking at one! Every believer is a priest."

You see, it is the great truth that we have direct access to the Father. We don't have to talk to someone else to confess our sins. We can confess directly to God.

Do you know what you and I are to be doing as priests? We are to be making God known to others so that they will learn, repent, and believe.

❦

Read 1 Peter 2:1-12 to learn what God wants from you as a member of His royal priesthood.

Spiritual concerns and prayer requests..

....

....

....

....

....

....

Today I will…..

....

FEBRUARY 20

"NOW ALSO WHEN I AM OLD AND GRAYHEADED, O GOD, FORSAKE ME NOT; UNTIL I HAVE SHOWED THY STRENGTH UNTO THIS GENERATION, AND THY POWER TO EVERY ONE THAT IS TO COME."
Psalm 71:18

The early Christians turned the world upside down. Their charge and ours today, is the same—to rescue the perishing and care for the dying, to go to the helpless ones and tell them Jesus saves.

I heard about a little girl who said to her mother, "Do you remember that priceless vase we all love so much that's been handed down to our family from one generation to another?" The mother said, "Yes." The little girl sheepishly revealed, "Well, this generation just dropped it."

Now friend, this generation cannot drop it. The faith we enjoy must be handed down from generation to generation. We must not drop this priceless heirloom that God has placed into our hands.

Ask yourself honestly, which is more precious to you—your possessions or the over two billion souls who do not know Jesus Christ? On which are you spending your talents, treasures, and time? Ask God to help you die to yourself in order that He may use ALL of you for His glory.

Spiritual concerns and prayer requests ....
....
....
....
....
....
Today I will... ....
....

"FINALLY, BE YE ALL OF ONE MIND, HAVING COMPASSION ONE OF
ANOTHER, LOVE AS BRETHREN, BE PITIFUL, BE COURTEOUS."
1 Peter 3:8

There are five qualities of friendship:

1. *Harmony.* We are to be of one mind, not necessarily singing the same note, but complimenting one another.

2. *Sympathy.* We hurt when friends hurt. The world is looking for friends like this.

3. *Fraternity.* We are to love one another like brothers. There is no brotherhood, like the brotherhood in Jesus Christ.

4. *Pity.* If you want to be a real friend, you're going to have to feel deeply. You'll need to put yourself in the place of the other person.

5. *Humility.* Genuine courtesy is thinking of the other person's needs before your own. You are less concerned with your rights, and more concerned about the relationship.

Begin to develop these characteristics of friendship in your life and watch God change your world!

Are you lonely and in need of a friend? Ask God to build these characteristics in your life and to lead you to someone with whom you can be a friend. Then, be a friend. In your weakness, He will show Himself strong.

Spiritual concerns and prayer requests ....

....

....

....

....

Today I will… ....

....

FEBRUARY 22

"ACCORDING AS HE HATH CHOSEN US IN HIM BEFORE THE FOUNDATION OF THE WORLD, THAT WE SHOULD BE HOLY AND WITHOUT BLAME BEFORE HIM IN LOVE." Ephesians 1:4

The Holy Trinity worked together for your salvation. God the Father thought it, God the Spirit wrought it, and God the Son bought it. Christians are God's special chosen ones.

Are you a believer? Then, you are a wanted child. Your salvation didn't just happen. Ephesians 1:4 tells you that God chose you before the foundation of the world. Before He swung the stars in space, before He planted the seeds, before He built the mountains, before all of that, you were in the heart and mind of God. How special you are to God!

God the Father sent His Spirit into the world to select and sanctify His children for His holy purpose. We are utterly dependent upon the Spirit for our salvation. And we seek Him because He first sought us!

Read Psalm 33. Praise God for calling you! Praise God for choosing you! Praise God for sanctifying you!

Spiritual concerns and prayer requests..

....

....

....

....

....

....

Today I will..

....

FEBRUARY 23

"THE WICKED FLEE WHEN NO MAN PURSUETH: BUT THE RIGHTEOUS ARE BOLD AS A LION." Proverbs 28:1

Our government has tried to judicially remove God from the public school. But do you know that will never be done? Because you can't keep Christianity out of schools unless you keep Christians out.

If you are a student, let me challenge you to speak out boldly and confidently about Jesus Christ. You are His special messenger of love to teachers, fellow students, custodians, cafeteria workers, and more. Some of these people may have gone to church on Sunday, but all they found was a cold, dead religion. They didn't find Jesus.

Will you be Jesus to them this week? Others may have never stepped into a church; will you invite them to your church?

❧

Invite a classmate or coworker to lunch. See if there are any needs in his/her life for which you can pray. Share how God has helped you in perhaps the same circumstance. Offer to pray for him/her before you go back to class or work.

Spiritual concerns and prayer requests...

....

....

....

....

....

....

Today I will…...

....

FEBRUARY 24

"But know that the LORD hath set apart him that is godly for Himself: the LORD will hear when I call unto Him." Psalm 4:3

If ever there were a reason for you and I to pray, it would be that Jesus *told* us to pray (see Luke 18:1b). Yet, you may wonder why you need to talk to God about your needs since, "your Father knoweth what things ye have need of, before ye ask Him" (Matthew 6:8).

Prayer is communion with God. It is part of God's grand scheme that we have been given the privilege to cooperate with God in prayer. Ephesians 6:18 tells us to pray "in the Spirit."

Any prayer that the Holy Spirit lays upon your heart will be answered, because the prayer that gets to heaven is the prayer that starts in heaven. We just close the circuit.

What are you talking to God about these days? Are you asking Him for something? Or are you just thankful for the privilege of communion with Him? Spend time in prayer today—*not asking Him for anything*—but simply praising Him and thanking Him for allowing you to have a relationship with Him.

Spiritual concerns and prayer requests ....

....

....

....

....

....

....

Today I will... ....

....

FEBRUARY 25

"AND HEREIN DO I EXERCISE MYSELF, TO HAVE ALWAYS A
CONSCIENCE VOID OF OFFENCE TOWARD GOD, AND TOWARD MEN."
Acts 24:16

What does it mean to have a clear conscience? As far as you know, there is nothing wrong between you and God. And there is nothing wrong between you and anybody else.

Do you jump every time the doorbell rings? Do you cringe when you see a police car approaching you? In Psalm 51:3, David knew the hounding of a bad conscience when he said, "My sin is ever before me." No torture the poets name can match that fierce unutterable pain of a bad conscience.

You know you've sinned and yet you have done nothing about it. The trials of life are easier to face when you have a clear conscience because when something bad happens, you can know that you haven't done anything wrong.

❖

Pray Psalm 139:23-24. Wait upon Him to reveal any hidden sins, then confess them and repent. And rejoice in His cleansing blood!

Spiritual concerns and prayer requests...

....

....

....

....

....

Today I will... ....

....

FEBRUARY 26

"NEVERTHELESS I HAVE SOMEWHAT AGAINST THEE, BECAUSE THOU HAST LEFT THY FIRST LOVE. REMEMBER THEREFORE FROM WHENCE THOU ART FALLEN, AND REPENT, AND DO THE FIRST WORKS; OR ELSE I WILL COME UNTO THEE QUICKLY, AND WILL REMOVE THY CANDLESTICK OUT OF HIS PLACE, EXCEPT THOU REPENT." Revelation 2:4-5a

The Sixties ushered in the sexual revolution. Now, tell me one more time how "free love" was to bring peace and harmony to our world? People are still being sucked into swirling sewers of sin. Homes are continuing to come apart at the seams. Precious little unborn babies are being put to death. Sexually transmitted diseases are rampant.

The time is half past late and we must return to our "first love." It's time to love the Lord our God with all our hearts, and with all our souls, and with all our minds; and love our neighbors as we love ourselves (see Matthew 22:36-39).

It's time to introduce people to the "free love" offered by our Savior when He died to forgive us our sins and purchase our salvation for eternity.

❦

How do you know if you have left your first love? Ask yourself: *Is there anything or anyone I serve more than God? Is there anyone or anything I love more than God?* If there is, then confess and repent of your sin of idolatry.

Spiritual concerns and prayer requests..

....

....

....

....

....

Today I will...

....

FEBRUARY 27

"HAVING YOUR CONVERSATION HONEST AMONG THE GENTILES: THAT, WHEREAS THEY SPEAK AGAINST YOU AS EVILDOERS, THEY MAY BY YOUR GOOD WORKS, WHICH THEY SHALL BEHOLD, GLORIFY GOD IN THE DAY OF VISITATION." 1 Peter 2:12

I often hear Christians complain about the immorality of movies and television, but who is doing something about it? Are you?

Are you a part of the solution? Do you have on your prayer list the names of producers, directors, writers, actors, or journalists? Are you witnessing to these people? Are you loving them to Christ? Are you writing letters to producers in support of good programming? Are you supporting advertisers who promote moral programming?

We are to be salt and light. Matthew 5:16 says, "Let your light so shine before men, that they may see your good works, and glorify your Father which is in heaven."

Ask yourself: *What impact is my life having upon immorality in the world? How am I laying down my life in order that others may know the salvation of Jesus Christ?* Now, lay down your life for the glory of God!

Spiritual concerns and prayer requests..
....
....
....
....
....
....

Today I will…..
....

FEBRUARY 28

"IF THE SON THEREFORE SHALL MAKE YOU FREE, YE SHALL BE FREE INDEED." John 8:36

Living a pure life means surrendering to Jesus Christ. But some people don't want to surrender because they say they want to be free.

What if a train said, "I don't want to run on these tracks, I want to be free." Then off through the field it would go. What if the kite said, "I want to be free. I don't want to be tied to a string." The string breaks and down it goes. What if a tree said, "I don't want to be planted in the earth. I want to be free." And it is jerked up from the earth and dies.

Everything that is truly free functions best when it functions as God made it. God made you to know Him and to love Him.

Write James 4:8 below and memorize and apply its truth to your life.

Spiritual concerns and prayer requests..

....

....

....

....

....

....

....

Today I will...

....

FEBRUARY 29

"WAIT ON THE LORD: BE OF GOOD COURAGE, AND HE SHALL
STRENGTHEN THINE HEART: WAIT, I SAY, ON THE LORD."
Psalm 27:14

Do you know the story of Joshua and how the wall of Jericho fell down after the Israelites marched around it once a day for six days, then seven times on the seventh day? Why not just walk around Jericho one time? I think it was because God was testing their faith.

God was teaching them that *waiting* time is not *wasted* time. Isaiah 28:16b says, "he that believeth shall not make haste." God is never in a hurry, like we are. We get upset when we miss a section in a revolving door!

God is also never late. He knows what He is doing. Do you know what our problem is? We've been around Jericho six times and we're ready to quit. Say with the psalmist: "My soul, wait thou only upon God; for my expectation is from Him" (Psalm 62:5).

❖

Are you single? Take comfort in knowing God knows your heart's desire. Take courage in knowing God's best is your purity. Though it may be hard to wait, God will honor your obedience.

Spiritual concerns and prayer requests..

....

....

....

....

....

....

Today I will… ....

....

MARCH 1

"FLEE ALSO YOUTHFUL LUSTS: BUT FOLLOW RIGHTEOUSNESS, FAITH, CHARITY, PEACE, WITH THEM THAT CALL ON THE LORD OUT OF A PURE HEART." 2 Timothy 2:22

Purity doesn't seem to be in vogue these days, but let me tell you what a father told his daughter one day.

She wrote him while away at college: "Dear Dad, My classmates make promiscuity sound so natural and so inevitable. There are times when I wonder what I am waiting for."

Her father wrote her back: "You are waiting to be free from the nagging voice of conscience and from the gray shadow of guilt, free to give all of yourself, not a panicky fraction. Some deep instinct in you knows what tremendous influence your first complete union will be. And that same instinct keeps telling you not to waste it."

Oh, how I wish more families were open enough to discuss this issue and to encourage young people to remain pure.

Are you a parent of a teenager? Then, schedule a time this week to discuss this issue with them. Why not start by sharing today's devotion?

Spiritual concerns and prayer requests ....
....
....
....
....
....
....

Today I will... ....
....

MARCH 2

"FOR THE WHICH CAUSE I ALSO SUFFER THESE THINGS:
NEVERTHELESS I AM NOT ASHAMED: FOR I KNOW WHOM I HAVE
BELIEVED, AND AM PERSUADED THAT HE IS ABLE TO KEEP THAT
WHICH I HAVE COMMITTED UNTO HIM AGAINST THAT DAY."
2 Timothy 1:12

It is a miracle that I know Jesus Christ. I didn't say it is a
miracle that I know *about* Jesus Christ. I *know* Him.

I can read a book about Abraham Lincoln, but I don't
know him. I know Jesus Christ because He has revealed Himself to
me. God saved me and now He has become real to me.

Is Jesus Christ real to you? The Holy Spirit reveals God to
each of us. Without Him, we would have no understanding of a
relationship with God through His Son Jesus Christ.

Hallelujah! How wonderful it is that God has chosen to know us
through His Son by the Holy Spirit. We have a constant
companion. The Holy Spirit is not only our Teacher, but He is our
Protector who is watching over the interests of God in His children
every day.

❈❈❈

Pray, "Lord, with all my heart, with all I am, I want to know
You. I want our relationship to be close and my faith to grow.
Cleanse me and make me all that You want me to be. I surrender my
life to You."

Spiritual concerns and prayer requests..

....

....

....

....

Today I will...

....

MARCH 3

"THE LORD GOD HATH GIVEN ME THE TONGUE OF THE LEARNED,
THAT I SHOULD KNOW HOW TO SPEAK A WORD IN SEASON TO HIM
THAT IS WEARY: HE WAKENETH MORNING BY MORNING, HE
WAKENETH MINE EAR TO HEAR AS THE LEARNED." Isaiah 50:4

D o you have difficulty remembering things? One little lady
said, "My memory is what I forget with."
Thankfully, we have the Holy Spirit who has a
ministry to our subconscious. He is there not only to teach you the
truth, but also to help you *recall* the truth and *apply* the truth in
every situation.

Over and over again, the Holy Spirit has done this for me in the
midst of preaching, witnessing, or counseling. The Lord has given us
the "tongue of the learned." Isn't that wonderful?

You may not have a formal education, but you can still be a
counselor to others in trouble. Why? Because when you walk in the
Spirit, He will give you the words to speak to someone who is weary.

But, He cannot remind you unless you first learn it. How we
need to open our hearts to what the Blessed Advocate is doing as He
tries to make Jesus real and vibrant in our lives.

※❈❈❈❈※

M aybe today you can begin a conversation with someone just by
offering a word of encouragement and share your faith. Who
knows where that spark of truth will lead? Ask God for the
opportunity.

Spiritual concerns and prayer requests...
....
....
....
Today I will…..
....

"But now being made free from sin, and become servants to God, ye have your fruit unto holiness, and the end everlasting life." Romans 6:22

In 1 Samuel 15, we read the story of how Saul failed to put to death the animals God said were to be utterly destroyed. Samuel confronted Saul about this and Saul told a lie—he was going to sacrifice them, but he just hadn't done it yet.

And Samuel said, "Hath the LORD as great delight in burnt offerings and sacrifices, as in obeying the voice of the LORD? Behold, to obey is better than sacrifice, and to hearken than the fat of rams. For rebellion is as the sin of witchcraft, and stubbornness is as iniquity and idolatry" (1 Samuel 15:22-23a).

To rebel against the Lord is as the sin of witchcraft because it puts you in the realm of the devil. When God gives a clear command from His Word, we are not to parade it past the judgment bar of our human wisdom. We are to obey whether or not we understand it or agree with it. It is either God's Word or it is not.

Is there a truth in God's Word you do not understand? Ask Him to give you understanding. Is there a truth to which you are not surrendered in obedience? Ask God to forgive you. Ask Him to meld and mold you into His servant for His glory.

Spiritual concerns and prayer requests ....

....

....

....

....

....

....

Today I will... ....

....

MARCH 5

"HE THAT BELIEVETH ON HIM IS NOT CONDEMNED: BUT HE THAT BELIEVETH NOT IS CONDEMNED ALREADY, BECAUSE HE HATH NOT BELIEVED IN THE NAME OF THE ONLY BEGOTTEN SON OF GOD."
John 3:18

The world doesn't really know what sin is. They think sin is lying, stealing, murder, adultery, or arson. No, those are sins, plural.

Do you know what *sin* is? Sin is the rejection of Jesus Christ that will damn a soul to hell. You don't go to hell because you steal, lie, or kill. I hear people say, "Sure, I lie every now and again, but God isn't going to send me to hell for that. I might fry a few years in purgatory, but to die in hell for lying doesn't make sense."

When a man talks that way, he doesn't understand sin. Sin is high treason against a holy God. Sin is a clenched fist in the face of God. Sin says to God, "I will not bow to You. I will not serve You. I will not trust You." That is sin.

The great commandment is to love God with all your heart, soul, and mind. The great sin is not to.

Have you realized that without Christ, you are destined for hell? Do you agree with Psalm 16:2 and Isaiah 43:11? If not, I encourage you to repent and believe upon Him today. Surrender your life in exchange for His.

Spiritual concerns and prayer requests...
....
....
....
....

Today I will…..
....

MARCH 6

"FEAR THOU NOT; FOR I AM WITH THEE: BE NOT DISMAYED; FOR I AM THY GOD: I WILL STRENGTHEN THEE; YEA, I WILL HELP THEE; YEA, I WILL UPHOLD THEE WITH THE RIGHT HAND OF MY RIGHTEOUSNESS." Isaiah 41:10

So many people want to know what the victorious life is, but let me first tell you what it is *not*.

It is *not* a life without ever committing a sin. It is *not* a life without ever having any failure. It is *not* a life without ever having any doubt. It is *not* a life without ever having discouragement.

Instead, the victorious life is the life of bringing our failures to the Lord Jesus and allowing Him to give us a brand new start. Day after day I tell the Lord I need a new start, I need to be anointed with fresh oil today, and I need forgiveness.

I thank God that He is a God of *grace*, a God of *glory*, and a God of the *second chance*. You're probably more prepared to serve God after failure and restoration, than perhaps at any other time in your life.

✦

Have you recently failed at something? There is no better time than right now to ask for His forgiveness for any unconfessed sin and ask Him to give you a new start.

Spiritual concerns and prayer requests...

....

....

....

....

....

....

Today I will...

....

MARCH 7

"IF ANY MAN WILL DO HIS WILL, HE SHALL KNOW OF THE DOCTRINE, WHETHER IT BE OF GOD, OR WHETHER I SPEAK OF MYSELF." John 7:17

There is an overriding principle taught in Scripture that will help us know and prove the will of God. It is the principle of surrender.

Many of us are absolutely afraid to pray, "Here I am. I am taking my hands off of my rights to my life...my desire to be married, have a family, live in a nice house, get a good job. I give it all to You." We don't come to God and say, "Lord, show me Your will, then I will make up my mind whether to do it or not."

You'll never know God's will that way.

Is there anything you would not do if you knew Jesus wanted you to do it? Is there any place you would not go if you knew Jesus wanted you to go? Is there anything you would not say if you knew Jesus wanted you to say it? Is there anything you would not be if you knew Jesus wanted you to be it? Is there anything you would not give if you knew Jesus wanted you to give it?

❀❀❀

Rededicate yourself to God today. Surrender your rights. Humble yourself. Then hand God a blank sheet of paper, sign your name at the bottom, and say, "Lord, You fill in the details."

Spiritual concerns and prayer requests...

....

....

....

....

....

Today I will..

....

"FOR IF YE FORGIVE MEN THEIR TRESPASSES, YOUR HEAVENLY
FATHER WILL ALSO FORGIVE YOU: BUT IF YE FORGIVE NOT MEN
THEIR TRESPASSES, NEITHER WILL YOUR FATHER FORGIVE YOUR
TRESPASSES." Matthew 6:14-15

A father came home one day and walked in on his two children
who were in the midst of a fight.

When the little girl looked up, she knew she was in
trouble. Right away, she turned on crocodile tears, and said,
"Daddy, I'm so sorry. We shouldn't have been fighting. Forgive me.
I love you, Daddy."

She was in her daddy's arms and he thought, *She really has a
good spirit about this.* But, out the corner of his eye he saw her and
she was sticking her tongue out at her little brother. Her father said,
"You can't hug my neck and stick your tongue out at the same time."

Do you have that kind of heart today? You're playing a game
with God and holding a grudge against somebody. Do you think God
receives your worship? Friend, it's time to get it right. Your
unforgiving spirit is going to do more damage to you than it will ever
do to the person you refuse to forgive.

❦

If there is someone who has sinned against you, forgive them. If
there is someone who has something against you, go to them and
reconcile. Then, spend some time in worship.

Spiritual concerns and prayer requests ....
....
....
....
....
....

Today I will... ....
....

MARCH 9

"Forasmuch as ye know that ye were not redeemed with corruptible things, as silver and gold, from your vain conversation received by tradition from your fathers; But with the precious blood of Christ, as of a lamb without blemish and without spot." 1 Peter 1:18-19

Emancipation. What picture does that word bring to mind? Many think about slaves. But, did you know the cross of Jesus Christ has emancipated every believer?

In 1 Peter 1:18, the word "redeemed" is the same word used to emancipate a slave. Jesus Christ has redeemed you and set you free from your "vain conversation."

That means "empty living"—drawing your breath, drawing your salary—not getting serious about this thing called the Christian life. Oh friend, it's time for you to take hold of the exciting life to which God has called you, and the abundant life for which Jesus died to give you.

It is a thrill to serve the One who has redeemed us with the silver of His tears and the gold of His blood.

How are you serving God today? You are a minister. You are a priest. You are His hands, His feet, and His mouthpiece to a world in need of a Savior. Ask Him to use you today? Then, step out in faith for the wonders He will perform.

Spiritual concerns and prayer requests...
....
....
....
....
....

Today I will…...
....

MARCH 10

"KNOWING THIS, THAT OUR OLD MAN IS CRUCIFIED WITH HIM, THAT THE BODY OF SIN MIGHT BE DESTROYED, THAT HENCEFORTH WE SHOULD NOT SERVE SIN." Romans 6:6

The word "sober" has become a one-definition word these days—to be free from alcohol.

But in Bible times, the word "sober" meant to be serious-minded about the things of God. It's half past late and Satan knows it. Now, you need to know it, too.

Do you think the closer we get to Christ's return Satan is just going to roll over and play dead? Absolutely not. Revelation 12:12 says that Satan is going to come in "great wrath" because he knows there is but little time left. You are going to see all of the artillery of hell let loose upon the believer as Christ readies for His return.

It's time to wake up, time is passing; look up, Jesus is coming; and sober up, Satan is working.

◄◄◆◆►►

Read 1 Thessalonians 5:6-8 and 1 Peter 1:13-16, 4:7, and 5:8-11. Are you serious-minded about the things of God?

Spiritual concerns and prayer requests ....

....

....

....

....

....

Today I will... ....

....

MARCH 11

"BECAUSE IT IS WRITTEN, BE YE HOLY; FOR I AM HOLY." 1 Peter 1:16

Why would you and I choose to live a holy life? One reason is that we anticipate His Second Coming. When we are looking for Christ's return at any moment, we desire to be clean and holy in preparation of seeing Him.

For example, if you knew Jesus was coming this afternoon, do you think you'd get some things right in your life? Would there be somebody with whom you've had a falling out that you'd want to make amends? Would there be some sins for which you would need to repent?

❦

If you answered yes to any of these questions, then act upon your answers in faith, bringing God glory in your obedience. Jesus may come today!

Spiritual concerns and prayer requests

Today I will…

"I REJOICE AT THY WORD, AS ONE THAT FINDETH GREAT SPOIL."
Psalm 119:162

Have you ever found a dollar bill on the sidewalk? Did you just leave it there? You probably picked it up, maybe asked people around you if it was theirs, and if it wasn't, maybe you rejoiced a little. Does that sound familiar?

Now, what happens with your Bible? You see it sitting on your desk and say, "Oh, the Bible is a wonderful book filled with good things for my life." But, what good is it going to do to just say nice things about the Bible? A dime and a gold Krugerrand are both of the same value when they are corroding on the ocean floor.

The promises in God's Word are of no value, unless you dig down deep and appropriate them into your life.

❧❧❧

Love Worth Finding offers a monthly online Bible study called Digging Deeper to help you study God's Word. Check it out today at www.lwf.org.

Spiritual concerns and prayer requests ....
....
....
....
....
....
....

Today I will... ....
....

MARCH 13

"WHO HATH SAVED US, AND CALLED US WITH A HOLY CALLING, NOT ACCORDING TO OUR WORKS, BUT ACCORDING TO HIS OWN PURPOSE AND GRACE, WHICH WAS GIVEN US IN CHRIST JESUS BEFORE THE WORLD BEGAN." 2 Timothy 1:9

You will only know the glory and honor God has prepared for you when you know Jesus as your personal Savior and Lord. Man was crowned with glory, charged with guilt, but can be changed by grace. When you are saved, God doesn't just put you back like you were before you were lost.

You have gained far more in Jesus than you ever lost in Adam (your old nature). Adam was only innocent. You are positively righteous. Adam could lose his relationship. You can never lose your relationship with God.

Angels do not even comprehend the joy of a sinner saved by grace. And the best is yet to be!

❧❦❧

Take time to meditate upon why God has saved you. Has He laid upon your heart a special area of ministry? Has He given you some relationships with lost people who need Jesus Christ? Could you use your gifts? Yes! He has saved you to bring glory to Himself.

Spiritual concerns and prayer requests ....

....

....

....

....

....

....

Today I will... ....

....

"WHEN JESUS THEREFORE HAD RECEIVED THE VINEGAR, HE SAID, IT IS FINISHED: AND HE BOWED HIS HEAD, AND GAVE UP THE GHOST." John 19:30

In the Old Testament, the priest would enter the temple to minister, burn incense, offer prayer and sacrifices.

But, there was one piece of furniture not in the Holy of Holies and that was a chair for the priest to sit upon. Why? Because his work was never finished.

But when Jesus bowed His head upon that cross and cried out, "It is finished!" He was finished and He sat down at the right hand of God, the Father. The first recorded words Jesus said were: "I must be about My Father's business." And His last words upon the cross were: "It is finished." He stayed until He finished His Father's work.

Nothing that you can do will add one measure to His completed work. It is finished! Hallelujah!

❦

Take time right now to pause and thank God for the finished work of Jesus. Do you try and "add" to your salvation by what you do? Repeat out loud, "It is finished!"

Spiritual concerns and prayer requests...

....

....

....

....

....

....

Today I will…..

....

MARCH 15

"BUT NONE OF THESE THINGS MOVE ME, NEITHER COUNT I MY
LIFE DEAR UNTO MYSELF, SO THAT I MIGHT FINISH MY COURSE
WITH JOY, AND THE MINISTRY, WHICH I HAVE RECEIVED OF THE
LORD JESUS, TO TESTIFY THE GOSPEL OF THE GRACE OF GOD."
Acts 20:24

Have you ever seen a triathlon? One time I watched on television the finish of an Ironman competition, which involved 2.4 miles of swimming, 112 miles of biking, and 26.2 miles of running. There was a young lady leading the pack, but suddenly within just a few feet of the finish line, she fell. Her legs were like noodles.

She tried to get up and walk, but fell again. I wept as I watched her end the race in agony. She literally clawed her way to the finish line and sadly did not finish first. If these men and women put themselves through this grueling race for a corruptible crown, God forbid we should be any less the strong, spiritual athletes to which God is calling us. We're dealing with life and death, heaven and hell, and the glory of God!

How are you doing in the race? Are you faithful to run when the going gets tough? Write Philippians 3:13-14 below and ask God to make you strong and faithful to the end.

Spiritual concerns and prayer requests...

....

....

....

....

....

Today I will..

....

MARCH 16

"GO YE THEREFORE, AND TEACH ALL NATIONS, BAPTIZING THEM IN THE NAME OF THE FATHER, AND OF THE SON, AND OF THE HOLY GHOST: TEACHING THEM TO OBSERVE ALL THINGS WHATSOEVER I HAVE COMMANDED YOU: AND, LO, I AM WITH YOU ALWAY, EVEN UNTO THE END OF THE WORLD. AMEN." Matthew 28:19-20

Have you ever shared with someone else the story of how God saved you? Some people are afraid of doing that because they are afraid they wouldn't know what to say. Or they are afraid someone will ask a question they cannot answer. Do you ever feel that way?

I believe it is okay for you to say, "I don't know." It's not a sin to be ignorant. It's a sin to be willing to stay that way, though.

God has called you to be His witness. Do you know what a Christian is? A witness—someone who has seen, heard, or experienced Jesus Christ—nothing more, nothing less.

Jesus did not call us to be lawyers to argue a case. He called us as His witnesses. Will you be His witness today?

Have you never shared your testimony because you didn't know what to say? The best way to start is to first, be a good listener. When someone shares their needs, step in to help meet that need if you can. Then ask if you can share what God has done in your life when you had a need.

Spiritual concerns and prayer requests ....

....

....

....

....

Today I will… ....

....

MARCH 17

"FOR WE WALK BY FAITH, NOT BY SIGHT." 2 Corinthians 5:7

In John 4, we read the story of a nobleman whose son was gravely ill. In this particular instance, Jesus chose not to go to the son to heal him. Other times, Jesus went to lay His hands on the sick and they recovered.

Why didn't He do that this time? I think for my sake and your sake He did not go. There are so many of us who think if only we had the physical presence of Jesus, then we will have the blessings of Jesus. We say to ourselves, "If only I lived back then." Or, "Won't it be wonderful when Jesus returns."

We don't have to live in the past or in the future, we have His Word today. And it's just as real and powerful as if He was here in the flesh. Distance makes no difference.

What are you waiting on before you step out in faith? It has been well said: When you can't trace His hand, trust His heart. Read Colossians 1:9-14.

Spiritual concerns and prayer requests...

....

....

....

....

....

....

Today I will...

....

MARCH 18

"JUDGE NOT, THAT YE BE NOT JUDGED." Matthew 7:1

What do you think "the beam" means in the question Jesus asked, "And why beholdest thou the mote that is in thy brother's eye, but considerest not the beam that is in thine own eye?" (Matthew 7:3).

Do you think Jesus is referring to a sin as heinous as adultery or murder? If you knew the crowd to whom Jesus was talking, you would know these weren't the temptations with which they struggled. You see, He was talking to the Pharisees. The beam in their eyes was their attitude toward the speck in their brother's eye. They were arrogant, prideful, and hypocritical.

God forbid that you and I become like those religious zealots who knew nothing of the loving humility of our Savior. God help us remove the sawdust from our own eyes before we ever think to judge another.

❧❧❧

Do you want to have the attitude of Christ toward others? Read and obey Philippians 2:1-16.

Spiritual concerns and prayer requests..

....

....

....

....

....

....

Today I will…..

....

MARCH 19

"MY VOICE SHALT THOU HEAR IN THE MORNING, O LORD; IN THE MORNING WILL I DIRECT MY PRAYER UNTO THEE, AND WILL LOOK UP." Psalm 5:3

Most Christians fail in their Christian life for one simple reason: They fail to have a quiet time. They fail to start the day with Jesus. It is so simple. They say, "Why am I failing? Why don't I have the victory? Why don't I understand?"

And I want to respond, "Why don't you get quiet before God at the beginning of your day and saturate your soul with His presence and bathe your heart with His Word?"

Someone has said, "Every morning lean thine arms a while upon the windowsill of heaven and gaze upon thy Lord. And then with the vision in thy heart, turn strong to meet the day."

Do you find excuses for not spending time alone with God every day? What can you do differently to make sure this is your first priority? Do you need someone to help you? Ask for help. Write your thoughts out below and then get accountable and have that daily time with God. Your life will forever change.

Spiritual concerns and prayer requests ....

....

....

....

....

....

....

Today I will... ....

....

"FOR BY HIM WERE ALL THINGS CREATED, THAT ARE IN HEAVEN, AND THAT ARE IN EARTH, VISIBLE AND INVISIBLE, WHETHER THEY BE THRONES, OR DOMINIONS, OR PRINCIPALITIES, OR POWERS: ALL THINGS WERE CREATED BY HIM, AND FOR HIM." Colossians 1:16

Jesus Christ is the power of creation. The little baby who was born in a manger was the great Creator talked about in Genesis, chapter one. In fact, that little baby created His mother Mary in the first place. When He was born, He was as old as His Father, and older than His mother.

If you look up the little word "for" in our passage today, you will discover it means "motion toward an object." The reason for everything was Jesus. Not only was everything made by Him, but it was made for Him.

And everything is coming back to Him. All of life will climax in Jesus Christ. He is the power of creation, the preserver of creation, and the purpose of creation.

❦❦❦

Find the Names of God, either in a book, at the library, or by visiting www.lwf.org. Look for the one that particularly speaks of the LORD Creator. Then read some of the Scriptures about His holy attribute.

Spiritual concerns and prayer requests..

....

....

....

....

....

....

Today I will…..

....

MARCH 21

"CAST THY BURDEN UPON THE LORD, AND HE SHALL SUSTAIN THEE: HE SHALL NEVER SUFFER THE RIGHTEOUS TO BE MOVED." Psalm 55:22

Have you ever wondered why Jesus "constrained His disciples to get into a ship, and to go before Him unto the other side" (Matthew 14:22), knowing that a storm was going to brew shortly after they set sail? Why would He send them right into the teeth of a stormy gale? Because He wanted them to know that He was sufficient for them. He wanted them to worship Him.

Your storm is nothing but a superhighway to bring you to Jesus. It is the vehicle that moves you from a head knowledge to an experiential understanding that God is Who He says He is.

It was Andre Crouch who said, "For if I never had a problem, I would never know that God could solve them. And I would never know what faith in His Word could do."

When was the last time you thanked God for the problems in your life? Today, reframe these problems and readjust your perspective to think of them as vehicles that drive you to the heart of the Lord.

Spiritual concerns and prayer requests ....

....

....

....

....

....

....

Today I will... ....

....

"ACCORDING AS HIS DIVINE POWER HATH GIVEN UNTO US ALL
THINGS THAT PERTAIN UNTO LIFE AND GODLINESS, THROUGH THE
KNOWLEDGE OF HIM THAT HATH CALLED US TO GLORY AND
VIRTUE." 2 Peter 1:3

A violinist stepped out onto stage one evening and drew the bow
across his violin. The room fell silent as out came the most
glorious music the audience had ever heard. When he
finished, the crowd leaped to their feet and gave ovation after ovation.

What happened next, shocked everyone speechless. The violinist
broke the violin on the podium into a thousand pieces. He looked at
the audience and said, "Ladies and gentlemen, don't be dismayed.
This was only a $3.50 violin. It is not so much the violin that makes
the music as it is the man who draws the bow."

Little is so much when God is in it. God can take a life that may
be comparable to a $3.50 violin and turn it into a masterpiece.

Substitute your name where you see the word "us" in today's
Scripture. Now, memorize that verse and may its truth transform
your life.

Spiritual concerns and prayer requests..

....

....

....

....

....

....

Today I will...

....

MARCH 23

"FOR THOUGH HE WAS CRUCIFIED THROUGH WEAKNESS, YET HE
LIVETH BY THE POWER OF GOD. FOR WE ALSO ARE WEAK IN HIM,
BUT WE SHALL LIVE WITH HIM BY THE POWER OF GOD TOWARD
YOU." 2 Corinthians 13:4

Are you facing a problem that you need to solve? We can learn
a lot about problem-solving by reading the miracle Jesus
performed in the feeding of the 5,000.

When Jesus and the disciples discovered thousands of hungry
people, He asked Philip, "Whence shall we buy bread, that these
may eat?" (John 6:5). Now, Jesus wasn't asking for information. He
already knew what He was going to do. Instead He was trying to give
Philip a revelation that we should never assess our problems in the
light of our own resources or strength.

We have no right to ask the world to believe our message unless
there is something about us that is unexplainable and supernatural.
There must be a divine dimension to our lives.

What does Proverbs 3:5-6 tell you to do when faced with a
problem?

Spiritual concerns and prayer requests...
....
....
....
....
....
....

Today I will...
....

MARCH 24

"O HOW LOVE I THY LAW! IT IS MY MEDITATION ALL THE DAY."
Psalm 119:97

D o you know the first words Paul uttered when he met the Lord Jesus on the Damascus Road? He said, "Lord, what wilt Thou have me to do?" (Acts 9:6). He didn't say, "Lord, what wilt others have me to do?" Or, "What will Thou have others to do?" God had a personal plan for his life.

He stayed on the course and didn't shirk his passion when the going got tough. Nothing could stop Paul. Will you be able to say that? The hounds of hell are mocking you even now.

Are you firmly focused on Jesus so that nothing can deter you from accomplishing His will, from loving Him with all your heart, from devoting every ounce of who you are to Him?

❦

H ow would someone know you are firmly focused on Jesus? What is there about your life that testifies you have a passionate love for God?

Spiritual concerns and prayer requests...
....
....
....
....
....
....

Today I will...
....

MARCH 25

"FOR IF BY ONE MAN'S OFFENCE DEATH REIGNED BY ONE; MUCH MORE THEY WHICH RECEIVE ABUNDANCE OF GRACE AND OF THE GIFT OF RIGHTEOUSNESS SHALL REIGN IN LIFE BY ONE, JESUS CHRIST." Romans 5:17

Why did God come down through the dark Judean night through the portals of a virgin's womb to be born a man? Why did He exchange His glory for flesh and blood?

One reason was to restore to us the dominion we lost as the people of God. You may not realize that God made you to rule, but He did. God created us to be kings and queens (see Genesis 1:26). But, how many people realize their God-given dominion today?

Jesus righteously regained our dominion and spoiled the principalities and powers of this world when He bowed His head and said, "It is finished" (John 19:30).

❧❦❧

Read the story of creation in the first chapter of Genesis. What distinctions can you make between the creations of God and the Creator called God? Go on a walk and thank God that He rules over creation and that He has given you dominion.

Spiritual concerns and prayer requests...
....
....
....
....
....
....
....

Today I will..
....

MARCH 26

"BEHOLD, I GIVE UNTO YOU POWER TO TREAD ON SERPENTS AND
SCORPIONS, AND OVER ALL THE POWER OF THE ENEMY: AND
NOTHING SHALL BY ANY MEANS HURT YOU." Luke 10:19

The word "power" is repeated twice in today's Scripture, but it has two different meanings. The first "power" is from the Greek word *exousia* and it has the meaning of authority. The second "power" is from the Greek word *dunamis*. We get the English word for "dynamite" from this word.

Jesus gives us authority over the force of the enemy. We do not defeat the devil with strength; we defeat him with authority. Is Satan wiser than you? Yes, with a perverted wisdom. Is he stronger than you? Yes, with a malevolent strength. Is Satan more powerful than you? Yes, but you can stop him when you stand against him with the authority God has given you. And he knows that.

When you begin to fight your battles, not in your strength, but in God's strength, then you are going to see Satan begin to cower before you.

⊱⊰

Is there someone in your life who is having a difficult time overcoming a certain area of sin? Pray for them, and then ask God for an opportunity to share what you've learned from today's devotion.

Spiritual concerns and prayer requests

Today I will…

MARCH 27

"BUT THE HOUR COMETH, AND NOW IS, WHEN THE TRUE
WORSHIPERS SHALL WORSHIP THE FATHER IN SPIRIT AND IN
TRUTH: FOR THE FATHER SEEKETH SUCH TO WORSHIP HIM."
John 4:23

The Father seeks to commune with you in worship. He is not looking for your money, your glory, or your strength. He is looking for your heart.

C.S. Lewis said, "It is in the process of being worshiped that God communicates His presence to men." If you are not worshiping God, but you are serving Him (or so you think), you are making a big mistake.

To pray without worship is mockery. To sing without worship is sounding brass. To work without worship is an insult to God. To teach without worship is ignorance. To serve without worship is hypocrisy. To witness without worship is perjury. God wants your worship.

❦

Begin the next seven days by reading Psalm 95 through 101. The first day, read Psalm 95 and finish with Psalm 101 on the seventh day.

Spiritual concerns and prayer requests..

....

....

....

....

....

Today I will...

....

"FOR WE WRESTLE NOT AGAINST FLESH AND BLOOD, BUT AGAINST PRINCIPALITIES, AGAINST POWERS, AGAINST THE RULERS OF THE DARKNESS OF THIS WORLD, AGAINST SPIRITUAL WICKEDNESS IN HIGH PLACES." Ephesians 6:12

So many times we have a falling out with someone and we want to argue with them rather than attacking the devil that caused the ruckus. Would to God that we would see that our battle is not with flesh and blood, but our battle is with Satan.

If we don't see that, we are going to lose the war—in a personal sense and global sense. Now, I'm not saying that our nation shouldn't be prepared and ready when we encounter a real enemy, but we cannot shoot down an idea with a bullet. The only thing that will kill an idea or philosophy is a better idea—the saving Gospel of Jesus Christ.

Martin Luther wrote in his hymn "A Mighty Fortress is Our God," "And though this world, with devils filled, should threaten to undo us. We will not fear, for God hath willed His truth to triumph through us: The prince of darkness grim, we tremble not for him; His rage we can endure, for lo, his doom is sure, one little word shall fell him."

Find the complete lyrics to this beloved hymn and worship God through singing praises to our Great Protector.

Spiritual concerns and prayer requests ....

....

....

....

....

Today I will... ....

....

MARCH 29

"AND THOU SHALT LOVE THE LORD THY GOD WITH ALL THINE HEART, AND WITH ALL THY SOUL, AND WITH ALL THY MIGHT."
Deuteronomy 6:5

I want you to reminisce about your spiritual journey for a moment. Recall the early days of when you were first learning about God. Remember the time you first understood how to pray.

Now, let me ask you: Was there ever a time in your life, when you loved the Lord Jesus more than you do at this moment? If there is, you are a backslider.

Friend, if you don't love Jesus now with a burning, glowing enthusiasm, you need to remember what it used to be like and return to your first love. Don't get the idea that the love bug bit you and you can fall in and out of love with Jesus. You choose to love Jesus—every day and every way.

❦

Write out Deuteronomy 6:5 below and make it personal by using "I" and "my" in the verse. Then ask God to make this a living reality in your life.

Spiritual concerns and prayer requests..

....

....

....

....

....

....

Today I will... ....

....

MARCH 30

"...OBEY MY VOICE, AND I WILL BE YOUR GOD, AND YE SHALL BE MY PEOPLE: AND WALK YE IN ALL THE WAYS THAT I HAVE COMMANDED YOU, THAT IT MAY BE WELL UNTO YOU." Jeremiah 7:23

In 2 Kings 5:10, we read that God chose to heal Naaman, who was a leper, in a very unique way. God told Elisha to tell Naaman to wash seven times in the Jordan and he would be healed.

Why seven times? Why not eight or five times? Because the number seven is the number of perfection in the Bible. One is the number of unity. Two is the number of witness. Three is the number of deity. Four is the earth number. Six is the number of man. When God told Naaman to dip seven times, He was saying, "If you want Me to bless you, not only must you obey, you must obey perfectly."

If you want God's blessing upon your life, you cannot just obey in part, you must obey perfectly. What person wants a friend who is 43% faithful?

❧❧❧

Why don't you determine today that you are going to get right with God and stay right with God? And why not take steps today to lead a life of obedience.

Spiritual concerns and prayer requests...

....

....

....

....

....

....

Today I will... ....

....

MARCH 31

"IF THOU, LORD, SHOULDEST MARK INIQUITIES, O LORD, WHO SHALL STAND? BUT THERE IS FORGIVENESS WITH THEE, THAT THOU MAYEST BE FEARED." Psalm 130:3-4

Samson, the mighty man of the Old Testament, learned three things about sin that I want to share with you today.

1. Sin will take you further than you want to go.
2. Sin will keep you longer than you want to stay.
3. Sin will cost you more than you want to pay.

Never has there been a greater failure than Samson, but in his remorse he began to think about the great God who loved him. And he thought of the fact that God is always willing to forgive. No matter how bad sin is, God is greater.

❖❖❖

Do you have a sin that you refuse to let go? Do you want victory? Do you want forgiveness? Ask Him to forgive your rebellious spirit. Ask Him for strength to repent. Let His Holy Spirit work His conviction, then seek His forgiveness. You can be reconciled to God today. He is always ready to forgive.

Spiritual concerns and prayer requests

Today I will...

"LET NO MAN DECEIVE HIMSELF. IF ANY MAN AMONG YOU SEEMETH TO BE WISE IN THIS WORLD, LET HIM BECOME A FOOL, THAT HE MAY BE WISE." 1 Corinthians 3:18

O ne day, Harry Ironside, the great preacher of yesteryear was traveling with friends on a ferry. They were having a glorious time singing praises to the Lord when someone critically interrupted them saying, "Who are you people? What are you doing?"

Dr. Ironside replied, "We're just some Christians having a good time praising the Lord." And the heckler replied, "You're a bunch of fools!" Ironside said, "You're right! We're fools for Christ's sake."

The way of the Christian is sometimes foolishness in the eyes of the world.

W hen was the last time you made a fool of yourself for Christ's sake? Ask God to help you die to yourself today so that your ego doesn't get in the way of His work.

Spiritual concerns and prayer requests..

....

....

....

....

....

....

Today I will... ....

....

APRIL 2

"But we all, with open face beholding as in a glass the glory of the Lord, are changed into the same image from glory to glory, even as by the Spirit of the Lord."
2 Corinthians 3:18

We are changed from glory to glory by the power of the Holy Spirit. That doesn't mean it happens overnight. It happens but one step at a time.

Today you ought to have a little more glory than yesterday. Today you ought to be a little bit more like Jesus than you were yesterday. And tomorrow, you ought to be even more like Jesus.

Are you becoming like Jesus? Not if you're not in the Word. Don't you think it's time for this generation to get serious about the Word of God?

Set aside a time and a place to get alone with Him today and pray Psalm 119:18.

Spiritual concerns and prayer requests..

....

....

....

....

....

....

Today I will...

....

"AND THE LORD SHALL HELP THEM, AND DELIVER THEM: HE SHALL DELIVER THEM FROM THE WICKED, AND SAVE THEM, BECAUSE THEY TRUST IN HIM." Psalm 37:40

In Old Testament days, when a tribe commenced war, they would sometimes hurl a spear into enemy territory.

It made no difference whether the enemy was there or not. It really wasn't for the enemy to see. It was an attitude of faith that was a declaration of war. Some would call it a throwing down of the gauntlet.

You may want the victory in something today, and yet you haven't let your arrow of faith fly into the enemy's territory. Faith that acts will bring the enemy to his knees.

We don't fight our enemy with actual bows and arrows, instead we fight him with the weapons of prayer and the Word. When we pray, we face the foe. By letting the arrow of prayer fly, God moves in, and our prayer becomes the Lord's deliverance. God does business with those who mean business.

What is the battle you are facing today? How are you preparing for battle? Spend some time in prayer and in God's Word before you face the day.

Spiritual concerns and prayer requests

....

....

....

....

....

....

....

Today I will... ....

....

APRIL 4

"AND HE SAID UNTO THEM, VERILY I SAY UNTO YOU, THERE IS NO MAN THAT HATH LEFT HOUSE, OR PARENTS, OR BRETHREN, OR WIFE, OR CHILDREN, FOR THE KINGDOM OF GOD'S SAKE, WHO SHALL NOT RECEIVE MANIFOLD MORE IN THIS PRESENT TIME, AND IN THE WORLD TO COME LIFE EVERLASTING." Luke 18:29-30

God has given you abilities and God wants you to take those abilities and invest them in Him.

Friend, it is a sin for you to be less than what God called you to be. Sure, you may not be the next Einstein, Tiger Woods, Betty Crocker, or Billy Graham. But, that is not the point.

The danger is that you will not do what you *can* do. There are three people inside you: (1) who you are right now, (2) who you could be for evil if you allowed the devil to get a hold of you, and (3) who you could be for God.

In a physical showing of your commitment, open wide your arms and lift them to God. Pray, *Father, I am letting go of this world with both hands. I am giving all of me to You. Use me for Your glory in whatever way You think is best.*

Spiritual concerns and prayer requests..
....
....
....
....
....
....

Today I will...
....

"BUT IT IS GOOD FOR ME TO DRAW NEAR TO GOD: I HAVE PUT MY TRUST IN THE LORD GOD, THAT I MAY DECLARE ALL THY WORKS." Psalm 73:28

We can be so protective of our reputations, can't we? I know of preachers who have lost their children because they were more concerned about what people thought than what God taught.

Maybe some of you are raising teenagers and they dress in a way that is modest, yet not your style. Maybe your church friends are saying some unpleasant things. Let them criticize! God knows your heart.

Those children are *yours*, not *theirs*. You need to love them with everything that God gives you. Stand by their sides. Never sacrifice your son or daughter on the altar of your reputation. Trust your children to the Lord.

Are you a parent? Ask God to give you His wisdom so you can see how He is fulfilling His promise of Romans 8:28 in every situation.

Spiritual concerns and prayer requests...

....

....

....

....

....

....

Today I will..

....

APRIL 6

"And hath raised us up together, and made us sit together in heavenly places in Christ Jesus." Ephesians 2:6

Why is the empty tomb so glorious? Because it signifies more than just the fact that God raised Jesus from the dead. He raised you, too, to walk "in newness of life" (see Romans 6:4).

I have come out of that grave. I have ascended. You have, too, if you are saved. Where is Christ today? Seated in the heavenlies. Where are you seated? In the same place. You don't have to die to go to heaven. In Christ, you are seated in the heavenlies *right now*.

We encourage our brothers and sisters by telling them to keep looking up, when we should be saying, "Keep looking down!" You're already seated in the heavenlies, so you can look down on your problems. You, dear friend, have a brand new life!

❦

Take a moment and ask God to give you a brand new life or thank Him for the one He has already given you.

Spiritual concerns and prayer requests...
....
....
....
....
....
....

Today I will..
....

APRIL 7

"NOT THAT I SPEAK IN RESPECT OF WANT: FOR I HAVE LEARNED,
IN WHATSOEVER STATE I AM, THEREWITH TO BE CONTENT."
Philippians 4:11

Paul came to a place in his life—not a physical place, but a spiritual place—where he felt divine contentment. Most people think they know what this word "contentment" means, but let me tell you what it means in God's Word..."self contained."

In the context of this passage, we learn that Paul was thanking people for their love gifts to him, but he wanted them also to know he was not dependent upon them because God had brought him to a place of sufficiency in Himself alone. That is, Paul was able to say, "I have learned that I don't need anything or anybody else, but the Lord. I have Him, and therefore, I am self-contained, not self-sufficient. I can do all things through Christ."

Perhaps you are single and desire to be married. Perhaps you are married and want a family. Perhaps you are in a job that feels like a dead-end. Seek the Lord with all your heart. Ask for His presence to be evident in your heart and mind so you are filled with His contentment.

Spiritual concerns and prayer requests..

....

....

....

....

....

....

Today I will... ....

....

APRIL 8

"TAKE THEREFORE NO THOUGHT FOR THE MORROW: FOR THE
MORROW SHALL TAKE THOUGHT FOR THE THINGS OF ITSELF.
SUFFICIENT UNTO THE DAY IS THE EVIL THEREOF." Matthew 6:34

Have you ever noticed that along with the command in
Matthew 6:34 not to worry, that correspondingly there
comes a promise from God to take care of us?

One of the most frequent promises is that we will be fed—God will
take care of our needs. Then, why does God promise that "all these
things will be added unto you." (Matthew 6:33)? *So, we will not
starve?* No. Friend, a lot of people who don't trust God have a pantry
full of food.

The average, unsaved person is thinking about money, homes,
cars, clothes, jewelry, etc. Jesus knows that we have a one-track mind
and we cannot serve two masters. If these are the things you are
seeking, then you are not seeking the Lord.

He is telling us, "You trust Me. Bring all of your attention into
trusting Me, and I'll take care of you."

❧⟨❦⟩❧

Are you seeking first His kingdom? How do you know? What is
it about your life that testifies He is your first priority?

Spiritual concerns and prayer requests..

....

....

....

....

....

....

Today I will…..

....

"BUT THEY THAT WAIT UPON THE LORD SHALL RENEW THEIR STRENGTH; THEY SHALL MOUNT UP WITH WINGS AS EAGLES; THEY SHALL RUN, AND NOT BE WEARY; AND THEY SHALL WALK, AND NOT FAINT." Isaiah 40:31

What does it mean to "renew" your strength? It literally means "changed," as if you changed clothes. You remove your rags of weakness and put on God's royal robes of strength.

God promises to exchange our strength with His strength. You see, the Christian life is not just simply a *changed* life, it is an *exchanged* life. God doesn't just change us from what we *were* to something *better*. He exchanges His life with ours.

He takes our sin. We take His holiness. He takes our weakness. We take His strength. He takes our anxiety. We take His peace. Sounds great. But, what's the problem? We get tired of waiting for the change. Friend, don't give up. The wait is never too long when God is in charge.

Read Psalm 62:5-8 and make it your prayer today.

*S*piritual concerns and prayer requests..

....

....

....

....

....

....

Today I will…..

....

APRIL 10

"DEARLY BELOVED, I BESEECH YOU AS STRANGERS AND PILGRIMS,
ABSTAIN FROM FLESHLY LUSTS, WHICH WAR AGAINST THE SOUL."
1 Peter 2:11

God saved you out of this world and sent you back into this world to tell the world Jesus saves. He is scattering you as precious seed. You are an ambassador upon foreign soil for the King of kings.

You are not only scattered as precious seed, you are also scattered as a persevering saint. You are a foreigner in a land where you march to a different drummer. You don't settle down in this world. It's not your home; you're only passing through.

You ought to pray, "Lord, if I am building a nest, put a thorn in it." If you dabble and delight in this world, yet your citizenship is in heaven, you're going to have one foot in the world and one in heaven—just enough religion to make you miserable in the world and just enough of the world to make you miserable in your spiritual life.

❖

Do you ever feel like a nomad? Maybe you are in the military, or in sales, or work in the transportation industry. Maybe you have moved often because of financial or relational reasons. God wants you to know that you always have a home with Him wherever you are. Read 1 Peter 1:12-21.

Spiritual concerns and prayer requests..

....

....

....

....

....

Today I will...

....

APRIL 11

"TO AN INHERITANCE INCORRUPTIBLE, AND UNDEFILED, AND THAT
FADETH NOT AWAY, RESERVED IN HEAVEN FOR YOU." 1 Peter 1:4

A man was sitting on a street corner weeping. A friend saw him
and asked, "Why are you crying?" He said, "Haven't you
read the papers? Rockefeller died." His friend responded,
"Why are you crying? You were no kin of his!" He said, "That's
why I'm crying."

You have an inheritance right now as a child of God. It is
incorruptible. The foul breath of decay and gnawing tooth of time
cannot take it away. It is undefiled. No high-power lawyer can find a
loophole. It will never fade away.

If you understood what you have in Jesus, you would never be
jealous of anybody.

Read Ezekiel 44:28, Matthew 25:34, Romans 8:16-17,
Galatians 4:7, Ephesians 1:11-14, and Colossians 3:24. You
have an inheritance that is faultless, flawless, fadeless, and reserved in
heaven for you!

Spiritual concerns and prayer requests...

....

....

....

....

....

....

Today I will…...

....

APRIL 12

"As every man hath received the gift, even so minister the same one to another, as good stewards of the manifold grace of God." 1 Peter 4:10

The Bible speaks of the "manifold" grace of God. What does that mean? It means we can experience God's grace in many ways.

For instance, there is *singing grace*. When Paul and Silas were in prison, God gave them grace to sing (see Acts 16:25). There is *speaking grace*. Colossians 4:6 says, "Let your speech be always with grace, seasoned with salt, that ye may know how ye ought to answer every man." God will give you the ability to talk about your troubles with His grace.

God also gives us *strengthening grace*. Timothy was often sick with many infirmities. Paul told him to "be strong in the grace that is in Christ Jesus" (2 Timothy 2:1). When you spend time in the Word of God, you too can draw from the manifold grace of God.

❦❦❦

Read about the other "manifold" ways that God has provided for His people: Nehemiah 9:19 and 27; Psalm 104:24; Luke 18:29-30; and Ephesians 3:8-12.

Spiritual concerns and prayer requests ....

....

....

....

....

....

....

Today I will... ....

....

"OF OLD HAST THOU LAID THE FOUNDATION OF THE EARTH: AND THE HEAVENS ARE THE WORK OF THY HANDS." Psalm 102:25

Even though I preached the Gospel of Jesus Christ for more than fifty years, I always felt I was just on the threshold of discovering Him. I wanted to move closer and closer to Him and learn more and more about Him.

Do you know what Paul said at the *end* of his ministry? That he may know God (see Philippians 3:10). Did he know God? Yes, but he knew so little *about* Him.

Let me ask you a question: Did Christopher Columbus discover America? Well, he touched on the shores of America. But even today there are thousands of unnamed lakes, forests, and more where no one has yet completely explored.

There is so much in Christ. You may have touched on Christ, but God's plan is that you know Him more and more each day.

Get to know God today. How do you do that? You can get outside and discover Him in His creation. You can dig into His Word by reading perhaps one of the Minor Prophets in the Old Testament. You can sit before Him in reverential silence as you meditate upon His holiness.

Spiritual concerns and prayer requests...

....

....

....

....

....

....

Today I will…...

....

APRIL 14

"I AM CRUCIFIED WITH CHRIST: NEVERTHELESS I LIVE; YET NOT I, BUT CHRIST LIVETH IN ME: AND THE LIFE WHICH I NOW LIVE IN THE FLESH I LIVE BY THE FAITH OF THE SON OF GOD, WHO LOVED ME, AND GAVE HIMSELF FOR ME." Galatians 2:20

The life of Joshua in the Old Testament is an illustration of Jesus. As a matter of fact, Joshua is the Hebrew name of Jesus.

The Lord Jesus is our heavenly Joshua who leads us into the land of promise and victory. And what is this victory? It is a victory of faith. There is nothing more, nothing less that will achieve the victory in our lives, but faith.

Victory is not achieved by fighting. Victory is received by faith. You see, when God has a gigantic task He wants us to perform, He gives the contract to faith. Your faith links your nothingness to God's almightiness and victory is yours for the taking!

❦

Are you losing the battle in an area of your life? Then, maybe it is because you have not completely died to yourself. The life God is calling you to live is not *your* life, it is *His* life through you. Put yourself upon the altar once again and die to self.

Spiritual concerns and prayer requests..

....

....

....

....

....

Today I will...

....

APRIL 15

"IN WHOM YE ALSO TRUSTED, AFTER THAT YE HEARD THE WORD OF TRUTH, THE GOSPEL OF YOUR SALVATION: IN WHOM ALSO AFTER THAT YE BELIEVED, YE WERE SEALED WITH THAT HOLY SPIRIT OF PROMISE." Ephesians 1:13

What does it mean to be sealed with the Holy Spirit? First, it is a *mark of authenticity*. If the Holy Spirit is not in you, then you are a fake. First John 3:24 says, "And he that keepeth His commandments dwelleth in Him, and He in him. And hereby we know that He abideth in us, by the Spirit which He hath given us."

Second, the seal is a *mark of ownership*, like the branding of a cow. You are His. Romans 8:9 says, "if any man have not the Spirit of Christ, he is none of His."

Third, the seal is a *mark of security*. Esther 8:8 tells about this type of seal, which "no man can reverse." The way I am kept saved, is because God sealed me. The way you are kept saved, is because God has sealed you.

❦

Praise God He has saved you, sealed you, and secured you for all eternity. Look up in a hymnal, online or rejoice by singing this beloved hymn from memory: "Hallelujah! What A Savior!" by Philip Bliss.

Spiritual concerns and prayer requests...

....

....

....

....

....

Today I will...

....

APRIL 16

"BUT WE PREACH CHRIST CRUCIFIED, UNTO THE JEWS A
STUMBLINGBLOCK, AND UNTO THE GREEKS FOOLISHNESS; BUT
UNTO THEM WHICH ARE CALLED, BOTH JEWS AND GREEKS,
CHRIST THE POWER OF GOD, AND THE WISDOM OF GOD."
1 Corinthians 1:23-24

Every man, woman, boy, and girl comes into contact with Jesus Christ. And He will be either a stepping stone into heaven or a stumbling stone into hell.

No one can be neutral about Jesus Christ. Either you rise on Him, or you fall on Him. You cannot walk around Him.

Either you're saved by Him or you're judged by Him. You will encounter Jesus Christ. He is inevitable. He is unavoidable. He is inescapable. What you do with Jesus Christ determines what Jesus Christ will do with you.

What are you doing with Jesus Christ today?

How is Jesus Christ involved in what I am doing right now? Answer this question below. May the application of that truth take hold of your life in a transforming way today.

Spiritual concerns and prayer requests..

....

....

....

....

....

....

Today I will... ....

....

"KNOW YE NOT THAT YE ARE THE TEMPLE OF GOD, AND THAT THE SPIRIT OF GOD DWELLETH IN YOU?" 1 Corinthians 3:16

I have had the privilege of pastoring churches in the midst of building campaigns. And it has been a faith-growing experience to watch God work.

In fact, I will never forget the first church where that happened in Fort Pierce, Florida. An elderly architect was overseeing the job and he said something I will never forget.

As we were looking over the plans I said, "It can't be expensive because we don't have much money." And he replied, "Oh, my boy. Good architecture is not an arrangement of beautiful materials. It is a beautiful arrangement of materials."

You see, the Lord can take people like you and me from the quarry of sin. And with His grace and His Word, He can fit us together into a majestic temple of God.

Do you feel like a mix-matched pile of bricks today? Maybe you're wondering if your life has any purpose. Or perhaps you question why you are even here. Meditate on today's Scripture until you are changed from uncertainty to faith, from sadness to joy, from helplessness to empowerment.

Spiritual concerns and prayer requests...

....

....

....

....

....

....

Today I will…..

....

APRIL 18

"I BESEECH YOU THEREFORE, BRETHREN, BY THE MERCIES OF
GOD, THAT YE PRESENT YOUR BODIES A LIVING SACRIFICE, HOLY,
ACCEPTABLE UNTO GOD, WHICH IS YOUR REASONABLE SERVICE."
Romans 12:1

In the Old Testament, the priests would offer an animal sacrifice
to God. What do believers offer today? Romans 12:1 tells us to
offer our bodies as living sacrifices.

And just as the altars of old had two flesh hooks to keep the
sacrifice from slipping off the altar, we have two hooks that hold our
bodies there—*discipline and devotion.*

In the Old Testament, the priests would burn incense as a
fragrant offering to the Lord. What do we do today? Hebrews 13:15
says that we continually offer to God a sacrifice of praise. Our incense
of praise should be going up out of our body, as we are the temple of
the Holy Spirit (see 1 Corinthians 3:16).

Are you disciplining and devoting yourself as a living sacrifice to
the glory of God? Put yourself upon the altar of God today as
a living sacrifice. Ask Him to give you the strength to be 100%
disciplined and devoted to His cause and glory.

Spiritual concerns and prayer requests..

....

....

....

....

....

Today I will…...

....

"FOR EVEN HEREUNTO WERE YE CALLED: BECAUSE CHRIST ALSO SUFFERED FOR US, LEAVING US AN EXAMPLE, THAT YE SHOULD FOLLOW HIS STEPS." 1 Peter 2:21

Christ suffered for us. *But, we don't want to suffer for Him.* We're going to suffer anyway—whether we are saved or lost. Hmmm?

When you submit to Jesus Christ and obey the Word of God, He is going to arch a rainbow of hope over your suffering. He is going to write Romans 8:28 over what you are going through. You will know that your current trial is for your good.

Surrender and submission to God is the only way to receive His grace and power over your life. Joy, peace, and worry-free days are ahead for the one who lays his life down for the glory of God. Suffering will come, but joy will follow.

What does it mean that Christ suffered for you? Read Isaiah 53 to get a prophetic glimpse of what He actually suffered on your behalf. How is your life going to be different today because of His sacrifice?

Spiritual concerns and prayer requests...

....

....

....

....

....

....

Today I will..

....

APRIL 20

"FOR IF YE LIVE AFTER THE FLESH, YE SHALL DIE: BUT IF YE THROUGH THE SPIRIT DO MORTIFY THE DEEDS OF THE BODY, YE SHALL LIVE." Romans 8:13

Preachers are fond of saying, "Get right with God. You may die!" It is far better to say, "Get right with God. You may live!"

The greatest joy in life is living for Jesus. Why waste more time? There is a life to live. Friend, the best thing you can say about a life lived without Christ is that it is a wasted life.

Billy Sunday, an early 20th Century revival preacher, said that a deathbed repentance is "burning the candle of life for the devil, and then blowing the smoke in God's face." If you are not saved, it's not too late for you to be saved. If you want to be saved—wherever you are, whoever you are, whatever you've done, Jesus wants to save you. Repent and believe and you will be saved.

If you are not sure whether you are saved or not, please turn to the "Closing Plea" at the back of this book or visit www.lwf.org and find more on assurance when you click on "Do you know Jesus?"

*S*piritual concerns and prayer requests...
....
....
....
....
....
....
....

Today I will... ....
....

"I MUST WORK THE WORKS OF HIM THAT SENT ME, WHILE IT IS DAY: THE NIGHT COMETH, WHEN NO MAN CAN WORK." John 9:4

Robert Moffett, a great missionary statesman said, "We shall have all eternity in which to celebrate our victories, but only one short hour before the sun sets in which to win them."

Life's setting sun is sinking low. There are only a limited number of days in which to tell others about Jesus Christ. Are you going to spend your days investing in the things of this world, or putting up treasures in heaven? *When?*

Are you going to start sowing seeds of salvation or are you going to plant happiness in this life alone? *When?* Are you going to do something nice for your wife? *When?* Are you going to write your father? *When?*

❦

Make a promise to yourself right now that you will not put off until tomorrow what you should be doing today.

Spiritual concerns and prayer requests...

....

....

....

....

....

....

Today I will…..

....

APRIL 22

"BRETHREN, I COUNT NOT MYSELF TO HAVE APPREHENDED: BUT
THIS ONE THING I DO, FORGETTING THOSE THINGS WHICH ARE
BEHIND, AND REACHING FORTH UNTO THOSE THINGS WHICH ARE
BEFORE, I PRESS TOWARD THE MARK FOR THE PRIZE OF THE HIGH
CALLING OF GOD IN CHRIST JESUS." Philippians 3:13-14

There are two days that can steal your joy and the fulfillment of today. One is *tomorrow* and the other is *yesterday*. Both are days in which we as Christians should refuse to live.

So many of us have never learned how to separate ourselves from yesterday. We are still dragging it around with us and it is stealing our joy. Paul could have lived there in the realm of guilt, but he refused.

Maybe you, like Paul and countless others, have committed some horrible sins. But friend, what God has called clean, let no man call unclean. If you have confessed that sin and given it to God, it is buried in the depths of God's forgetfulness.

Don't let it contaminate your day. Learn to live in the present.

If you are experiencing guilt over unconfessed sin, then confess and repent. If you are experiencing guilt over confessed sin, refuse that guilt. The Holy Spirit convicts, He does not condemn. Read Romans 8:1 and 1 John 1:19.

Spiritual concerns and prayer requests...

....

....

....

....

....

....

Today I will..

....

APRIL 23

"THERE IS NEITHER JEW NOR GREEK, THERE IS NEITHER BOND NOR FREE, THERE IS NEITHER MALE NOR FEMALE: FOR YE ARE ALL ONE IN CHRIST JESUS." Galatians 3:28

If we are going to survive in the tough times of our lives, we must learn to submit. That's right. Now, I know that sounds like an oxymoron, but let me explain.

The Word of God teaches us that no one is inferior to anyone else. We are one in Jesus Christ. Submission is something we do to one another "in the fear of God" (Ephesians 5:21). Through submission comes power and victory.

Do you want to know a good definition of submission? Here it is: Submission is one equal willingly placing himself under another equal that God may therefore be glorified.

We are never more like Jesus than when we submit. And never more like the devil than when we rebel.

Are you struggling with someone right now? Could the answer be in your submission? Ask God and break through to the abundant life today.

Spiritual concerns and prayer requests...

....

....

....

....

....

....

Today I will…...

....

APRIL 24

"BE SOBER, BE VIGILANT; BECAUSE YOUR ADVERSARY THE DEVIL, AS A ROARING LION, WALKETH ABOUT, SEEKING WHOM HE MAY DEVOUR." 1 Peter 5:8

Your adversary, the devil, is prowling about like a roaring lion. Don't underestimate his power.

Satan is an enemy you need to respect like an electrician who has respect for wires that carry deadly voltage. He knows where the insulation is and he knows how to handle electricity. If an electrician loses his respect for this power, he is going to be in serious trouble.

Everything may be going great for you right now. You've got money in the bank, a good job, good health. You're dancing through the forest and picking wildflowers. But, behind a bush is a lion so deadly that he can pounce on you and swallow you whole. You've got to be vigilant.

❧❦❧

Read 1 Corinthians 10:12. Is there any unguarded area in your life where you are feeling self-confident? Submit to God. Die to self. Be on your guard.

Spiritual concerns and prayer requests...
....
....
....
....
....
....

Today I will..
....

APRIL 25

"For whom He did foreknow, He also did predestinate to be conformed to the image of His Son, that He might be the firstborn among many brethren." Romans 8:29

God's wisdom is supreme. Now, we know *after* the fact, but God knows *before* the fact. The word "foreknow" is from the Greek word *proginosko*.

God's foreknowledge can be illustrated in a limited way like the viewing of a parade. If you watch a parade from the ground level, you will see the floats as they come past one at a time. But suppose you could go up in a 30-story building and look down upon the parade? Then, you would not only see the float directly in front, but quite possibly the first and last float. You now have a different vantage point.

We see events as they come by one at a time. But, God dwells in eternity. He sees everything. He sees the beginning, the end, and everything in between. But, more than that He has *foreknowledge* of everything that happens.

❦❦❦

Knowing can also imply that there is a relationship, as we discover when we examine the word "know" in marital relationships in the Old Testament (see Genesis 4:1, 17, 25; 19:8; 24:16). Read these for further study on what "foreknowledge" means: Acts 2:23; Romans 11:2; 1 Peter 1:20.

Spiritual concerns and prayer requests ....

....

....

....

....

....

Today I will... ....

....

APRIL 26

"Blessed is the man to whom the Lord will not impute sin." Romans 4:8

God has imputed His righteousness to every believer. That means instead of your sin being on *your* account, it is *His righteousness* on your account.

Not only has He forgiven you and covered your sins, but He has given you His righteousness. You will fail, but God will not impute that to you. If God were to impute sin to you, then when you fail you would be lost again.

How much sin would it take to make you lost? Just one half of one sin. You see, you are not going to heaven because you are perfect. No one is perfect. But, we have received Christ as our righteousness. And in His eyes, we are perfect.

❦

Read Isaiah 29:15. Have you tried to hide something from God—thinking He won't find out? Read Psalm 32. God desires a relationship with you, but your sin will keep you separated from Him until you confess and repent.

Spiritual concerns and prayer requests ....
....
....
....
....
....
....

Today I will... ....
....

APRIL 27

"BUT GOD HATH CHOSEN THE FOOLISH THINGS OF THE WORLD TO CONFOUND THE WISE; AND GOD HATH CHOSEN THE WEAK THINGS OF THE WORLD TO CONFOUND THE THINGS WHICH ARE MIGHTY; AND BASE THINGS OF THE WORLD, AND THINGS WHICH ARE DESPISED, HATH GOD CHOSEN, YEA, AND THINGS WHICH ARE NOT, TO BRING TO NOUGHT THINGS THAT ARE: THAT NO FLESH SHOULD GLORY IN HIS PRESENCE." 1 Corinthians 1:27-29

What wisdom is there in dying on a cross? The Greeks couldn't understand it, and yet that is the wisdom of God. God is so wise that the person with the highest IQ cannot figure Him out.

If you could come to God with your intellect, then God is not fair because all of the smart people would have a head start and the rest of us would be left standing in the shadows. Your spirituality would be based upon your intellect.

I'm so glad God has "hid these things from the wise and prudent, and hast revealed them unto babes" (Matthew 11:25). God is not so high that few can figure Him out; it is that God has placed Himself at such a level few of us will get down low enough to see God revealing Himself to us.

⟨❈⟩

Praise God for choosing you! Praise God for His wisdom!

Spiritual concerns and prayer requests..

....

....

....

....

Today I will… ....

....

APRIL 28

"HE THAT BELIEVETH ON THE SON HATH EVERLASTING LIFE: AND HE THAT BELIEVETH NOT THE SON SHALL NOT SEE LIFE; BUT THE WRATH OF GOD ABIDETH ON HIM." John 3:36

There was a preacher who kept a painting in his study of a shipwreck. There were sailors in lifeboats reaching out their hands to people floating on debris from the ship. A little boy looked at the painting and asked, "Are the ones in the lifeboats trying to save those people or are they just shaking hands?"

I wonder about us. It is all right to have friends; in fact, I encourage you to do that. But, are you doing more than just socializing? Wouldn't it be a shame if all you did was shake the hands of those around you, when you could be serving and showing them the way to God through Jesus Christ?

We don't pray, live, and witness as if people are dying and going to hell or heaven every day around us. May God have mercy on us. The need of the hour is for men and women to have a servant's heart.

Ask God to give you courage and the opportunity to share your faith with friends with whom you have only socialized.

Spiritual concerns and prayer requests...

....

....

....

....

....

Today I will...

....

"I CALL HEAVEN AND EARTH TO RECORD THIS DAY AGAINST YOU, THAT I HAVE SET BEFORE YOU LIFE AND DEATH, BLESSING AND CURSING: THEREFORE CHOOSE LIFE, THAT BOTH THOU AND THY SEED MAY LIVE." Deuteronomy 30:19

Years ago, I was witnessing to a young lady in Florida. I asked her if she had received Jesus as her Lord and Savior. She became teary-eyed and said, "I just don't seem...no...I can't do it today."

I asked her, "Don't you realize that if you don't receive Him, you're going to deny Him?" She said, "Oh, I wouldn't deny Him for anything." I said, "But there's no middle ground." And yet she refused.

I said, "Before you go, would you shake hands with me?" And she said, "Well, certainly." And so I said, "If you'll take Christ as your Savior, take my right hand. If you'll take hell and refuse Christ, take my left hand." She refused to take either of my hands.

Every person has a choice. There is no neutral ground.

You are either crowning Jesus as Lord of your life or you are not. Which is it my friend? Crown Him with many crowns! And if that moves you to praise Him, then praise Him in song with the hymn, "Crown Him With Many Crowns" by Matthew Bridges.

Spiritual concerns and prayer requests..

....

....

....

....

....

Today I will... ....

....

APRIL 30

"HEREBY PERCEIVE WE THE LOVE OF GOD, BECAUSE HE LAID DOWN HIS LIFE FOR US: AND WE OUGHT TO LAY DOWN OUR LIVES FOR THE BRETHREN." 1 John 3:16

The rich man asked Jesus, "Good Master, what shall I do that I may inherit eternal life?" (Mark 10:17). Then Jesus asked him if he had kept the law. He said yes. In love Jesus responded, "One thing thou lackest: go thy way, sell whatsoever thou hast, and give to the poor, and thou shalt have treasure in heaven: and come, take up the cross, and follow Me" (Mark 10:21b).

But, the rich man was "sad at that saying, and went away grieved: for he had great possessions" (Mark 10:22). Jesus let him go. Jesus didn't run after him.

And there's another important thing you should notice: Jesus didn't lower His standards.

Ask God to show you if there is anything or anyone you love more than Him. You must willingly lay it down.

Spiritual concerns and prayer requests...

....

....

....

....

....

....

Today I will...

....

"O TASTE AND SEE THAT THE LORD IS GOOD: BLESSED IS THE MAN THAT TRUSTETH IN HIM." Psalm 34:8

I am filled with joy, but I don't take any credit for it. It is Jesus who gives me joy and satisfaction. I couldn't have found it had I been searching for it. But by finding, knowing, and growing in Christ, He has filled me with an overflowing joy.

Do you know what the devil will tell you? That holiness and happiness don't go together. He will tell you that if you make up your mind to live a holy life, then you will not have any fun.

Friend, the devil is a liar. You'll never know satisfaction and joy until you find it in the right place. You will never enjoy the good things of life until you know Jesus. Oh, how sweet to know the Lord Jesus Christ.

A sk yourself if the hunger of your heart is met in Christ. If it is not, ask God to turn your heart hunger back to Him.

Spiritual concerns and prayer requests..

....

....

....

....

....

....

Today I will... ....

....

MAY 2

"FOR THE MOUNTAINS SHALL DEPART, AND THE HILLS BE
REMOVED; BUT MY KINDNESS SHALL NOT DEPART FROM THEE,
NEITHER SHALL THE COVENANT OF MY PEACE BE REMOVED, SAITH
THE LORD THAT HATH MERCY ON THEE." Isaiah 54:10

Sometimes the grandest revelations come through confrontation.
Why did God bring the Israelites to the Red Sea? That
they might have a confrontation with Him and discover His
greatness and deliverance.

Many times the things we think are tragedies and problems are
God's way of drawing us to Himself. God shuts this door. God shuts
that door. It seems that there is no way out.

But, we must cling to the fact that God makes Himself known to
us in the storm and He plants His footsteps in the sea.

❦

Think of three things you can do today to bring the light of God's
Son to someone who may be struggling with his or her faith.
Then go do it!

Spiritual concerns and prayer requests...

....

....

....

....

....

....

Today I will..

....

"AND YE SHALL BE HATED OF ALL MEN FOR MY NAME'S SAKE: BUT HE THAT ENDURETH TO THE END SHALL BE SAVED." Matthew 10:22

Have you ever read God's hall of fame in Hebrews 11? These men and women of faith did miraculous things. "Who through faith subdued kingdoms." Hallelujah! "Wrought righteousness." Praise the Lord! "Obtained promises." Amen! "Stopped the mouths of lions." Glory! And how did they do it? Faith.

"And others [men and women of faith] had trial of cruel mockings and scourgings, yea, moreover of bonds and imprisonment: They were stoned, they were sawn asunder…" (Hebrews 11:36-37). "And these all, having obtained a good report through faith, received not the promise" (Hebrews 11:39). Some had faith to escape; others had faith to endure.

If it is God's will for you, faith to endure may be the kind of faith God wants you to have. Will God be enough if He lets you go into the fiery furnace?

Read Hebrews 11 and pray how God can use you as a hero of faith.

Spiritual concerns and prayer requests...
....
....
....
....
....
....
....

Today I will… ....
....

MAY 4

"BUT YE ARE A CHOSEN GENERATION, A ROYAL PRIESTHOOD, AN HOLY NATION, A PECULIAR PEOPLE; THAT YE SHOULD SHOW FORTH THE PRAISES OF HIM WHO HATH CALLED YOU OUT OF DARKNESS INTO HIS MARVELOUS LIGHT." 1 Peter 2:9

Christians are a kingdom of priests, so in order to understand what that means, let's look at what someone had to do to become a priest in the Old Testament.

The first thing the priest did was bathe from head to toe. This symbolized that he was saved (see Titus 3:5). When we are saved, we are bathed from head to toe in Christ's cleansing blood.

After his bath, the priest received a linen garment, which symbolized the righteousness that is provided by our Lord.

Then he was anointed with oil, which is symbolic of the Holy Spirit. How encouraging to discover God's Word flowing from the Old Testament to the New to describe such essential details of the believer.

❦❦❦❦

You are chosen to serve and share. Share the message of salvation with someone by telling them the good news of Christ or inviting them via email to visit www.lwf.org. They may be eternally grateful!

Spiritual concerns and prayer requests...

....

....

....

....

....

....

Today I will...

....

"THOU HAST ALSO GIVEN ME THE SHIELD OF THY SALVATION: AND THY RIGHT HAND HATH HOLDEN ME UP, AND THY GENTLENESS HATH MADE ME GREAT." Psalm 18:35

Do you know what our churches could use a little bit more of? Courtesy among the brethren—love in the little things, love that says "please" and "thank you," love that steps back and gives the other person first place.

It never ceases to amaze me how people so quickly lose their religion when they leave church on Sunday morning. They go to their cars in the parking lot, then cut people off in traffic. And don't ever take someone's "regular" seat in church. You're seen as stealing their "rightful" place in the worship service!

May God cleanse our churches of self-righteousness and pride. May He purify us from anything that seeks to elevate self over others.

※◆※

Reread the Scripture for today and answer these questions: Who has saved you? Who holds you up? Who has made you great? Finish out today's devotion by reading and meditating upon Micah 6:8.

Spiritual concerns and prayer requests ....

....

....

....

....

....

....

Today I will... ....

....

MAY 6

"IF WE CONFESS OUR SINS, HE IS FAITHFUL AND JUST TO FORGIVE US OUR SINS, AND TO CLEANSE US FROM ALL UNRIGHTEOUSNESS."
1 John 1:9

What does it mean to "confess your sins"? It doesn't mean to simply admit your sin. There are a lot of people who have admitted their sins, but have never confessed their sins.

I have spoken to people many times and asked them, "Do you know that you're a sinner?" And they respond, "Yes, I know. We have all sinned." But, those people aren't confessing; all they are doing is admitting.

There is a difference. The word "confess" is a compilation of two words "con" and "fess," which means "to agree with." To confess your sins is to say with God what God says about it.

❦❦❦

Read Proverbs 28:13. Ask God to reveal your sin. Confess, repent, and receive His forgiveness.

Spiritual concerns and prayer requests...

....

....

....

....

....

Today I will...

....

"FOR UNTO EVERY ONE THAT HATH SHALL BE GIVEN, AND HE SHALL HAVE ABUNDANCE: BUT FROM HIM THAT HATH NOT SHALL BE TAKEN AWAY EVEN THAT WHICH HE HATH." Matthew 25:29

In Matthew 25, we read the parable of the talents. When the master who distributed the talents came to see the stewardship of those talents, one man had taken his and hid it in the ground.

You may have a buried talent, but you have been covered up with the sinister minister of fear who keeps you from achieving your dreams. You say, "But what if I fail?" You can be so afraid of making a mistake that your entire life will be a mistake.

The fear of failure keeps so many from competing that they never even get in the race. They just lose by default! Sir Walter Scott was called a "dunce" by his teachers. Napoleon Bonaparte was next to last in his military class. Walt Disney was fired as a cartoonist because the newspaper said he couldn't draw!

It's not bad to fail. We all will fail. But, may God deliver you from the spirit of failure, which is a spirit of fear.

❦

Read and meditate upon Psalm 56 and 57.

Spiritual concerns and prayer requests ....
....
....
....
....
....
....

Today I will... ....
....

MAY 8

"YE THAT LOVE THE LORD, HATE EVIL: HE PRESERVETH THE
SOULS OF HIS SAINTS; HE DELIVERETH THEM OUT OF THE HAND
OF THE WICKED." Psalm 97:10

This may come as a surprise to you, but just because you are a
Christian doesn't mean you are supposed to love everything.
Now, we hear that Christians are to be a people of love, and
that is true.

But, did you know that if you're a Christian, not only must you
learn to love, but you also must learn to hate? If you love God, then
you are to hate what God hates. It is true in every realm.

If you love flowers, you hate weeds. If you love health, you hate
germs. If you love God, you hate evil. It is just that plain.

Romans 12:9b tells us in even stronger terms to "abhor that which
is evil." A hypocrite, which is something none of us want to be, is
someone who says he loves God, but then he doesn't hate sin. Don't
tell others you love God, if you don't hate that which nailed His Son
on the cross.

Ask God to break your heart with the things that break His
heart. Ask God to teach you to hate sin, yet love the sinner.

Spiritual concerns and prayer requests...
....
....
....
....
....
....

Today I will...
....

"EXAMINE ME, O LORD, AND PROVE ME; TRY MY REINS AND MY HEART. FOR THY LOVINGKINDNESS IS BEFORE MINE EYES: AND I HAVE WALKED IN THY TRUTH." Psalm 26:2-3

How do automobile manufacturers make sure their vehicles are safe for people to drive? They put their vehicles onto a proving ground. They drive it hundreds of miles over rough roads and through water and heat—screeching, turning, twisting, hitting the brakes, accelerating to top speeds. They want to see if that automobile will stand the test.

It is the same with our spiritual lives. God gives the test first, and the lesson afterwards. Read throughout Scripture and you will find this to be true. Joseph was tested. David was tested. Moses was tested. Peter was tested.

When God gets ready to prove you, He is not going to test you in the good times because that is not a test. Anybody can serve God in the sunshine. The test is not how you behave when there is victory all around; the test is how you behave when God brings you to the wilderness. He wants to know what is in your heart. Are you fully devoted to God?

Pray Psalm 26:2-3 and thank God for what you will learn in the wildernesses of your life.

Spiritual concerns and prayer requests..

....

....

....

....

....

Today I will…..

....

MAY 10

"FOR I AM THE LORD THAT BRINGETH YOU UP OUT OF THE LAND OF EGYPT, TO BE YOUR GOD: YE SHALL THEREFORE BE HOLY, FOR I AM HOLY." Leviticus 11:45

Are you a parent? Then, you have probably told your children to do something and they asked why. And what did you say? "Because I told you. Period."

I believe there are some times when parents want their children to do things and they need to explain their rationale. It is important to teach principles for living instead of mere commands and rules.

But, sometimes children are not able to understand, so the answer "because I told you" is one that simply communicates parental authority to a child.

Leviticus is a book full of laws that no one understood logically. And yet did God stop to explain the law? No. He simply said, "I am the Lord, your God." He is above our need for explanations and deserving of our full obedience.

Meditate upon the holiness of God by reading Psalm 47 and Psalm 111.

Spiritual concerns and prayer requests...
....
....
....
....
....
....

Today I will... ....
....

"AND THEN SHALL THEY SEE THE SON OF MAN COMING IN THE CLOUDS WITH GREAT POWER AND GLORY." Mark 13:26

When we come to a place where we don't understand what is happening...when everything seems to be caving in, there is Jesus. We always have the forgiveness of the cross, the victory of the empty tomb, and the hope of Christ's imminent return.

When circumstances occur like going to the doctor and learning of a life-threatening illness. Or when a couple is told they are are infertile and cannot bear a child. When we have to declare bankruptcy. When we are laid off work. When we read a note that our spouse has left. When a loved one dies because of a terrorist act. We have a Savior...and we have a choice to believe or not to believe!

At that time we can begin to murmur, criticize, grumble, or despair. Or we can yield to the Savior and hear Him say, "My child, no matter what is happening, this is how much I love you. Look to the cross. Look to the empty tomb. Look for Me. I'm coming again."

Get in a position of humility. If you can, drop to your knees. If you cannot, bow your head and close your eyes. Imagine the cross of Christ. Meditate upon the shame Christ experienced, the pain He endured, and the victory He secured in His death just for you.

Spiritual concerns and prayer requests

Today I will...

MAY 12

"THEREFORE TO HIM THAT KNOWETH TO DO GOOD, AND DOETH IT
NOT, TO HIM IT IS SIN." James 4:17

Procrastination. Just seeing the word, makes me want to put off
saying anything else. That's because I find myself under
conviction in that area. And God has taught me that
procrastination is a form of disobedience.

When God tells us to do something and we don't do it, we can
label our actions with all kinds of fancy words, but the bottom line is
that it is sin.

The days are passing and time cannot be stopped. You can't call a
"time out" in life. And time cannot be stored like money in the bank.
Really, the only thing you can do with time is use it or lose it.
Someone has said, "Lost: One golden hour, studded with sixty
diamond minutes. No reward offered, for it is lost forever." Redeem
the time.

Have you been procrastinating about doing something? Maybe
you are putting off telling someone about Christ out of fear they
will reject you. Maybe you are delaying asking someone to forgive you
because you are feeling ashamed. Friend, it's time.

Spiritual concerns and prayer requests..

....

....

....

....

....

....

Today I will…..

....

"THE LIGHT OF THE BODY IS THE EYE: THEREFORE WHEN THINE
EYE IS SINGLE, THY WHOLE BODY ALSO IS FULL OF LIGHT; BUT
WHEN THINE EYE IS EVIL, THY BODY ALSO IS FULL OF DARKNESS."
Luke 11:34

Joshua 14 tells us something very interesting about a man named
Caleb. Three times, the Holy Spirit tells us that Caleb
"wholly followed the Lord God" (verses 8, 9, and 14). Every
ounce of Caleb was given to the Lord.

This is the kind of heart you and I should have if we call
ourselves Christians. The devil is going to intimidate a fainthearted
man. And, there's only one way to stand against the devil and that is
to give everything to Jesus Christ.

Indeed, God does not accept half-hearted religion. It would be
better for you to say there is no God, than for you to say He doesn't
mean that much to you; or He doesn't make a difference in your life;
or He doesn't stir your heart to love Him.

※※※

Read Revelation 3:14-18. Can you make application in your life
from this admonition to the church in Laodicea?

Spiritual concerns and prayer requests...

....

....

....

....

....

....

Today I will... ....

....

MAY 14

"PRAY WITHOUT CEASING." 1 Thessalonians 5:17

Did you know it's possible to pray during your daily routine? You are to pray when you are adding up prices in the grocery store line. You are to pray when you are changing a tire. You are to pray when you are singing a song. You are to pray when you are teaching a little one how to read. You are to pray when you are working at your desk.

We are commanded to pray all the time, but how do we do this? Think of a mother who has a child who is ill with a fever. Finally, the fever breaks and the mother and child settle down for some much-needed sleep. Not a noise from the television, from the street, or from the phone could awaken that mother.

But one whimper from her child and she's awake, right? That's because even when she is asleep, she is in tune with that child—just as we are to be with God...constantly communing and attuned to His voice.

※◆※

Make a conscious endeavor to make it through your day in a state of watchful, unending prayer.

Spiritual concerns and prayer requests...

....

....

....

....

....

Today I will...

....

"WHO IS AMONG YOU THAT FEARETH THE LORD, THAT OBEYETH THE VOICE OF HIS SERVANT, THAT WALKETH IN DARKNESS, AND HATH NO LIGHT? LET HIM TRUST IN THE NAME OF THE LORD, AND STAY UPON HIS GOD." Isaiah 50:10

We can endure almost anything if we know why it is happening. Wouldn't you agree? But, we don't always get the luxury of knowing why things happen.

You can't be a pastor as long as I have been without having heartbroken questions asked of you. *Why did my baby die? Why did I lose my business? Why am I so sick?* Job felt this way. He said, "I deserve an answer as to why this is happening to me! The bottom has fallen out of my life. And I don't know why."

Have you ever been plunged into darkness? Don't get the idea that if you're right with God, you'll have all the answers. Never doubt in the dark, what God has shown you in the light.

Are you in the middle of heartbreak? Write out your feelings to the Lord. Pour out your heart to Him. Now, fold up that piece of paper and on the outside write these words, "I will trust God to help me. I will keep my focus upon Him." Keep that piece of paper and every time you think about your hurt, repeat this promise to the Lord.

Spiritual concerns and prayer requests..

....

....

....

....

....

....

Today I will… ....

....

MAY 16

"For thou shalt be His witness unto all men of what thou hast seen and heard." Acts 22:15

What is more important in your life today? Seeing your daytime soap opera or asking an unsaved neighbor over for a chance to love them to Jesus? Joining your buddies in a round of golf, or visiting your unsaved father? Going shopping with your friends, or taking time to read the Bible to a lost person in a nursing home?

Friend, your time is running out. And you will not be witnessing in heaven. This is your earthly duty and privilege now. None of us knows how many hours we have left.

We must seize the golden opportunities that God daily gives us to witness. A line from "The Battle Hymn Of The Republic" is our challenge: "Oh, be swift, my soul to answer Him! Be jubilant, my feet! Our God is marching on."

⋘⋙

Imagine today is your last day on earth. Now, live as if it is!

Spiritual concerns and prayer requests..
....
....
....
....
....
....
....

Today I will...

....

"BE CAREFUL FOR NOTHING; BUT IN EVERY THING BY PRAYER AND SUPPLICATION WITH THANKSGIVING LET YOUR REQUESTS BE MADE KNOWN UNTO GOD." Philippians 4:6

Do you ever worry? Don't look around and point your finger at someone else. Do you ever worry—even the least little bit?

And yet the Bible so clearly tells us not to worry about anything, but to pray about everything. There are really only two classes of things for which we ought not to worry—those things we cannot do anything about and the things we can do something about.

The best thing you can say about worry is that it is useless. The worst thing you can say about it is that it dishonors God. Worry is the opposite of faith.

❧❧❧

Read Hebrews 11:6. Turn this verse into a prayerful commitment to God.

Spiritual concerns and prayer requests..

....

....

....

....

....

Today I will…..

....

MAY 18

"BEHOLD, HOW GOOD AND HOW PLEASANT IT IS FOR BRETHREN TO DWELL TOGETHER IN UNITY!" Psalm 133:1

Do you know what God wants from you today? Reconciliation. That's far more important than singing in the choir, preaching a sermon, serving in the nursery, or giving an offering.

When we learn this, God is going to bring great revival to our churches. Revival always begins when people begin to confess their faults to one another, pray for one another, and forgive one another.

Revival isn't raising the roof with a lot of emotion. It is getting the walls down. It is not just saying, "I am going to get right with God." It is saying, "I want to get right with my brothers and sisters." When we are reconciled, revival will come.

And rejoicing will surely follow. And not any kind of rejoicing, there will be Holy Spirit joy when you know there is nothing between your soul and the Savior and nothing between your soul and a brother! Joy unspeakable!

Read Matthew 5:23-26. Have you had a falling out with a sibling and are no longer speaking? Are you and your spouse estranged? Have you broken ties with a friend? Be reconciled today.

Spiritual concerns and prayer requests..
....
....
....
....
....
....

Today I will...
....

MAY 19

"BUT WHOSO LOOKETH INTO THE PERFECT LAW OF LIBERTY, AND
CONTINUETH THEREIN, HE BEING NOT A FORGETFUL HEARER, BUT
A DOER OF THE WORK, THIS MAN SHALL BE BLESSED IN HIS DEED."
James 1:25

James 1:23-24 paints a picture of a man in a hurry. He has a lot
on his mind. He takes a casual glance at himself ("he is like
unto a man beholding his natural face in a glass:" James 1:23b)
and rushes on. If the Bible is like a mirror, then this man is simply
getting a glimpse into the Word and not really applying it to his life.

Most Christians I know today are this kind of Bible student.
They are like a gnat bouncing here and there instead of being like a
bee and diving in and staying long enough to extract the sweetness.

Contrastingly, the man in verse 25 gazes into the Word. This is
someone who delights in God's Word, who applies God's Word,
who cherishes God's Word.

Are you like that? Or do you take a passing glance at God's
Word and move on to the next thing on your TO DO list?
How do you know? Spend one hour in God's Word not once, but
twice this week. That will be a great start.

Spiritual concerns and prayer requests

Today I will…

MAY 20

"I AM ALPHA AND OMEGA, THE BEGINNING AND THE ENDING, SAITH THE LORD, WHICH IS, AND WHICH WAS, AND WHICH IS TO COME, THE ALMIGHTY." Revelation 1:8

A boy was reading a murder mystery one day and he became anxious about whether the heroine was going to live. To alleviate his anxiety, he read the last chapter and discovered that she survived.

Afterwards, when he read the villain was planning a dastardly plan, he chuckled to himself and thought, *If you knew what I know, you wouldn't be so haughty.*

Christians know the last chapter and that helps us cope with the present. Indeed, the glories of the future can help dilute the sorrows of the present. The devil's gloom is pronounced in Genesis, and executed in Revelation.

D o you know someone who could use this good news today? Take time to let them know the victory is won!

Spiritual concerns and prayer requests...

....

....

....

....

....

Today I will..

....

"AND LET US CONSIDER ONE ANOTHER TO PROVOKE UNTO LOVE AND TO GOOD WORKS." Hebrews 10:24

One area where Christians can shed the light of Christ is in our school system. We have a generation who has no standards of right and wrong—everything is relative. In our schools our children are being taught they have descended from animals. Is it any wonder many have begun to act like animals?

What can you and I do? We must "love" our way back in! We must get involved by becoming active in our schools. Become members of the PTA or encourage teachers and tell them we are praying for them.

We must go to school board meetings and find out about policies and curricula. We must seek to be holy people in a godless world. And if we don't, we are contributing to the demise of the next generation.

❧❧❧

Are you a parent of a school-age child? Get involved in your child's school. Are you a grandparent? Ask God to send you to a teacher so you can be an encouragement to him or her through prayer and ministry. Are you a single person? Learn about becoming a tutor or mentor in a nearby school.

Spiritual concerns and prayer requests..

....

....

....

....

....

....

Today I will…..

....

MAY 22

"BEING CONFIDENT OF THIS VERY THING, THAT HE WHICH HATH BEGUN A GOOD WORK IN YOU WILL PERFORM IT UNTIL THE DAY OF JESUS CHRIST." Philippians 1:6

In Scotland some men were sitting around drinking tea and swapping fishing stories. One man, with a flamboyant gesture of his hand, knocked the other man's hand and his tea splattered on the white plastered wall creating an ugly brown stain.

He was horrified, but the man said, "Never mind." And he took out his crayons and started to sketch around that stain. Suddenly there emerged a royal stag with his antlers spread. The artist was Sir Edwin Lancier—England's foremost painter of animals.

He was able to take that old stain and make something beautiful out of it. Jesus Christ is that kind of an artist. He can take a life that has been stained and by His transforming power He can make something beautiful out of it.

Have you or someone you know endured a tragic childhood and are now saved? Encourage yourself and someone else with today's Scripture.

Spiritual concerns and prayer requests...
....
....
....
....
....
....

Today I will…..
....

MAY 23

"AND THOU SHALT TEACH THEM DILIGENTLY UNTO THY CHILDREN, AND SHALT TALK OF THEM WHEN THOU SITTEST IN THINE HOUSE, AND WHEN THOU WALKEST BY THE WAY, AND WHEN THOU LIEST DOWN, AND WHEN THOU RISEST UP." Deuteronomy 6:7

Have you ever tried to take a tasty bone away from a dog? It's a good way to get bitten! But what if you put a steak down on the ground? The dog will drop the bone to get the steak.

This is the mistake so many parents are making today. They spend all of their time telling their children, "Don't do this. Don't do that. That's wrong." By such behavior, these parents are failing an entire generation.

Many times, children are never shown the riches of Jesus Christ. Children must be shown that what they have in the Lord Jesus Christ is so much better than what this world has to offer.

Are you a parent or grandparent? Think about the ways you negatively discipline your kids. Ask God to show you positive ways to reward and teach them and then put it into practice.

Spiritual concerns and prayer requests...

....

....

....

....

....

....

Today I will... ....

....

MAY 24

"CREATE IN ME A CLEAN HEART, O GOD; AND RENEW A RIGHT SPIRIT WITHIN ME. CAST ME NOT AWAY FROM THY PRESENCE; AND TAKE NOT THY HOLY SPIRIT FROM ME. RESTORE UNTO ME THE JOY OF THY SALVATION; AND UPHOLD ME WITH THY FREE SPIRIT."
Psalm 51:10-12

So many people have the idea that being a Christian is like taking foul-tasting medicine—it tastes awful, but you know you'll feel better one day.

Or they're like the young man who prayed at a prayer meeting with few in attendance: "Oh God, be with us now, and help us while the rest of the people are out there having a good time."

Do you ever feel that going to church or having a quiet time is like going to the dentist? Then, you are getting your satisfaction in life outside of a relationship with God.

Be honest...how do you really feel about church attendance and quiet time? Today is a great day to celebrate the joy of your salvation in prayer, in Bible study and in church attendance.

Spiritual concerns and prayer requests...

....

....

....

....

....

....

Today I will...

....

MAY 25

"Do all things without murmurings and disputings: That ye may be blameless and harmless, the sons of God, without rebuke, in the midst of a crooked and perverse nation, among whom ye shine as lights in the world."
Philippians 2:14-15

Do you know the problem with many of us when we obey God?

We murmur about it while we are doing it. And God is taking notes because half-hearted obedience isn't obedience at all. Remember God is looking at the heart, not the deed (see 1 Samuel 16:7).

Do you know why we murmur? Because we have taken our eyes off of Calvary. Jesus didn't murmur on the way to the cross. Oh no. Do you thank God for the pains in life? Or only the gains?

Read Ephesians 5:20. For what should you be giving thanks?

Spiritual concerns and prayer requests ....
....
....
....
....
....
....

Today I will… ....
....

MAY 26

"IF ANY OF YOU LACK WISDOM, LET HIM ASK OF GOD, THAT GIVETH TO ALL MEN LIBERALLY, AND UPBRAIDETH NOT; AND IT SHALL BE GIVEN HIM." James 1:5

Today's Scripture tells us if we lack wisdom, we are to ask God. Let me tell you what it literally means. If you lack wisdom, ask of the "giving" God. Have you thought of God as the "giving" God?

What does it mean to you that God yearns to pour out His blessing upon you? Do you say to yourself, "Oh goodie, goodie, let me see what I can get from God"?

Or does it humble you to know that the Almighty God who created the air you breathe, the ground you walk upon, and the body you are draped in…this God loves you and wants to bless you? I pray it is the latter, for that is the heart of a child of God.

Humble yourself before Almighty God and ask Him to create in you the heart of a child who longs for the Father more than anything else.

Spiritual concerns and prayer requests..
....
....
....
....
....
....

Today I will…..
....

MAY 27

"BUT THE NATURAL MAN RECEIVETH NOT THE THINGS OF THE
SPIRIT OF GOD: FOR THEY ARE FOOLISHNESS UNTO HIM: NEITHER
CAN HE KNOW THEM, BECAUSE THEY ARE SPIRITUALLY
DISCERNED." 1 Corinthians 2:14

God made the mind of man. All true discoveries and all true knowledge in this world come from God. It is God's truth and we do not have to be afraid of it.

But, that doesn't mean we are to casually stroll down the devil's lane of godless philosophies. God's truth doesn't change like philosophies. Malachi 3:6a says, "For I am the LORD, I change not." I don't know whether that means anything to you, but it means an awful lot to me, dear friend.

The same God who loved us enough to put His Son on the cross two thousand years ago still loves us with that same love today. We don't have to worry when we come to God in prayer that we might catch Him in a bad mood. Now, if that doesn't start your motor, you don't have one!

Read Psalm 145. Let it start your motor running in praise to God.

Spiritual concerns and prayer requests..

....

....

....

....

....

....

....

Today I will… ....

....

MAY 28

"GOD IS FAITHFUL, BY WHOM YE WERE CALLED UNTO THE FELLOWSHIP OF HIS SON JESUS CHRIST OUR LORD." 1 Corinthians 1:9

Discipleship is fellowship with Christ, knowing Christ, loving Christ, abiding in Christ. I'm afraid too many have joined the *movement* of Christianity rather than having surrendered to the *Man* of Christianity.

Those in the movement of Christ are doing things for Christ, rather than sitting at the feet of Christ. Now, there's nothing wrong with service and we ought to serve God, but we need to learn that we must minister to Jesus Christ as His disciple before we can minister to others.

Jesus values the time you spend with Him far more than the things you do for Him. Do you know that?

Before you head out this morning or go to bed tonight, make sure that you make a date with Jesus—sit with Him, think upon His love for you, talk to Him.

Spiritual concerns and prayer requests..

....

....

....

....

....

....

Today I will…..

....

"WHO CAN UNDERSTAND HIS ERRORS? CLEANSE THOU ME FROM SECRET FAULTS." Psalm 19:12

I believe in church attendance, but if your relationship with the Lord and with others is suffering, then you need to stay at home and get on your face before God.

Sometimes a businessman will get very prosperous in his business, and at first, it seems a good thing. He tells his wife, "Honey, you know how I couldn't give you much when we got married? Well, now I can."

But soon, the pursuit of a nice home and nice things consumes him. A sadness descends upon his wife and children, and they lament, "Oh Daddy. Oh Husband…what we would give to just have you spend time with us." What tragedy it would be if what you do *for* Jesus keeps you *from* Jesus.

⁂

Stop the cycle today. If you know you're a workaholic, stop it. If you know your walk is far from God, get it right.

Spiritual concerns and prayer requests ....

....

....

....

....

....

....

Today I will… ....

....

MAY 30

"YEA, THOUGH I WALK THROUGH THE VALLEY OF THE SHADOW OF DEATH, I WILL FEAR NO EVIL: FOR THOU ART WITH ME; THY ROD AND THY STAFF THEY COMFORT ME." Psalm 23:4

Psalm 23 is perched between Psalm 22, which tells about the crucifixion of Jesus and Psalm 24, which is a prophecy of the coronation of Jesus. It is beautiful trilogy about the Savior's cross, the Shepherd's crook, and the Sovereign's crown.

Psalm 23 is the valley between the blood-drenched slopes of Mount Calvary and the sunlit peaks of Mount Zion. Thank God for every valley, because there must be a mountain.

If you are in the valley today, remember you wouldn't be there had there not been mountains to cross. There is vision in the valley and hope in the hills.

❦

Read the trilogy—Psalms 22, 23, and 24.

Spiritual concerns and prayer requests...

....

....

....

....

....

....

Today I will... ....

....

"FOR HE LOOKETH TO THE ENDS OF THE EARTH, AND SEETH UNDER THE WHOLE HEAVEN; TO MAKE THE WEIGHT FOR THE WINDS; AND HE WEIGHETH THE WATERS BY MEASURE." Job 28:24-25

There are certain things God is not going to reveal. And that is good news. Who wants to believe in a God they can put in a box and completely understand? Not me.

You can take a bucket down to the ocean and dip out a bucket full of water. Everything in that bucket is ocean, but all of the ocean is not in that bucket. Amen?

And with our bucket-size minds, we are never going to know all there is about God. I'm not. You're not. Nobody is.

※◆◆◆◆◆※

Read Deuteronomy 29:29. What belongs to God? What belongs to you? What are you doing with the things God has given to you?

Spiritual concerns and prayer requests...

....

....

....

....

....

....

Today I will...

....

JUNE 1

"FOR THOUGH I BE FREE FROM ALL MEN, YET HAVE I MADE
MYSELF SERVANT UNTO ALL, THAT I MIGHT GAIN THE MORE."
1 Corinthians 9:19

There are three reasons for obedience. A slave obeys because he has to. An employee obeys because he needs to. But a loving son obeys because he wants to.

So many of us live like slaves, when Jesus has said, "Henceforth I call you not servants; for the servant knoweth not what his lord doeth: but I have called you friends; for all things that I have heard of My Father I have made known unto you" (John 15:15). I don't work for my salvation—that work has been done by my Lord.

But, I will work like any slave for the love of God. What about you?

❦

Are you trying to do something today to earn God's salvation for your soul? Jesus' atonement for your sin was complete on the cross over 2,000 years ago. Today, praise God for sending His Son to die on your behalf.

Spiritual concerns and prayer requests ....

....

....

....

....

....

Today I will... ....

....

JUNE 2

"AND EVERY MAN THAT HATH THIS HOPE IN HIM PURIFIETH HIMSELF, EVEN AS HE IS PURE." 1 John 3:3

Some girls were talking in school one day and one of them said to the other, "I hear our school is having important visitors this week." And the other girl looked at her messy desk and said, "I'll clean it up tomorrow."

But her friend said, "What if they come today?" Her friend said, "You know, I think I'll clean it up right now and keep it clean."

If you knew that Jesus was coming to your house this afternoon, would there be any cleaning you would need to do? Any magazines or videos you would need to trash? Any pictures on the walls you would need to take down? Friend, perhaps it's time you did a little cleaning—and keep it clean.

❦

Have you considered some cleaning mentally and spiritually too? Read Matthew 12:43-45. Rid yourself of those strongholds in your thought life and spiritual life. Recognize the dangers of not keeping it clean!

Spiritual concerns and prayer requests ....

....

....

....

....

....

....

Today I will… ....

....

JUNE 3

"HE THAT FINDETH HIS LIFE SHALL LOSE IT: AND HE THAT LOSETH HIS LIFE FOR MY SAKE SHALL FIND IT." Matthew 10:39

We have nothing that God needs. Think about that. If I were to give God my riches, I couldn't make Him richer. He owns everything.

If I were to give God my wisdom, I wouldn't make Him wiser. He is the all-wise God.

If I were to give God my power, I couldn't make God more powerful. He is omnipotent.

God wants only one thing from His children—our hearts. If we pray to God without giving Him our heart, we are mocking Him. If we preach without giving God our hearts, we are preaching in ignorance.

❦

God is saying to you today, "Give Me your heart." How will you respond? Read Luke 9:23-27. What are you holding onto that keeps you from fully surrendering your life to Him?

Spiritual concerns and prayer requests...

....

....

....

....

....

....

Today I will...

....

JUNE 4

"I WILL WORSHIP TOWARD THY HOLY TEMPLE, AND PRAISE THY NAME FOR THY LOVING-KINDNESS AND FOR THY TRUTH: FOR THOU HAST MAGNIFIED THY WORD ABOVE ALL THY NAME."
Psalm 138:2

There was a man who loved to study the Bible and every time he came to something he didn't understand, he asked his friend Charlie, "What does this verse mean?" One day in his Bible study the Holy Spirit said, "Why don't you ask me? I'm the one who taught Charlie."

Now, I thank God for the Bible scholars who teach God's Word, but the same God who teaches these men and women is the One who wants to teach you.

As you read the Bible, I want you to ask God to help you answer these questions: (1) Is there a lesson to learn? (2) Is there a sin to avoid? (3) Is there a blessing to enjoy? (4) Is there a promise to claim? (5) Is there a new thought to carry with me?

❦❦❦

Read Psalm 138 and answer the questions above related to the truths in that passage.

Spiritual concerns and prayer requests...

....

....

....

....

....

....

Today I will…..

....

JUNE 5

"I WILL MEDITATE IN THY PRECEPTS, AND HAVE RESPECT UNTO THY WAYS." Psalm 119:15

Psalm 119:9 says, "Wherewithal shall a young man cleanse his way? By taking heed thereto according to Thy word." That word "way" really means a "rut" like a chariot wheel would make in the road.

Have you ever heard of a "one track" mind? The devil plants a thought in our minds, and over time it becomes a belief. Before we know it, he has captured a stronghold. Thank God there is a way of deliverance. God's Word will cleanse you (see John 15:3 and Ephesians 5:26).

Picture the Lord Jesus walking through your mind, filling up a wheelbarrow full of filth, and throwing it out. Hallelujah! God's cleansing powers can sweep over your soul today. And fresh winds of the Holy Spirit can blow through the temple of your body and make you clean and pure.

❦

Read 2 Corinthians 10:3-6. What strongholds are there in your life that need God's deliverance? Pray in His name, in His authority, and for His glory that He will deliver you today!

Spiritual concerns and prayer requests...

....

....

....

....

....

....

Today I will..

....

"ALL WE LIKE SHEEP HAVE GONE ASTRAY; WE HAVE TURNED EVERY ONE TO HIS OWN WAY; AND THE LORD HATH LAID ON HIM THE INIQUITY OF US ALL." Isaiah 53:6

Jesus suffered like you will suffer. But He suffered more than that because He took not only your suffering, but He also took upon Himself the suffering of the world. The sins of the world were compressed and distilled upon the Lord Jesus Christ.

Hebrew scholars tell us there is an intensive plural in Isaiah 53 that speaks of the death of Christ. They say it literally means that He died a thousand deaths.

Do you know what that means? It means Jesus being infinite suffered for a finite amount of time; what you being finite would suffer for an infinite amount of time. He suffered upon the cross an eternity of hell for every one of us.

Jesus died to appease the wrath of God so that His justice and holiness will be satisfied. The Bible calls this "propitiation". Write Romans 3:23-24 and 1 John 2:2 in your journal and meditate upon its humbling, life-changing truth throughout the day.

Spiritual concerns and prayer requests...
....
....
....
....
....
....

Today I will…..
....

JUNE 7

"LOOKING UNTO JESUS THE AUTHOR AND FINISHER OF OUR FAITH; WHO FOR THE JOY THAT WAS SET BEFORE HIM ENDURED THE CROSS, DESPISING THE SHAME, AND IS SET DOWN AT THE RIGHT HAND OF THE THRONE OF GOD." Hebrews 12:2

What does it mean that Jesus is the "Author" and "Finisher" of our faith? The Greek word *archegos* means He is the Captain, Leader, or Prince of our faith. The Greek word *teleiotes* means finisher. He is the Completer of our faith.

Jesus paid the price, so that you could be saved. But He also is our example. Do you want to know how to run the race? Keep your eyes on Him.

He is the Savior who not only shows you how to run the race, but then He enters into you through the Holy Spirit, and runs the race through you. Praise God—we are never alone!

Worship God in prayerful praise that not only did He author your faith by giving it to you as an umerited gift, but He also finished your faith by securing your salvation in the atoning blood of His Son! Read Philippians 1:6 for this truth.

Spiritual concerns and prayer requests..

....

....

....

....

....

....

Today I will...

....

JUNE 8

"BUT PUT YE ON THE LORD JESUS CHRIST, AND MAKE NOT
PROVISION FOR THE FLESH, TO FULFILL THE LUSTS THEREOF."
ROMANS 13:14

One of my favorite stories about temptation is about a father who leaves his son at home one Saturday afternoon because his son isn't feeling well. The father tells his son, "Don't go swimming with your buddies." And the son says, "Yes sir!"

The dad returns by way of the swimming hole and notices his son frolicking with the other boys. He stops the car, calls his son over and says, "I told you not to go swimming."

The son responds, "But, I didn't intend to go swimming. I just came down to watch and I fell in." By the time the dad began feeling sorry for his son, he noticed his son had his bathing suit on. And the son said, "I brought my suit along in case I was tempted." Friend, don't make any provision for the flesh.

Ask God to prevent you from being tempted today. Ask Him to give you strength to overcome temptation, should He allow it. And not just when the temptation occurs, but along the way as you make choices.

Spiritual concerns and prayer requests ....

....

....

....

....

....

....

Today I will... ....

....

JUNE 9

"NOW FAITH IS THE SUBSTANCE OF THINGS HOPED FOR, THE
EVIDENCE OF THINGS NOT SEEN." Hebrews 11:1

A nobleman's son became ill, so he sought Jesus to heal him.
When he found Jesus, he asked Him to come see his son.
Instead of going to him, Jesus healed him by His word.
And John 4:50b says, "And the man believed the word that Jesus
had spoken unto him, and he went his way."

Not a wonder, not a sign, not a vision, not angels playing tic-tac-
toe on his ribs, or cold chills going up and down his spine. The man
believed Jesus' Word and went on his way.

Faith sees the invisible, believes the incredible, and receives the
impossible. Doubt sees the obstacles; faith sees the way. Doubt sees
the darkest night; faith sees the day. Doubt dreads to take a step; faith
soars on high. Doubt questions who believes; faith answers I believe.
Life follows faith like night follows day. There is no life without faith.

❈❈❈

A sk God to forgive you for the times when you have doubted
Him, when you have not trusted Him, when you have chosen
to believe something other than what He says. Ask Him to help you
believe.

Spiritual concerns and prayer requests..

....

....

....

....

....

....

Today I will...

....

JUNE 10

"AND I WILL GIVE UNTO THEE THE KEYS OF THE KINGDOM OF HEAVEN: AND WHATSOEVER THOU SHALT BIND ON EARTH SHALL BE BOUND IN HEAVEN: AND WHATSOEVER THOU SHALT LOOSE ON EARTH SHALL BE LOOSED IN HEAVEN." Matthew 16:19

Many of us who are praying for our unsaved friends, family, and neighbors are directing our prayers in the wrong way. We are saying, "Oh God, help them to see." But, they are blind and cannot see.

Second Corinthians 4:3-4 says, "But if our gospel be hid, it is hid to them that are lost: In whom the god of this world hath blinded the minds of them which believe not, lest the light of the glorious gospel of Christ, who is the image of God, should shine unto them."

We must first bind the blinder. We are not in a battle of flesh and blood. We are in a battle with Satan himself and we will never rob his house until we first bind him.

❦

Ask God to set the captives free. Ask Him to cause them to repent and believe upon His Son Jesus Christ. Ask Him to give you a praying spirit and to give you His boldness and passion to witness to the lost.

Spiritual concerns and prayer requests..

....

....

....

....

....

....

Today I will... ....

....

JUNE 11

"AND HE IS THE HEAD OF THE BODY, THE CHURCH: WHO IS THE BEGINNING, THE FIRSTBORN FROM THE DEAD; THAT IN ALL THINGS HE MIGHT HAVE THE PREEMINENCE." Colossians 1:18

When we look at creation, we must realize there are two beginnings.

The first beginning occurred when God created the heavens and the earth. When God created the first beginning, He spoke and just like that—from His fingertips flew this vast, measureless universe. How simple it was for God to create this universe.

The second beginning is when His creature, man, becomes a new creation in Christ (see 2 Corinthians 5:17). When God reconciled us through His Son, it took every drop of His blood. There was no other way to be saved apart from the death of Jesus—*the perfect sacrifice.*

◈◈◈

What does it mean that God has preeminence in your life? If we were to ask your neighbor if God has preeminence in your life, what do you think they would say? Do they even know He is Lord of your life? If not, why not?

Spiritual concerns and prayer requests ....
....
....
....
....
....
....

Today I will... ....

....

"I SOUGHT THE LORD, AND HE HEARD ME, AND DELIVERED ME FROM ALL MY FEARS." Psalm 34:4

The times that will most strengthen and enrich your life are those times when you go barehanded, armed with only the Spirit of God against the red lion of hell and prevail. Like Samson, who killed a lion with his bare hands, then ate honey out of its carcass (see Judges 14:6-9).

Whatever is hounding and threatening your life right now, you *must* hold fast to the Word of God that promises deliverance and hope, power and strength, wisdom and guidance. Look beyond the physical evidence to the spiritual promise of God. Problems are opportunities for God's power to be manifest in your life.

Read what the LORD said to Zerubbabel in Zechariah 4:6. How are you going to be free from fear?

Spiritual concerns and prayer requests..
....
....
....
....
....
....

Today I will…...
....

JUNE 13

"BUT OF HIM ARE YE IN CHRIST JESUS, WHO OF GOD IS MADE
UNTO US WISDOM, AND RIGHTEOUSNESS, AND SANCTIFICATION,
AND REDEMPTION." 1 Corinthians 1:30

The church is not an organization with Jesus Christ as its president. The church is an organism with Jesus Christ as its head. We are in Him and He is in us.

The victory He won on the cross was for us. When Jesus went to the cross, He wasn't fighting the battle for Himself. He didn't need to overcome Satan. He fought it on your behalf.

Jesus became the Son of man that you might become a child of God. He took your sins that you might take His innocence. He became guilty that you might become acquitted. He was filled with despair that you might be filled with joy. He took your shame that you might take His glory. He suffered the pains of hell that you might know the joys of heaven.

❖❖❖

So many people think salvation comes from the *inside out* by asking Jesus into their hearts. But, did you know it is equally correct to say that you are saved from the *outside in*? Read Colossians 3:3. Your salvation is "in Christ" just like Noah was saved by being in the ark? Ask God to help you understand these truths today.

Spiritual concerns and prayer requests...

....

....

....

....

....

....

Today I will...

....

"I LOVE THE LORD, BECAUSE HE HATH HEARD MY VOICE AND MY SUPPLICATIONS. BECAUSE HE HATH INCLINED HIS EAR UNTO ME, THEREFORE WILL I CALL UPON HIM AS LONG AS I LIVE." Psalm 116:1-2

Here's the recipe for a miracle: Take a problem, transfer it to Christ, and it will be transformed by Christ. The ingredient most of us keep missing or taking back is when we are to transfer the problem to Christ.

Have you given your all to Jesus Christ? I am being serious and honest with you. It may sound simple, but ask yourself that question. Do you truly want a miracle? You've got one—the new birth!

❧❦❧

Have you literally given everything to Jesus Christ? If not, do so today and note it in today's journal page. Then you will begin to see God's miracle-moving power transform your life.

Spiritual concerns and prayer requests...

....

....

....

....

....

....

....

Today I will…..

....

JUNE 15

"IT IS OF THE LORD'S MERCIES THAT WE ARE NOT CONSUMED, BECAUSE HIS COMPASSIONS FAIL NOT. THEY ARE NEW EVERY MORNING: GREAT IS THY FAITHFULNESS." Lamentations 3:22-23

Do you know what today's Scripture means? It means that God never runs out of compassion.

Have you ever gone to Niagara Falls and watched the water rampaging with torrential force? I've thought, *surely the water is one day going to dry up.* But, it hasn't. Friend, greater than Niagara is the compassion of the Lord.

His compassions fail not. In 1923, Thomas O. Chisholm wrote one of the greatest hymns of all time and this stanza is the refrain of this truth, "Great is Thy faithfulness, O God my Father; There is no shadow of turning with Thee; Thou changest not, Thy compassions, they fail not; As Thou hast been, Thou forever will be."

❧❦❧

Find the words to the song "Great Is Thy Faithfulness" and meditate upon its great truths. Meditate on times of God's faithfulness in your own life.

Spiritual concerns and prayer requests...
....
....
....
....
....
....

Today I will...
....

JUNE 16

"Let Thy tender mercies come unto me, that I may live: for Thy law is my delight." Psalm 119:77

How does God unite a law book with a song book? I'll tell you how. With liberty and harmony. God never intended His laws to be burdensome. He meant for them to be a blessing.

The piano operates according to laws. When a person masters those laws, the drudgery of learning turns to delight. Piano practice enables a person to sit at the piano in perfect liberty and let the melody dance off the ivory keys.

Every law has a song written on the back of it. And you will discover this when you keep the law. Your duty will turn to delight.

❦

Read Psalm 1 and ask God to give you the delight the psalmist talks about in verse 2, and the strength to meditate upon His truth throughout the day.

Spiritual concerns and prayer requests

Today I will…

JUNE 17

"FOR THOU SHALT WORSHIP NO OTHER GOD: FOR THE LORD, WHOSE NAME IS JEALOUS, IS A JEALOUS GOD." Exodus 34:14

God is a jealous God. Now, to you and I that may sound like a bad attribute. But, to God it is a holy attribute. You see, I have no right to be jealous of another preacher because I am not the only preacher in the world. I do not *own* preaching.

On the other hand, there is only one God. Exodus 20:2-3 says, "I am the LORD thy God, which have brought thee out of the land of Egypt, out of the house of bondage. Thou shalt have no other gods before Me." And when asked what the greatest commandment was, Jesus replied, "Thou shalt love the Lord thy God with all thy heart, and with all thy soul, and with all thy mind" (Matthew 22:37).

When you die to self and worship God, you will begin to experience the fullness of God in a way that transforms your life.

What is an idol? It is anything you love, serve, or desire more than God. Ask God to convict you of idols you may have in your life. Then, ask His forgiveness and ask Him to help you to love Him with all your heart, soul, and mind.

Spiritual concerns and prayer requests..
....
....
....
....
....
....
....

Today I will...
....

"THE LORD IS NIGH UNTO ALL THEM THAT CALL UPON HIM, TO ALL THAT CALL UPON HIM IN TRUTH." Psalm 145:18

Psalm 23 speaks of the "valley of the shadow of death." For every shadow, there must be light. Christ said, "I am the light of the world" (John 8:12).

A shadow may frighten you, but a shadow cannot really hurt you. I dare say that a shadow at one time or another has spooked many of us. But, thank God, death is but a shadow if you know the Lord Jesus Christ. If you keep your face toward the light, the shadow will fall behind you. You won't even see the shadow.

God doesn't bring us to a valley to leave us there. He always brings us through. God is never closer to you than when you are in a dark valley. He is especially near.

❦

Are you in a state of confusion or perhaps despair today? Do you feel hopeless about a situation you are in? Read Psalm 23:4, and praise God that He takes you "through" the valley and doesn't leave you there. Ask Him to give you wisdom to learn what He wants you to learn, to stay focused on Him, and to witness to others of His strength in the valley.

Spiritual concerns and prayer requests...

....

....

....

....

....

Today I will...

....

JUNE 19

"YE SHALL WALK AFTER THE LORD YOUR GOD, AND FEAR HIM, AND KEEP HIS COMMANDMENTS, AND OBEY HIS VOICE, AND YE SHALL SERVE HIM, AND CLEAVE UNTO HIM." Deuteronomy 13:4

When we read a command in the Bible, whether we understand it or not, we ought to obey it. The Bible is not first and foremost a book to be explained, it is a book to be believed and obeyed.

So many times we want to tell God how He ought to do things. I can imagine those early apostles when they first met Paul persecuting believers. Those well-meaning Christians could have been praying for God to strike Paul dead, but what did God do? He struck Paul alive! And, aren't you glad He did? Don't substitute human reasoning for obedience.

Read Isaiah 55:8-9 and Proverbs 3:5-6. Ask for God's forgiveness if you are trusting in *your* way instead of *His* way to do something. Ask for His strength to fully trust in Him.

Spiritual concerns and prayer requests ....
....
....
....
....
....
....
....

Today I will... ....
....

"GRACIOUS IS THE LORD, AND RIGHTEOUS; YEA, OUR GOD IS MERCIFUL." Psalm 116:5

Just imagine yourself in a plane on the runway. The pilot has come on the intercom and told you there is a delay because of the fog. You glance out your window and it looks so gloomy and dark. You wonder if the sun is shining.

The fog then lifts enough for the control tower to give the pilot the green light and the plane takes off. It's still cloudy, but the plane starts climbing, climbing, and climbing. Suddenly, the plane bursts through the clouds and it is so gloriously bright that you have to blink your eyes. Now, you realize the sun has been there all the time.

That's the way it is with Jehovah God, the Sun of righteousness with healing in His wings (see Malachi 4:2-3). He is always loving, always giving. He is waiting for you to see Him now.

Are you worrying about something today? What is it? Name it and give it to God. He is more than able to carry your burden. Ask Him to give you faith to trust Him with your burden.

Spiritual concerns and prayer requests...

....

....

....

....

....

....

Today I will..

....

JUNE 21

"IN WHOM WE HAVE BOLDNESS AND ACCESS WITH CONFIDENCE BY THE FAITH OF HIM." Ephesians 3:12

One of the grandest privileges you and I have is the privilege of prayer. I believe when we get to heaven one of the things which will amaze us is that we prayed so poorly, and we prayed so little while we were here on earth.

You do not have a failure in your life but what is a prayer failure. You do not have a need in your life but what prayer could supply that need. There's not a sin in your life that a proper prayer life couldn't overcome.

Hymn writer Joseph M. Scriven penned these words, "O what peace we often forfeit, O what needless pain we bear, All because we do not carry everything to God in prayer." Friend, rather than wringing our hands, we ought to be bending our knees.

※⊰⊰⊱⊱※

Spend some time in prayer—offering praise to God for hearing and answering every prayer you offer to Him. He may answer, "Yes." He may answer, "No." He may answer, "Wait." But, He *will* answer.

Spiritual concerns and prayer requests ....

....

....

....

....

....

....

Today I will... ....

....

"HOW THEN SHALL THEY CALL ON HIM IN WHOM THEY HAVE NOT BELIEVED? AND HOW SHALL THEY BELIEVE IN HIM OF WHOM THEY HAVE NOT HEARD? AND HOW SHALL THEY HEAR WITHOUT A PREACHER?" Romans 10:14

Y ou are either a helper or a hurter when it comes to reaching the world for Christ. Why? Because whether you like it or not, the world is watching your Sunday "go to church" behavior and wondering how it compares to your Monday "go to work" behavior or your Saturday "rest and relaxation" behavior.

I've said on more than one occasion that the greatest argument for Christ and the greatest argument against Christ is the life of a Christian. "Let the lower lights be burning! Send a gleam across the wave! Some poor fainting struggling seaman you may rescue, you may save" (Philip P. Bliss).

D o your neighbors see you give your time and resources to help them when they need help? Do they witness how you treat your family or how you entertain your friends? Do you even know their names? Let's bring a soul to Jesus for Him to save today!

Spiritual concerns and prayer requests..

....

....

....

....

....

....

Today I will…...

....

JUNE 23

"GIVE UNTO THE LORD THE GLORY DUE UNTO HIS NAME; WORSHIP THE LORD IN THE BEAUTY OF HOLINESS." Psalm 29:2

There was a man who had lived a long life with Jesus and now he was dying. His loved ones came to him and asked him to sign his name to a legal document.

They said, "Daddy, if you would sign this, it would help us with a lot of legal difficulties. We hate to mention it, but it needs to be done." With the old man facing eternity, he lifted his quivering hand and signed the paper.

Before long, he went to be with the Lord. When the family picked up the document, to their amazement he had signed, "Jesus." More than likely, it was the only name that meant anything to him at the time. There is coming a time when the only name that will mean anything to you is Jesus.

What name means the most to you right now? If you want to learn more of the names of God, why not visit www.lwf.org to read and meditate on them.

Spiritual concerns and prayer requests..

....

....

....

....

....

....

Today I will…..

....

"IN THE FEAR OF THE LORD IS STRONG CONFIDENCE: AND HIS CHILDREN SHALL HAVE A PLACE OF REFUGE." Proverbs 14:26

T he devil hates families who worship together. He will allow parents to be religious, but he does not want them to take their children to heaven with them. As a result, we are losing an entire generation. Our children are being left behind to die and go to hell because we are compromising with Satan.

Catherine Booth, wife of the founder of the Salvation Army, prayed, "Oh God, I will not stand before Thee without all my children." There are many fathers and mothers today who need to say that. Stand firm, Mom. Stand firm, Dad. Gather those children close to you and love them to Jesus.

A re you a parent? Then, make a daily, weekly, or monthly date with your children to discuss their relationship with God. Are you a grandparent, aunt or uncle? Why not start today by praying for the salvation and protection of that child?

Spiritual concerns and prayer requests..

....

....

....

....

....

....

Today I will..

....

JUNE 25

A former president of the American Psychiatric Association said, "Premarital [physical] relationships resulting from the so-called new morality have greatly increased the number of young people in mental hospitals."

Dr. Billy Graham said at one time he talked to the head psychiatrist at one of our great universities. The psychiatrist said over fifty percent of students at the university were suffering psychological problems because of immoral relationships.

Friend, why does God tell us to live a pure and holy life? It's not only so we can have fellowship with Him, but also it is for our own mental health! He knows holiness brings life to our bones, healing to our hearts, and joy to our steps!

What do you think of when you hear you need to lead a holy life? You'll have a good start if you start applying the exhortation of God's Word from Colossians 3:12-14.

Spiritual concerns and prayer requests

Today I will...

JUNE 26

"AND YE NOW THEREFORE HAVE SORROW: BUT I WILL SEE YOU AGAIN, AND YOUR HEART SHALL REJOICE, AND YOUR JOY NO MAN TAKETH FROM YOU." John 16:22

When I was a boy and living on the Florida coastline, my brother and I were a little disappointed when a hurricane passed us by. We experienced such exhilaration leaning into the wind and tasting the salty air! I can remember waves sometimes reaching fifty feet in the air. What a sight!

But, did you know there has never been a storm to move the ocean floor? There will be storms that will course across the surface of our lives with raging torment, but the child of God can know a deep-down joy that nothing can take away.

If you keep your eyes on Jesus, He will bring a joy no man can take from you. Oh, thank God for the steadfastness of His power, love, and mercy.

❖❖❖

Is your heart full of the joy of the Lord today? If not, why not? Who or what are you allowing to steal away your joy today? Confess this to the Lord and ask Him to cleanse you and restore His joy to you.

Spiritual concerns and prayer requests..

....

....

....

....

....

....

Today I will...

....

JUNE 27

"THEREFORE IF ANY MAN BE IN CHRIST, HE IS A NEW CREATURE: OLD THINGS ARE PASSED AWAY; BEHOLD, ALL THINGS ARE BECOME NEW." 2 Corinthians 5:17

Our backyard had a number of trees in it. During the autumn, Joyce and I would enjoy watching the leaves fall. However there were certain trees that would hold their leaves until spring. Their leaves whither and turn brown, but they wouldn't drop. Not until spring did those trees lose their leaves when the new leaves push out the old leaves.

That is exactly what happens to our old habits and our old lives when we find the Lord Jesus. The new life pushes that old life off. It is not a matter of plucking off this leaf and knocking off that leaf. The Christian life is not forged in that manner. Our new life replaces our old life when we are born again.

Did you know it is impossible to live the Christian life? That is, it is impossible to live the Christian life apart from the Holy Spirit. Ask God to show you where you may be trying to live the Christian life in your own strength. Ask His forgiveness and surrender your will to His today.

Spiritual concerns and prayer requests..

....

....

....

....

....

....

Today I will... ....

....

JUNE 28

"WASH ME THOROUGHLY FROM MINE INIQUITY, AND CLEANSE ME FROM MY SIN." Psalm 51:2

Before a priest could enter the Holy of Holies, he had to stop by the basin and wash his hands and feet. He had already been washed from head to toe, but there was no floor in the tabernacle, only dirt. There were also no utensils, so his hands became dirty.

This final preparation before he entered God's presence was the washing away of the defilement of this world by washing his hands. As you and I come into contact with the world, we are going to become defiled. We don't need a bath all over. We are already saved.

But, each day we must ask God to search our hearts and cleanse us from our sins. Wouldn't it be wonderful if each of us came into the presence of God as seriously as the Old Testament priests? We should.

Have you been to the basin this morning? If not, bow before Him right now. Make Psalm 139:23-24 your prayer. He is waiting to forgive you.

Spiritual concerns and prayer requests...

....

....

....

....

....

....

Today I will…..

....

JUNE 29

"ACCORDING TO MY EARNEST EXPECTATION AND MY HOPE, THAT IN NOTHING I SHALL BE ASHAMED, BUT THAT WITH ALL BOLDNESS, AS ALWAYS, SO NOW ALSO CHRIST SHALL BE MAGNIFIED IN MY BODY, WHETHER IT BE BY LIFE, OR BY DEATH." Philippians 1:20

Moderation is good in some things like eating, sleeping, recreation, exercise, and finances. But when it comes to spiritual warfare, moderation is a sin. When it comes to believing the Bible, moderation is a sin. When it comes to loving the Lord, moderation is a sin!

Suppose a wife asked her husband, "Honey, do you love me?" And he said, "Well, moderately." She'd fix his wagon, don't you think? Friend, if the world considers you a "moderate" when it comes to your Christianity, you are riding the fence of lukewarmness. May God forgive those who will not go the second mile.

Ask God to help you be passionate in your worship and a bold evangelist in a sea of lukewarm apathy. Friend, if your Christian life is worth anything, it's worth everything. Just look at the cross. Take what you see there and let it ignite a flame of holy boldness in your heart. Go forth and proclaim the good news...Jesus saves!

Spiritual concerns and prayer requests ....

....

....

....

....

....

....

Today I will... ....

....

JUNE 30

"AND JABEZ CALLED ON THE GOD OF ISRAEL, SAYING, OH THAT
THOU WOULDEST BLESS ME INDEED, AND ENLARGE MY COAST, AND
THAT THINE HAND MIGHT BE WITH ME, AND THAT THOU
WOULDEST KEEP ME FROM EVIL, THAT IT MAY NOT GRIEVE ME!
AND GOD GRANTED HIM THAT WHICH HE REQUESTED."
1 Chronicles 4:10

Jabez wanted his influence to be enlarged. God can stretch you,
as well. Psalm 4:1 says that God enlarged the psalmist when he
was "in distress." If you ask to be enlarged, you can expect that
God may use distressing circumstances to do that. And the pain will
be worth it all.

When God enlarges you, He does so to fill you with more of
Himself. Don't be satisfied with God's filling a small place if God
wants to fill a larger place. Are you ready to say, "God I want more.
I want You to enlarge my coasts. I don't want a blessing. I want a
blessing indeed."? We need to pray big prayers to a big God.

❧❦❧

Ask God to keep you aware of His presence all day, to bless your
witness for His glory, to keep you from evil.

Spiritual concerns and prayer requests..
....
....
....
....
....
....

Today I will… ....
....

JULY 1

"FOR THIS IS MY BLOOD OF THE NEW TESTAMENT, WHICH IS SHED FOR MANY FOR THE REMISSION OF SINS." Matthew 26:28

In 1829, George Wilson was adjudicated guilty and given the death sentence for murder. But, Wilson had some friends who petitioned President Andrew Jackson for a pardon. Jackson granted the pardon and it was brought to prison and given to Wilson.

To everyone's surprise, Wilson said, "I am going to hang." There had never been a refusal to a pardon, so the courts didn't know what to do. Discussion went all the way to the Supreme Court and Justice John Marshall gave this ruling: "A pardon is a piece of paper, the value of which depends upon the acceptance by the person implicated. If he does not accept the pardon, then he must be executed."

God loves you and wants to pardon you, but if you refuse Him, you will die and go to hell. Cast yourself upon Him completely, and receive the free gift of His forgiveness today.

Have you repented of your sin and believed upon the atoning work of Christ's blood on the cross? If not, turn to the "Closing Plea" at the end of this devotional journal. Being good doesn't get you to heaven. It is only Jesus.

Spiritual concerns and prayer requests..

....

....

....

....

....

....

Today I will...

....

JULY 2

"Only rebel not ye against the LORD, neither fear ye the people of the land; for they are bread for us: their defense is departed from them, and the LORD is with us: fear them not." Numbers 14:9

Joshua and Caleb faced formidable foes in the Promised Land, and yet what was their response to their enemies? "They are bread for us" (Numbers 14:9).

What is bread? It is the staff of life. What happens when you eat bread? You are strengthened by it and you grow by it. Paul even said, "For a great door and effectual is opened unto me, and there are many adversaries" (1 Corinthians 16:9).

Why isn't the door to victory easy? Because if it were easy, then you would become weak in your effort to work out your faith in God. God places obstacles in your path to give you strength. Wheaties is not the breakfast of champions; giants are. God wants you to feed upon your difficulties and depend upon Him to make you a conqueror.

❦

What does it take to strengthen your body? What does it take to build your intellect? What does it take to grow love in relationships? Work. Read Philippians 2:12-13 and apply it to your life today.

Spiritual concerns and prayer requests ....

....

....

....

....

....

Today I will... ....

....

JULY 3

Is there stirring a spirit of rebellion in your heart today? Maybe you don't even recognize it. But if you do, let me plead with you to do something about it right now.

Ask God to cleanse you from your desire to rebel. Ask Him to root out the rebel in you. He is not going to remove it until you renounce it. It is your choice. Ask Him to forgive you for the foolish and careless words you have spoken. Ask Him to take out that spirit of rebellion against authorities. Ask Him to teach you how to lovingly respect people when they are in the wrong.

Either you crown Jesus as Lord, or you crucify Him. Are you with Jesus today or are you against Him?

❦

Is there someone who has wronged you and you seek revenge? Do you have a need to have your rights exalted above others? Read and apply the truth of Philippians 2:3-11.

Spiritual concerns and prayer requests..

....

....

....

....

....

....

Today I will…...

....

"WILT THOU NOT REVIVE US AGAIN: THAT THY PEOPLE MAY REJOICE IN THEE? SHOW US THY MERCY, O LORD, AND GRANT US THY SALVATION." Psalm 85:6-7

When I was a Boy Scout, a buddy and I took a seven-mile hike to earn a merit badge and we decided to camp out. We pitched our tent, built a fire, cooked our dinner, and then went to sleep.

The next morning we kindled another fire, fixed breakfast, and set out to explore. When we came back, the woods were on fire! A wind was blowing and I thought we'd never put out that fire.

Have you ever thought about the fire that came on the day of Pentecost? The Bible says there was a sound of a rushing mighty wind that spread His flame (see Acts 2:2). Let me ask you a question: Is America going to burn by the fires of rebellion or by the fires of revival? How I pray God will cause a mighty Pentecostal wind to sweep across America. Whether it does or not lies in the hands, hearts, minds, wills, prayers, ambitions, and aspirations of people like you and me.

❦

Pray for America—for those who make and adjudicate the law of the land. Pray for preachers and teachers of God's Word. Pray for those who call themselves Christians. Pray for the lost. Pray 2 Chronicles 7:14. Ask God to save. Ask God to humble His people where we need humbling so His glory may be known.

Spiritual concerns and prayer requests ....
....
....
....
....

Today I will… ....
....

JULY 5

"FOR THE LORD YOUR GOD IS HE THAT GOETH WITH YOU, TO
FIGHT FOR YOU AGAINST YOUR ENEMIES, TO SAVE YOU."
Deuteronomy 20:4

Do you remember the miracle God performed when He
brought the Israelites through the Red Sea, when they
were being hunted down by Pharaoh's army? It was
incredible.

Now, let me ask you: What happened three days later? The
Israelites began grumbling because there was no water. Do you think
God would invest such a miraculous deliverance for them, and then
abandon them just days later? Absolutely not!

But, what happens to you and me when we are down in the
dumps and wondering where God is taking us? We become just like
the Israelites! And yet God did something more for you than He did
for them! He sent His precious and only Son to die on Calvary's
tree for you. *God redeemed you.*

More than God bringing you out of a watery grave, He delivered
you from eternal damnation into glorious communion with Him
forever! God saved you! What more could you possibly want?

❦❦❦

Are you despondent today? Do you feel like the victim of a bad
situation? Do you feel like God has abandoned you? Memorize
today's Scripture and meditate on it until you believe it.

Spiritual concerns and prayer requests ....
....
....
....
....
....
Today I will... ....
....

JULY 6

"WHO FED THEE IN THE WILDERNESS WITH MANNA, WHICH THY
FATHERS KNEW NOT, THAT HE MIGHT HUMBLE THEE, AND THAT
HE MIGHT PROVE THEE, TO DO THEE GOOD AT THY LATTER END."
Deuteronomy 8:16

There are three categories of people reading this: those who are in trouble; those who are just getting out of trouble; and those who are going into trouble. Job 14:1 says, "Man that is born of a woman is of few days, and full of trouble." The Spanish have a proverb: "There's no home without its hush."

Sooner or later, we will all know sorrow, heartache, and trouble. What we need to know is that troubles are not a sign that things have gone wrong or things have gotten out of hand. We must believe in the providence, plan, and purpose of Almighty God.

When the Israelites were delivered from Pharaoh's army through the Red Sea, they went into the wilderness. Had God lost control? No. God led them there by a pillar of cloud by day and a pillar of fire by night. In the unfailing providence of God, we are often led into a place of trouble. The wilderness is God's proving ground for your faith. How are you doing?

Are you in the middle of a trial? Where is your focus—on God, on the situation, or on yourself? When you get your focus right, you will find wisdom, strength, hope, and peace.

Spiritual concerns and prayer requests

Today I will...

JULY 7

"FOR GOD HATH NOT GIVEN US THE SPIRIT OF FEAR; BUT OF POWER, AND OF LOVE, AND OF A SOUND MIND." 2 Timothy 1:7

God has endowed us with His power and enriched us with His love. Not only that, He has enlightened us with a sound mind. Now, this phrase "sound mind" does not mean the opposite of insanity. It actually means discipline and self-control. Along with that, it is the ability to discern between truth and falsehood.

So often, the devil gets us running from shadows. Proverbs 28:1 says, "The wicked flee when no man pursueth: but the righteous are bold as a lion." Have you ever heard of phobias? That is what this verse is talking about.

We must pull back the mask of darkness from the devil's ploys and expose them for what they are and see the things that count in eternity. God has given you a sound mind by trusting in His Word, not in the devil's schemes.

Do you ever get defensive or has someone ever told you that you had a chip on your shoulder? If you answered yes to either you may have responded this way because you are afraid of someone taking advantage of you. Reread today's Scripture and ask God to give you the faith to believe and apply this truth in your life today.

Spiritual concerns and prayer requests...
....
....
....
....
Today I will...
....

"BLESSED BE THE GOD AND FATHER OF OUR LORD JESUS CHRIST,
WHO HATH BLESSED US WITH ALL SPIRITUAL BLESSINGS IN
HEAVENLY PLACES IN CHRIST." Ephesians 1:3

Did you know fear can cause you to forget things? Now, I'm not talking about forgetting a phone number or someone's name.

Instead, I'm referring to fear that causes you to forget the blessings, the anointing, the power of God—all these possessions you have because you are saved! It happened to Timothy, who was mightily gifted and graced by God for the ministry God had given him. Yes, he forgot this in the midst of fear, and Paul had to remind him (see 2 Timothy 1:6).

He had taken his eyes off God and focused on fear so much so he couldn't see anything else. Let me tell you something friend: You are *tremendously blessed*! If you get your mind distracted by fear, then you will fail to see your blessings in Christ. Fear will blow out every light in your soul, take the blue out of your sky, and the joy out of your life.

❧❖❧

It's time to wake up and count your blessings. It's time to claim what you already have in Christ! Spend a few minutes going through the alphabet and thank God for something that begins with each letter, i.e., the *A*tonement of *J*esus, the *B*eauty of the Creator, the *C*omforter called the Holy *S*pirit.

Spiritual concerns and prayer requests...

....

....

....

....

Today I will... ....

....

JULY 9

"NEVERTHELESS I TELL YOU THE TRUTH; IT IS EXPEDIENT FOR YOU THAT I GO AWAY: FOR IF I GO NOT AWAY, THE COMFORTER WILL NOT COME UNTO YOU; BUT IF I DEPART, I WILL SEND HIM UNTO YOU. AND WHEN HE IS COME, HE WILL REPROVE THE WORLD OF SIN, AND OF RIGHTEOUSNESS, AND OF JUDGMENT." John 16:7-8

The devil accuses you of sin. The Holy Spirit convicts you of sin. Do you know the difference? The devil accuses you to drive you *from* Christ. The Holy Spirit convicts you to draw you *to* Christ. The devil wants you to get under a load of guilt, so you'll say, "I'm no good. I can't live the Christian life. There's something wrong with me. God doesn't hear my prayers. It doesn't do me any good to go to church."

When you believe those lies, you let the devil drive you away from God! He accuses you to destroy you. The Holy Spirit convicts you to reclaim you. He is trying to correct you and bring you back, so you may know the fullness of joy. The Holy Spirit draws you to Christ so you may confess your sins and be cleansed!

Ask God to show you if you have been listening to the accusations of Satan. Ask Him to silence those accusations and give you discernment to only hear the conviction of the Holy Spirit.

Spiritual concerns and prayer requests...

....

....

....

....

....

....

Today I will...

....

JULY 10

"Thou hast also given me the shield of Thy salvation: and Thy right hand hath holden me up, and Thy gentleness hath made me great." Psalm 18:35

Can a person donate to the poor and not have love? Can a person work in a soup kitchen for the homeless and not have love? Yes.

Now, you may say, "A person wouldn't do that!" Oh yes they would if they had a guilty conscience. Sometimes it is neater to write a check or donate some used things than to give of our time. Do you know what the world needs? Not more money, though I'm sure they'd be glad to take it. First Corinthians 13:3 says, "And though I bestow all my goods to feed the poor, and though I give my body to be burned, and have not charity, it profiteth me nothing." You can give without loving, but you cannot love without giving of yourself to others.

How about you? Are you serving others out of a guilty conscience? Are you tithing out of a guilty conscience? Ask God to look at your heart and teach you how to love others by dying to self and living for Him.

Spiritual concerns and prayer requests..

....

....

....

....

....

Today I will…...

....

JULY 11

"TRULY GOD IS GOOD TO ISRAEL, EVEN TO SUCH AS ARE OF A CLEAN HEART." Psalm 73:1

Asaph, the author of Psalm 73, started his psalm by talking about the purity of a person's heart and the goodness of God. Then he says, "But as for me, my feet were almost gone; my steps had well nigh slipped" (Psalm 73:2). He had the idea that when he got right with God, he wouldn't have any more troubles. *Are you sure about that?*

Psalm 73:13-14 says, "Verily I have cleansed my heart in vain, and washed my hands in innocency. For all the day long have I been plagued, and chastened every morning." He said, "I got right with God and I still have problems!" He had a false expectation that the Bible doesn't necessarily give. Christians are not due preferential treatment. The presence of God is enough even in the midst of our trials.

◈

Has this false view been something under which you have been living? If so, then it's time you believed in God's Truth. Read 1 Peter 4:12-16 and commit your situation to the glory of God today.

Spiritual concerns and prayer requests..

....

....

....

....

....

....

Today I will...

....

"WITH LONG LIFE WILL I SATISFY HIM, AND SHOW HIM MY
SALVATION." Psalm 91:16

One day, I was eating in a cafeteria in New York when the
door of the restaurant opened and a man ran in. He rushed
to a table that had been abandoned by patrons just shortly
before.

He began to stuff his mouth with the leftovers when the
management discovered him. He rushed out like a squirrel scurrying to
safety. No pride. He didn't care what people thought.

A man who is starving is dead serious about the matter of getting
food. He's focused. He's only got one thing on his mind—where is his
next meal? He's not concerned about popularity, position, or
possessions. When a person is thirsty or hungry enough, he will pay
any price.

Oh that we would hunger and thirst after righteousness (Matthew
5:6) and the things of God. What are you hungry for today?
Is Jesus enough to satisfy your appetite?

Spiritual concerns and prayer requests...

....

....

....

....

....

Today I will..

....

JULY 13

"OPEN THOU MINE EYES, THAT I MAY BEHOLD WONDROUS THINGS OUT OF THY LAW." Psalm 119:18

Have you ever thought you could just go to the Bible and pull some truth out of it for your life? Let me tell you friend, *you* cannot do that.

That is, your mind will never comprehend the things of God apart from the Holy Spirit illuminating you. If you want to understand God's Word, you must lay your intellect in the dust, and with open arms and a heart of faith, approach God's Word for wisdom, discernment, and knowledge, then He will teach you.

It took a supernatural miracle to write the Word of God. It takes a supernatural miracle for you to understand it. When God begins to write His Word upon your heart, you are going to lead a supernatural life!

Pray Psalm 119:18 to God today. Expectantly await His answer with an open Bible in front of you. Then, share what He shows you with someone else.

Spiritual concerns and prayer requests..

....

....

....

....

....

Today I will…..

....

"I WILL GREATLY REJOICE IN THE LORD, MY SOUL SHALL BE JOYFUL IN MY GOD; FOR HE HATH CLOTHED ME WITH THE GARMENTS OF SALVATION, HE HATH COVERED ME WITH THE ROBE OF RIGHTEOUSNESS, AS A BRIDEGROOM DECKETH HIMSELF WITH ORNAMENTS, AND AS A BRIDE ADORNETH HERSELF WITH HER JEWELS." Isaiah 61:10

There are some who may be reading this, who are going to be absolutely speechless when they stand before the King of heaven. They are church members, but they're not saved. Instead, they're dressed in the rags of self-righteousness, rather than the wedding garment of His righteousness.

In 1834, hymn writer Edward Mote wrote this timeless pledge, "When He shall come with trumpet sound, Oh may I then in Him be found. Dressed in His righteousness alone, Faultless to stand before the throne."

It would be tragic indeed for those who acted in every conceivable religious way, to think they can come to the wedding without Christ's righteousness. *Are you saved? How do you know?*

❧❦❧

If you are relying on anything other than the blood of Jesus Christ to save you, then friend, you need to repent and believe upon Jesus Christ. It's time to crown Him Lord of your life.

Spiritual concerns and prayer requests ....

....

....

....

....

....

Today I will... ....

....

JULY 15

"BUT WE ARE ALL AS AN UNCLEAN THING, AND ALL OUR RIGHTEOUSNESSES ARE AS FILTHY RAGS; AND WE ALL DO FADE AS A LEAF; AND OUR INIQUITIES, LIKE THE WIND, HAVE TAKEN US AWAY." Isaiah 64:6

There is none good, no not one. If you asked every single human being on planet earth to deposit in a cup all of his or her goodness, there would not be enough goodness in that cup to save even *one* person!

Isaiah 64:6 says our righteousness is as "filthy rags" in the sight of God. The cross of Jesus Christ is our only hope. Without Jesus, you are going to face the wrath of God. Jesus paid the debt of your sin that God's justice required. And now as His child, you share in His righteousness.

In 1906, Jessie Brown Pounds wrote these words: "I must needs go home by the way of the cross, there's no other way but this; I shall ne'er get sight of the gates of light, if the way of the cross I miss."

How do you see yourself right now? Worthy? Or unworthy? What does John 3:36, 5:24 and Romans 3:23-26 say?

Spiritual concerns and prayer requests...

....

....

....

....

....

....

Today I will...

....

JULY 16

"KNOW THEREFORE THAT THE LORD THY GOD, HE IS GOD, THE FAITHFUL GOD, WHICH KEEPETH COVENANT AND MERCY WITH THEM THAT LOVE HIM AND KEEP HIS COMMANDMENTS TO A THOUSAND GENERATIONS." Deuteronomy 7:9

When I talk about eternal security, inevitably I will hear, "Well, maybe your sins can't take you out of the hand of God, but Satan can." In all due respect, I respond, "Pardon me. But that is foolishness. If Satan could take you out of the hand of God, why hasn't he done it yet? Do you think he's just being nice to you?"

That would be a strange doctrine if you were going to heaven by the grace of the devil. How absurd! God saves us. God keeps us. What has been settled in eternity can never be undone by the ways of men _or_ the schemes of the devil."

❦

Do you have an assurance in your heart that you are going to heaven when you die? If you do not, spend some time talking to God right now. Ask Him to give you the gift of faith right now to believe in the surety of what His Son did on the cross on your behalf over 2,000 years ago.

Spiritual concerns and prayer requests...

....

....

....

....

....

....

Today I will…...

....

JULY 17

"For whom He did foreknow, He also did predestinate to be conformed to the image of His Son, that He might be the firstborn among many brethren. Moreover whom He did predestinate, them He also called: and whom He called, them He also justified: and whom He justified, them He also glorified." Romans 8:29-30

D r. Scofield, who edited the Scofield Bible says that "predestination is the effective exercise of the will of God by which things before determined by Him are brought to pass." That is, God says He is determined to do something and then He does it. God's wisdom is sovereign.

What did God predestinate? That those whom God foreknew will be conformed to the image of Jesus Christ who is the Firstborn. God had one Son and He said, "I want more just like Him." And so God is redeeming a whole race of people, that all of these people might be conformed to the image of God's Son.

If you are saved, you are predestined to be like Jesus. When you received Jesus as your Lord and Savior, then God said, "It is settled. You will one day be like My Son."

P raise God that He predestined you to be like His Son, that He called you, that He justified you, that He glorifed you! Jesus said, "It is finished!" Hallelujah! Praise the Lamb who was slain!

Spiritual concerns and prayer requests...
....
....
....
....

Today I will...
....

"KNOW YE NOT THAT THEY WHICH RUN IN A RACE RUN ALL, BUT
ONE RECEIVETH THE PRIZE? SO RUN, THAT YE MAY OBTAIN."
1 Corinthians 9:24

God has given you a race to run. In fact, God has given each one of us a race to run, and everyone must run his own race. We're not racing against each other to win the victor's crown. We are in a pilgrimage together. I'm not trying to outrun you. And you're not trying to outrun me. That is good news!

God has a plan for your life with particular speed bumps, detours, and hurdles to cross. And you are to stay in the race until it is over. But, you are not alone. Though we are not in the same race, we are in the journey together so we encourage one another to win. And I want you to win the victor's crown today! Run, my friend, run!

"Wherefore seeing we also are compassed about with so great a cloud of witnesses...let us run with patience the race that is set before us." (Hebrews 12:1)

Ask God to shod your feet with the preparation that comes from the gospel of peace (see Ephesians 6:14-15) so you can run the race in confidence. Ask God to cause your feet to take you places where you can declare God's plan of salvation (see Romans 10:15). Thank God that the victor's crown awaits you at the end of the race because of His power upon your life.

Spiritual concerns and prayer requests

Today I will…

JULY 19

"THEREFORE I TAKE PLEASURE IN INFIRMITIES, IN REPROACHES,
IN NECESSITIES, IN PERSECUTIONS, IN DISTRESSES FOR CHRIST'S
SAKE: FOR WHEN I AM WEAK, THEN AM I STRONG."
2 Corinthians 12:10

What does Paul mean when he says that he "takes pleasure" in all of these difficult circumstances? When Paul was placed in solitary confinement in prison, he wasn't alone—Jesus was near. His weakness became his strength.

If they beat him and he hurt, then he had the fellowship of Christ's suffering—his weakness became his strength. If his body became crippled and he was not able to lean upon his own arm, then he had to lean on the Everlasting Arms. Paul took pleasure in these things.

God is waiting to make you strong. There is power in our suffering. Suffering is not going to hurt you, it is going to strengthen you.

❧❦❧

Are you suffering today? What does God have to say about your attitude in what you are going through? Ask God to forgive you if you are viewing your circumstances in any other way than through His eyes. Ask for His strength to see that when you are weak, He is strong!

Spiritual concerns and prayer requests..

....

....

....

....

....

Today I will..

....

"I WILL PRAISE THE LORD ACCORDING TO HIS RIGHTEOUSNESS: AND WILL SING PRAISE TO THE NAME OF THE LORD MOST HIGH."
Psalm 7:17

Did you know that joy is a choice? A man said to a beggar one day, "Good day, my friend." The beggar answered, "Well, thank you, but I never have a bad one." He said, "Well, may God give you a happy life, my friend." And the beggar replied, "I thank God that I am never unhappy."

The man was speechless. And the beggar continued, "When I have plenty to eat, I thank God. When I am hungry, I thank God. If it is God's will for me to endure this, then whatever is God's will for me makes me happy." He chose to be happy.

Do you want to be happy? Then, choose to be happy by praising God today no matter your circumstances. It's not going to be easy, but victory awaits if you do.

Spiritual concerns and prayer requests ....

....

....

....

....

....

....

Today I will… ....

....

JULY 21

"BOAST NOT THYSELF OF TOMORROW; FOR THOU KNOWEST NOT WHAT A DAY MAY BRING FORTH." Proverbs 27:1

Some time ago, I read some research by William Morriston, a psychologist, who reported that 94% of the 3,000 persons he surveyed were *enduring today* in order to *get to tomorrow*.

Do you know anyone like that? Perhaps you are one of those. Tomorrow, you're going on vacation. Tomorrow, you're going to get the house cleaned. Tomorrow, you're going to start your diet. Tomorrow, you're going to balance your checkbook. Tomorrow, tomorrow, tomorrow. The only problem is tomorrow never arrives.

When it gets here, it is today. And today is the tomorrow you worried about yesterday. It is always today.

What are you worrying about? It's time to ask His forgiveness and give Him your concern. He is more than able to handle it. Worry is pulling tomorrow's clouds over today's sunshine.

Spiritual concerns and prayer requests..

....

....

....

....

....

....

Today I will..

....

"AND ABOVE ALL THINGS HAVE FERVENT LOVE AMONG
YOURSELVES: FOR LOVE SHALL COVER THE MULTITUDE OF SINS."
1 Peter 4:8

Why is love so important? First, because *love is the greatest virtue*. First Corinthians 13:13 tells us that love supercedes faith and hope.

Second, because *love is the greatest command*. Jesus said, "Thou shalt love the Lord thy God with all thy heart, and with all thy soul, and with all thy mind" (Matthew 22:37).

Third, *love is the greatest testimony*. What is really going to make your community wake up and believe that your church is really the church of the Lord Jesus Christ? The size of your building? The way your lawn looks? The signage at the street? No. The way you love God and show love to others. Nothing can motivate a lost sinner like the heartfelt love of Jesus Christ.

❦

Make a commitment to God right now, that you will seek to love Him with all your heart, soul, and mind, and love your neighbor as yourself. Ask for His strength to do this. Anything less is sin.

Spiritual concerns and prayer requests...
....
....
....
....
....
....

Today I will...
....

JULY 23

"BUT SANCTIFY THE LORD GOD IN YOUR HEARTS: AND BE READY ALWAYS TO GIVE AN ANSWER TO EVERY MAN THAT ASKETH YOU A REASON OF THE HOPE THAT IS IN YOU WITH MEEKNESS AND FEAR."
1 Peter 3:15

B e ready to give an answer when someone asks you about your faith. In seminary, we call this *apologetics*. Contrary to what you might think, this does not mean you are to apologize for your faith. Instead, "apologetics" comes from the Greek word that means to give a defense—as in front of a judge.

Can you defend your faith? It is not enough for you to *demonstrate* your faith, you must also *defend* your faith. If you ran into someone who was dying and he asked you to share your faith with him, could you? You need to be ready. You need to also be reasonable. You need to study God's Word and know what it says about salvation, sin, heaven, and hell. Are you ready? If not, get ready today. There's no better time.

D o you know why you believe? Do you know what you believe? If not, then spend some time each day in God's Word and ask Him to show you His Truth. Ask God to send you an older Christian who will disciple you, and commit to a lifetime of loving God and sharing His Truth with others. It is why you are here.

*S*piritual concerns and prayer requests..

....

....

....

....

....

Today I will... ....

....

"SERVANTS, OBEY IN ALL THINGS YOUR MASTERS ACCORDING TO THE FLESH; NOT WITH EYESERVICE, AS MENPLEASERS; BUT IN SINGLENESS OF HEART, FEARING GOD." Colossians 3:22

Do you work for a difficult person? *Yes! That slave driver, penny pincher, and bully!* Well, let's see what the Bible says about that slave driver. "Servants, be subject to your masters with all fear; not only to the good and gentle, but also to the froward [harsh]" (1 Peter 2:18). *You mean I am supposed to submit to that two-legged devil?* That's right. And you are to serve him.

You can shut the mouth of criticism and bring that one to Jesus Christ when you practice the mightiest force upon the face of the earth—submission through obedience.

❦

Ask God to give you a spirit of submission towards the authorities in your life. Ask Him to give you strength to do the impossible, to rise above your circumstances, and to reflect His Spirit of trust and obedience.

Spiritual concerns and prayer requests...

....

....

....

....

....

....

Today I will…..

....

JULY 25

"WHICH HOPE WE HAVE AS AN ANCHOR OF THE SOUL, BOTH SURE AND STEADFAST, AND WHICH ENTERETH INTO THAT WITHIN THE VEIL; WHITHER THE FORERUNNER IS FOR US ENTERED, EVEN JESUS, MADE AN HIGH PRIEST FOR EVER AFTER THE ORDER OF MELCHIZEDEK." Hebrews 6:19-20

The Old Testament temple had three parts: the outer court, the inner court, and the innermost court. The innermost court was called the "inner sanctum" or the "Holy of Holies." Only the priest could go in there.

Once a year, the high priest would enter the Holy of Holies to make atonement for the people. He would lift up a corner of the heavy veil and slip under. Then, he would sprinkle blood upon the Mercy Seat. If anyone went into the Holy of Holies without the blood, there was sudden death.

When the veil of the temple was torn at Jesus' death, it was torn from top to bottom so no one would think a person did this. By His death, Jesus was saying there were no more animal sacrifices necessary. Now, every believer can enter the Holy of Holies.

Have you been there today? It's time to enter in and praise Him for sending His Son to make atonement for your sin. It's time to bow before His Mercy Seat and thank Him for His grace towards you that saved you from eternal separation from God's presence.

Spiritual concerns and prayer requests...

....

....

....

....

Today I will...

....

JULY 26

"FOR NO MAN EVER YET HATED HIS OWN FLESH; BUT NOURISHETH
AND CHERISHETH IT, EVEN AS THE LORD THE CHURCH: FOR WE
ARE MEMBERS OF HIS BODY, OF HIS FLESH, AND OF HIS BONES."
Ephesians 5:29-30

Many believers think they don't have to go to church.
They say, "Yes" to Jesus but "No" to the church.
Now, this happens for many reasons. But, if you love
God, you will love Jesus. And if you love Jesus, you will love what
He loves, and Jesus loves the church.

*Well, can't I be a Christian without being a member of the
church?* Let me answer that question with another. Can a bee be a bee
without a hive? Can a sailor be a sailor without a ship? Can a person
be a parent without a family? We need one another. We were made
for one another. Jesus didn't say, "I will build *you* a church" or
"*You* will build My church." Instead, Jesus said, "*I* will build
My church."

Are you a member of a church that preaches the Word of God?
If not, you can visit the web site of the Southern Baptist
Convention (www.sbc.net) and find the church search feature to help
you select churches in your area to visit. Then ask God to direct your
path to the church He wants for you.

Spiritual concerns and prayer requests

Today I will…

Practicing *the* Presence *of* God   211

JULY 27

A coin is minted for a purpose. It is meant to be spent, treasured, and valued, but not to be lost. When a coin is lost, it is worthless to the owner and the creator. It doesn't matter how valuable it may be intrinsically. If it is lost, it is lost.

Which is worth more on the ocean floor, a hundred-dollar gold piece or a five-cent nickel? As long as they are both on the ocean floor, both have the same value.

Lost people are like lost silver. As long as a person is lost, he or she is out of circulation. God made you for a purpose. He wants you in circulation to spend and be spent for His glory.

Think about the relationships you have in your family, neighborhood, and community. Ask God to put you in circulation as His salt and light to tell others about salvation through Jesus Christ.

Spiritual concerns and prayer requests...
....
....
....
....
....
....

Today I will..
....

"WHO HATH ALSO SEALED US, AND GIVEN THE EARNEST OF THE
SPIRIT IN OUR HEARTS." 2 Corinthians 1:22

God has given us the "earnest of the Spirit in our hearts."
What does that mean? When a man in Jesus' day intended
to buy something he couldn't afford to purchase at that
moment, he would put down "earnest" money. The greater the down-
payment, the greater the indication that the full payment will be made.

For instance, if a person were selling their home for $100,000 and
a prospective buyer gave him earnest money of $50, the owner would
probably not look for that person again. But, if that person gave
$10,000 in earnest money, then he means business and the owner
would know he was coming back.

In today's terminology, we would say that God has given us a
down payment of the Spirit. Do you think God is going to forfeit
His Holy Spirit? No. God is not going to forsake you because He
has too much invested in you.

❦

Praise God your salvation was paid in full when Jesus died on the
cross. Praise God He has sealed you for all eternity in the
atoning blood of His Son. Praise God you are not alone, but that
His Spirit dwells within you to sanctify you.

Spiritual concerns and prayer requests..

....

....

....

....

....

....

Today I will...

....

JULY 29

"HE THAT HATH MY COMMANDMENTS, AND KEEPETH THEM, HE IT IS THAT LOVETH ME: AND HE THAT LOVETH ME SHALL BE LOVED OF MY FATHER, AND I WILL LOVE HIM, AND WILL MANIFEST MYSELF TO HIM." John 14:21

A little boy fell out of bed and was crying. His mother came, picked him up, and said, "Honey, what's wrong? How did you fall out of bed?" He said, "Well, I guess I went to sleep too close to where I got in."

I think there are a lot of people who have done exactly that. They get into Christ and somehow they just seem to go to sleep right there. They say, "I'm saved and that's it."

But friend, that's not it. It's just the beginning of a relationship that will last through all eternity. God wants to move you further into a knowledge of Himself. I don't know about you, but I'm not satisfied with the status quo of my life. I want to go deep into the heart of Jesus. I hope you desire the same.

What evidence would there be in a court of law to convict you of living the Christian life? What evidence would your neighbors, family, or church friends give that you have kept God's commands? Ask God to forgive you and make you faithful to obey Him.

Spiritual concerns and prayer requests

Today I will…

JULY 30

"AND IF CHILDREN, THEN HEIRS; HEIRS OF GOD, AND JOINT-HEIRS WITH CHRIST; IF SO BE THAT WE SUFFER WITH HIM, THAT WE MAY BE ALSO GLORIFIED TOGETHER." Romans 8:17

How do you enlist suffering to make it your servant? First, *you receive it as a gift from God.* Job said, "the LORD gave, and the LORD hath taken away; blessed be the name of the LORD" (Job 1:21b).

Second, *rely on God's grace* because with the gift comes His grace. Second Corinthians 9:8 promises, "And God is able to make all grace abound toward you; that ye, always having all sufficiency in all things, may abound to every good work." God is going to be near you in a special way.

Finally, *reflect on the glory of God.* There is no greater Christian who ever lived than the Apostle Paul. His greatest motive in all he endured was the glory of God. His pain became a platform from which he declared the glory of God.

If you are suffering today for whatever reason, post this truth on a piece of paper and carry it with you wherever you go: "Whatever I am going through, Jesus has already experienced and He will bring me through."

Spiritual concerns and prayer requests ....

....

....

....

....

....

....

....

Today I will... ....

....

JULY 31

"BURIED WITH HIM IN BAPTISM, WHEREIN ALSO YE ARE RISEN
WITH HIM THROUGH THE FAITH OF THE OPERATION OF GOD,
WHO HATH RAISED HIM FROM THE DEAD." Colossians 2:12

People often ask me, "Why do Baptists immerse people in baptism?" The answer is simple...because that is what God's Word teaches.

When you go under the water, that is a picture of your death and burial. When you come up out of the water, that is a picture of your resurrection.

If someone died and you took him to the cemetery and sprinkled a few granules of dirt on his head, has that person truly been buried? No. The very word "baptism" means to immerse. And the devil doesn't like that. Your baptism is a funeral service. The baptismal is a liquid tomb and the mourner who comes to that funeral is the devil.

Have you been baptized? If not, then call your church and make an appointment for your baptism today.

Spiritual concerns and prayer requests...

....

....

....

....

....

....

Today I will... ....

....

AUGUST 1

"THAT I MAY KNOW HIM, AND THE POWER OF HIS
RESURRECTION, AND THE FELLOWSHIP OF HIS SUFFERINGS, BEING
MADE CONFORMABLE UNTO HIS DEATH; IF BY ANY MEANS I MIGHT
ATTAIN UNTO THE RESURRECTION OF THE DEAD." Philippians 3:10-11

Did you know you can backslide with a Bible under your arm? I had more difficulty maintaining my spiritual life when I was in seminary than any other time in my life. I'm not putting down seminary. It wasn't their fault. It was my fault.

I started reading the Bible like a math book instead of a love story. You can know the letter, but the letter kills if you are not clean. The test of your Bible study is not how many facts you know or how fast you can take apart a Greek verb and put it back together.

The test is: *Are you becoming like Jesus because you spent time in His Word?* May God help us as teachers, soul winners, disciples, and deacons to be using the Word of God to clean us, convict us, and challenge us to be more like Christ.

Read 2 Corinthians 3:5-6. How does this verse convict or exhort you in your current study of God's Word and ministry to others?

Spiritual concerns and prayer requests...

....

....

....

....

....

....

Today I will… ....

....

AUGUST 2

"AND HE SAID UNTO ME, MY GRACE IS SUFFICIENT FOR THEE: FOR MY STRENGTH IS MADE PERFECT IN WEAKNESS. MOST GLADLY THEREFORE WILL I RATHER GLORY IN MY INFIRMITIES, THAT THE POWER OF CHRIST MAY REST UPON ME. THEREFORE I TAKE PLEASURE IN INFIRMITIES, IN REPROACHES, IN NECESSITIES, IN PERSECUTIONS, IN DISTRESSES FOR CHRIST'S SAKE: FOR WHEN I AM WEAK, THEN AM I STRONG." 2 Corinthians 12:9-10

Have you ever felt too weak to win the battle? Friend, you may not be weak enough. God identifies Himself with our obedient weakness. It is when we stop trying and start trusting that God's power can be manifest.

You see, your weakness is not a liability; your weakness is an asset. The battle is not yours; it is the Lord's! If only we could learn that God does not need our strength. God calls for our obedience!

God has the strength. And He wants to give you that supernatural strength in place of your own. It is not your ability; it is your availability. It is not your fame; it is your faith. It is not who you are; it is Whose you are!

You may think that doing something in your own strength is something of which to be proud. But read 1 Corinthians 1:26-31. In what should you boast?

Spiritual concerns and prayer requests...

....

....

....

....

....

....

Today I will...

....

"But it shall not be so among you: but whosoever will be great among you, let him be your minister." Matthew 20:26

In Jesus' day, the pagan Gentile princes had many servants—this was a mark of their greatness. To be great in God's eyes, on the other hand, we are to be servants.

Do you want to be great? Then, minister to others. There are some people who are great because they have servants. That is the pagan way. Jesus said the Christian way of greatness is not measured by the number of servants, but by how many men he serves.

Now, don't miss this point. Jesus did not say for us not to be great. He said, "Be great, but just be certain your greatness is measured in God's economy." That is sanctified ambition.

It's time to look at your life and ask yourself, "How am I spending my time? Is it mostly on myself, or am I ministering to others?" Is there balance in your life—loving God and loving others as you love yourself? Talk to God about the answer you get. Ask for His forgiveness if He reveals any selfishness within you. And ask Him to give you opportunities to be His minister.

Spiritual concerns and prayer requests ....
....
....
....
....
....
....

Today I will… ....
....

AUGUST 4

"BLESSED IS THE MAN THAT HEARETH ME, WATCHING DAILY AT MY GATES, WAITING AT THE POSTS OF MY DOORS." Proverbs 8:34

Tick, tock. Tick, tock. Tick, tock. We twiddle our thumbs. We watch the clock. Is this what God means for us to do when He tells us to wait on Him?

Sometimes, but not always. When you sit down in a restaurant and someone approaches your table to take your order, what do you call this person? A waiter. Does that mean he spends his time doing nothing? Not if he wants a job! He is to be busy serving you.

In the same way, we are to be busy in our waiting upon the Lord. Waiting on God involves longing for the Lord, listening to the Lord, looking to Him, and living for Him. If you do this type of waiting, you will receive His power, provision, and peace.

❦

Perhaps you have asked God to bring you a spouse or a child and years have gone by without an answer. Maybe you are simply waiting in the airport for your flight. How are you redeeming your time? Ask God to tell you what He wants you to do right now for His glory.

Spiritual concerns and prayer requests...

....

....

....

....

....

....

Today I will...

....

"LIKEWISE RECKON YE ALSO YOURSELVES TO BE DEAD INDEED
UNTO SIN, BUT ALIVE UNTO GOD THROUGH JESUS CHRIST OUR
LORD." Romans 6:11

We are to "reckon" ourselves dead to sin, but alive to
Jesus Christ. What does that mean? In the south
when someone says, "I reckon so," it means they think
so. But that's not what this word means.

"Reckon" is a legal term that means "to count upon" or
"calculate." When you repented of your sin and asked God to save
you, you reckoned upon what Jesus did on the cross to atone for your
sins. And now, you depend upon His righteousness.

Just as you reckon upon Him for victory over the *penalty of sin*,
you also reckon upon Him for victory over the *power of sin*. Count
on it! Reckon yourself to be dead unto sin and alive unto God!

❦

Do you want to walk in victory today? As you go about your
day, repeat the following: "I am crucified with Christ:
nevertheless I live; yet not I, but Christ liveth in me: and the life
which I now live in the flesh I live by faith of the Son of God, who
loved me, and gave Himself for me" (Galatians 2:20). Die to self and
live for Christ.

Spiritual concerns and prayer requests..

....

....

....

....

....

....

....

Today I will…...

....

AUGUST 6

"AND THE MULTITUDE OF THEM THAT BELIEVED WERE OF ONE HEART AND OF ONE SOUL: NEITHER SAID ANY OF THEM THAT AUGHT OF THE THINGS WHICH HE POSSESSED WAS HIS OWN; BUT THEY HAD ALL THINGS COMMON." Acts 4:32

You can tell a lot about a person by what makes him sad, what makes him glad, and what makes him mad. Amen? Many times this can be the lack or the abundance of possessions or wealth.

However, when a person has joy in the Lord, nothing can steal that joy. Have you learned to have joy in the Lord and not in the things of this world? Are you holding the things of this world loosely? If you don't, then God may teach you to do this. To fully trust in the Lord, there must be a *confidence that relies on the Lord.*

Secondly, there must be a *communion that rejoices in the Lord.* And thirdly, there must be a *commitment that rolls burdens onto the Lord.*

Where is your confidence—your possessions, your position, your personal esteem? How much time do you spend communing with the Lord every day? How would you define your commitment to trust God in every area of your life?

Spiritual concerns and prayer requests ....

....

....

....

....

....

....

Today I will... ....

....

"WHEREFORE HE IS ABLE ALSO TO SAVE THEM TO THE UTTERMOST THAT COME UNTO GOD BY HIM, SEEING HE EVER LIVETH TO MAKE INTERCESSION FOR THEM." Hebrews 7:25

If you are a child of God, I have some good news for you! Because Jesus lives, you live. Because you are part of Him and He will never die, you will never die. Jesus Christ is more than Savior, He is Intercessor and High Priest.

I have often said that I will get worried about losing my salvation, when Jesus dies. And He is not going to die! Where is He today? At the right hand of God to make intercession for you. You can be secure in this world because your salvation is rooted in the Father's mercy, obtained by the Son's obedience, and made possible by the regenerating power of the Holy Spirit!

Read Hebrews 7:26-27 and 8:1-2. Praise God for the provision of His Son as your Savior and High Priest.

Spiritual concerns and prayer requests..

....

....

....

....

....

....

Today I will...

....

AUGUST 8

"HAVING PREDESTINATED US UNTO THE ADOPTION OF CHILDREN
BY JESUS CHRIST TO HIMSELF, ACCORDING TO THE GOOD
PLEASURE OF HIS WILL, TO THE PRAISE OF THE GLORY OF HIS
GRACE, WHEREIN HE HATH MADE US ACCEPTED IN THE BELOVED."
Ephesians 1:5-6

In the Old Testament, there were three types of persons who were anointed by God: the prophet, the priest, and the king.

As a believer, you are also a prophet, a priest, and a king because God has anointed you. As prophet, you are to receive the Word from God and share that Word with others. As priest, you have direct access to God, so you can worship Him and offer spiritual sacrifices to Him. As king, you are to reign with Christ.

What an awesome responsibility plus an awesome privilege!

As you face the cares of the day, ask yourself, "What would a prophet say?" "How would a priest respond?" and "Would a king do this?"

Spiritual concerns and prayer requests

Today I will…

"FOR WHERE TWO OR THREE ARE GATHERED TOGETHER IN MY NAME, THERE AM I IN THE MIDST OF THEM." Matthew 18:20

One day, the secret service visited a church to check it out for the President of the United States. For some reason the President decided not to come, but the news was already out around town. Soon people were calling the church to find out if anyone could come that Sunday.

A lady called to say that she wasn't a member, but she wanted to see the President. She asked the pastor, "Is it true that the President of the United States is going to be in your services on Sunday?" The preacher said, "No madam, he will not be here, but the King of kings will and that ought to be good enough for you."

Jesus meets with His people, and He doesn't care about the credentials of the guest list. He is in their midst.

❦❦❦

What credentials do you bring to the table when you meet with God? Have you ever read of Paul's credentials in Philippians 3:4-6? What was his response in verses 7-14? What should be yours?

Spiritual concerns and prayer requests ....

....

....

....

....

....

....

Today I will... ....

....

AUGUST 10

"My little children, these things write I unto you, that ye sin not. And if any man sin, we have an Advocate with the Father, Jesus Christ the righteous: And He is the propitiation for our sins: and not for ours only, but also for the sins of the whole world." 1 John 2:1-2

The headline of an article read "Tail Was Short. Snake Was Not." Needless to say, it caught my attention and so I read the entire article.

It seems that there was a lady in South Africa who passed a haystack one day, and saw the tail of a snake. She took a stick to kill it and before she knew it she was wrestling with a 17-foot python! Gratefully, a man quickly came along to kill the snake with a fence post; otherwise it would have crushed her to death.

You may think your sin is just a little sin, but I want to tell you that it is part of the same snake. Sin murdered Jesus, and sin will crush you. Your only hope is salvation through Jesus Christ.

❈❈❈

How would you define these words: sin, advocate, propitiation? If you need some help, read these verses: 1 John 3:4, Hebrews 13:6, and Romans 5:6-8.

Spiritual concerns and prayer requests ....

....

....

....

....

....

....

Today I will... ....

....

"CAST THY BURDEN UPON THE LORD, AND HE SHALL SUSTAIN
THEE: HE SHALL NEVER SUFFER THE RIGHTEOUS TO BE MOVED."
Psalm 55:22

I have a preacher friend who was on an airplane when the weather got really rough. The lady next to him was whimpering a little from fear and so he turned to her and tried to comfort her.

She said, "Do you mean to tell me you're not afraid?" And he replied, "Well, I have committed my life into the keeping of my heavenly Father. And I will have to be honest, I have reminded Him about that fact several times since we've been up here."

Cast your burden upon the Lord, and leave it there. Don't pick it back up. He is able. In fact, He is *more* than able.

W hen trials or disappointments come your way, remind yourself that God WILL sustain you. Write out below and memorize 1 Peter 5:7.

Spiritual concerns and prayer requests..

....

....

....

....

....

Today I will...

....

AUGUST 12

"FOR IT IS GOD WHICH WORKETH IN YOU BOTH TO WILL AND TO DO OF HIS GOOD PLEASURE." Philippians 2:13

I can't do anything like Jesus, can you? At least not in my strength. But, aren't you glad that the *Example* of our obedience is also the *Enabler* of our obedience? God is responsible for not only the *desire*, but also the *doing*.

The word "worketh" in Philippians 2:13 is the word from which we get our English word "energy." God energizes us to do His will. It is like the power steering in your automobile. The power steering is there to work for you, but it waits on you to turn the wheel. The moment you turn the wheel, you will notice the wonderful power.

The moment you decide to serve God, His power takes over. God is waiting on you right now to serve Him. What are *you* waiting for?

❧❧❧

Today, I challenge you to attempt something so great for God that it is doomed to failure without God in it. Attempt the impossible. Reach for the unreachable. Dream the improbable.

Spiritual concerns and prayer requests...
....
....
....
....
....
....

Today I will… ....
....

AUGUST 13

"THIS IS THE DAY WHICH THE LORD HATH MADE; WE WILL REJOICE AND BE GLAD IN IT." Psalm 118:24

Have you ever heard someone say, "He has more time than I have." That's not true. No one has more time. There are only 86,400 seconds in a day.

Nobody has more time than that. Even the man who bought the most expensive watch ever—an $11 million watch at a Sotheby's auction in 1999—doesn't have more time!

He doesn't have one more second than you have. You have a day that God has made. It is a gift from God. That is why it is called the present. Every morning, His mercies are new. Every day God gives you enough time to learn, enough time to work, enough time to laugh, enough time to love. He gives you enough time to do gracefully everything He wants you to do. It is a gift.

What kind of steward are you of that gift today?

Have you ever been micromanaged? That is a negative term to most everyone in business, but I challenge you to micromanage yourself for one month, but just in one area. That is the area of evangelization. Set a goal to spend time in prayer daily for your lost friends. Set a goal for the number of times each day you are going to talk to others about Jesus Christ. All these things are part of your witness. When the month is over, see how you did!

Spiritual concerns and prayer requests..
....
....
....
....
Today I will…..
....

AUGUST 14

"FOR GOD SO LOVED THE WORLD, THAT HE GAVE HIS ONLY BEGOTTEN SON, THAT WHOSOEVER BELIEVETH IN HIM SHOULD NOT PERISH, BUT HAVE EVERLASTING LIFE." John 3:16

A boy was having difficulty living the Christian life. He went to his pastor who told him to go see a painting. The caretaker at the gallery took him to a large room where the painting adorned an entire wall.

The young man was repulsed at what he saw. It was a painting of Christ on the cross but the perspective from which the artist painted it was off balance. It looked grotesque. The caretaker said, "Son, you need to get closer." The young man came closer. "Son, you need to get lower." The young man got lower. "No, closer and lower."

Before the young man knew what was happening, he was kneeling at the foot of the cross and when he looked up, he understood the entire painting. Until you are willing to take your place at the foot of the cross, the Christian life will never make sense to you.

S pend some time meditating on what Jesus experienced as He suffered the anguish, accusations, scourging, mocking, and actual crucifixion to make atonement for your sin.

Spiritual concerns and prayer requests...

....

....

....

....

....

....

Today I will...

....

AUGUST 15

"ALTHOUGH THE FIG TREE SHALL NOT BLOSSOM, NEITHER SHALL FRUIT BE IN THE VINES; THE LABOR OF THE OLIVE SHALL FAIL, AND THE FIELDS SHALL YIELD NO MEAT; THE FLOCK SHALL BE CUT OFF FROM THE FOLD, AND THERE SHALL BE NO HERD IN THE STALLS: YET I WILL REJOICE IN THE LORD, I WILL JOY IN THE GOD OF MY SALVATION." Habakkuk 3:17-18

So many times we say, "Oh, I love the Lord because He has given me a wonderful family." Or, "I love the Lord because of the beautiful day He has given." I call this "because" kind of love.

And that kind of love can be threatening. *How can that be?* What if a woman told her husband, "Honey, I love you *because* you're so rich." Then, he loses his health and ability to earn an income for the family. What if a husband told his wife, "I love you *because* you're such a great cook." And she loses her ability to cook.

These would be threats to the future of their love for one another. They could say, "Well, since I can no longer do this, I have lost his (her) love." There are a lot of people who love God this way. They love Him as long as He is blessing them.

Read Job 1:20-22 and ask yourself, "Would you still love God if He took your family, your home, and your health away?" If you don't think you would, then read Job 40:3-5 and 42:1-6 and determine what steps are you going to take to love Him no matter what.

Spiritual concerns and prayer requests ....
....
....
....
....

Today I will... ....
....

Practicing *the* Presence *of* God   231

AUGUST 16

"AND THE WORLD PASSETH AWAY, AND THE LUST THEREOF: BUT HE THAT DOETH THE WILL OF GOD ABIDETH FOR EVER." 1 John 2:17

The only things that are going to last are the things of God. Period. The world is passing away and our days are fleeting. One day we will all be gone from this earth as we know it. You see, we're not citizens of earth trying to get to heaven. We're citizens of heaven sojourning here on earth. This earth is not our home.

Are you living for the pleasures of the flesh or the joy of the Spirit? Are you living for the praise of men or the glory of God? Are you living for today? Or are you living for eternity? Are you living for the things that can be seen or the things that cannot be seen?

One of these days, this old world and all of its vaulted culture, proud philosophies, egocentric intellectualism, and godless materialism is going to be forgotten. But he that "doeth the will of God abideth for ever."

❖❖❖

Be candid—if all you have is taken away, would you still do the will of God? Why or why not?

Spiritual concerns and prayer requests ....
....
....
....
....
....
....

Today I will... ....
....

AUGUST 17

"BUT THIS THING COMMANDED I THEM, SAYING, OBEY MY VOICE, AND I WILL BE YOUR GOD, AND YE SHALL BE MY PEOPLE: AND WALK YE IN ALL THE WAYS THAT I HAVE COMMANDED YOU, THAT IT MAY BE WELL UNTO YOU." Jeremiah 7:23

I have always enjoyed a good debate. But, when it comes to what God tells us to do, there's no debate.

Let me give you some of the best advice I have ever read. It was what Jesus' mother, Mary, said at the wedding feast in Cana when the wedding party ran out of wine. She said, "Whatsoever He saith unto you, do it" (John 2:5b). Oh, that we would live at that level of obedience!

Jesus touched the water pots with His divine finger of omnipotence, and the water turned to wine. The Bible tells us the people didn't understand where it came from but it also tells us "the servants which drew the water knew" (John 2:9b).

❦

Do you want insight into God? You will never know God by studying the Bible. You will know God when you obey the Bible.

Spiritual concerns and prayer requests...

....

....

....

....

....

....

Today I will..

....

AUGUST 18

"UNTO THE PURE ALL THINGS ARE PURE: BUT UNTO THEM THAT
ARE DEFILED AND UNBELIEVING IS NOTHING PURE; BUT EVEN
THEIR MIND AND CONSCIENCE IS DEFILED." Titus 1:15

Have you ever heard someone say, "Let your conscience be
your guide?" Well, that is not always the best saying
because a conscience can be defiled.

I heard a quote by a Christian American Indian about our
conscience: "In my heart there is an arrowhead with three points to it.
If I do wrong, the arrowhead turns, and cuts me. If I do wrong too
much, I wear out the points and it doesn't hurt me quite so much.
But when the pain is gone, watch out!"

A person can be numb or blinded to what he has done, thereby
making him oblivious to his wrongdoing. You can only let your
conscience be your guide, when God guides your conscience.

◄◄◄❖►►►

Read 2 Chronicles 16:9. Live today knowing the eyes of the
Lord are upon you. At the end of the day, ask yourself, "Did
I find favor in the eyes of the Lord by the way I talked, the things I
did, and the places I went?"

Spiritual concerns and prayer requests...

....

....

....

....

....

....

Today I will..

....

"COME NOW, AND LET US REASON TOGETHER, SAITH THE LORD:
THOUGH YOUR SINS BE AS SCARLET, THEY SHALL BE AS WHITE AS
SNOW; THOUGH THEY BE RED LIKE CRIMSON, THEY SHALL BE AS
WOOL." Isaiah 1:18

Years ago an account was reported of soldiers at Fort Dix who
were fighting a raging forest fire. Soon, they could see fire all
around with no route of escape.

Unexpectedly a plane flew overhead and dropped notes which said
they were surrounded by fire except for one narrow corridor. The note
gave instructions on how to find it, which the firefighters did and they
escaped. They could not see the way out, but the pilots could.

Thankfully, these soldiers did not question the authenticity or
reliability of the note and were saved. What a picture of our society
today! We are in a firestorm of trouble and an inferno of problems.
God has given us clear directions from above to help us escape with
our lives. What will you do?

Psalm 19:12 and 90:8 tells us we have "secret faults." Ecclesiastes
12:14 says God will bring even those secret things into judgment.
Confess to God that you don't even know all the ways you have
sinned against Him. Ask Him to reveal your secret faults so you can
confess them and be cleansed.

Spiritual concerns and prayer requests...

....

....

....

....

....

Today I will... ....

....

AUGUST 20

"DEARLY BELOVED, LET US CLEANSE OURSELVES FROM ALL FILTHINESS OF THE FLESH AND SPIRIT, PERFECTING HOLINESS IN THE FEAR OF GOD." 2 Corinthians 7:1

Satan tricks many people today by making them think they will become religious fanatics if they live a holy life. They want to see how close to the world they can live. They do not necessarily want to drink, but they will go to a bar, sit with their friends, and sip ginger ale so no one will know the difference.

Why can't they just go ahead and be holy? Why don't they just take a stand for Jesus Christ? I believe Jesus would rather have us on the wrong side of the fence than sitting on the fence! He says so in Revelation 3:15-16, "I know thy works, that thou art neither cold nor hot: I would thou wert cold or hot. So then because thou art lukewarm, and neither cold nor hot, I will spew thee out of My mouth."

❧

Open yourself to accountability. Ask God to lead you to a Christian with whom you can be accountable for the places you go, the people you spend time with, the way you spend your money. Enter into a covenant with that person to cleanse yourselves from "all filthiness of the flesh and spirit, perfecting holiness in the fear of God."

Spiritual concerns and prayer requests..

....

....

....

....

....

....

Today I will..

....

"For to me to live is Christ, and to die is gain." Philippians 1:21

I want you to finish this sentence: "For me to live is _____." Now, don't just give the answer you think you should. I want you to think of the thing that means the most to you because that is what it means for you to live.

You might fill in the blank with money, family, pleasure, finishing your education, fame, popularity, your children, your spouse, closing the next big deal, or even church work.

"For me to live is _____, to die is _____." If you put anything other than Christ in the first blank, then you must finish the second sentence with the word "loss" because you can't take anything else with you when you die.

※《❖》※

So, what word did you mentally put in the blank? Still can't think of anything? Then, spend some time with God—ask Him to show you if there is anything that you are putting above Him.

J Spiritual concerns and prayer requests ....
....
....
....
....
....
....
Today I will... ....
....

AUGUST 22

"HE IS THE ROCK, HIS WORK IS PERFECT: FOR ALL HIS WAYS ARE
JUDGMENT: A GOD OF TRUTH AND WITHOUT INIQUITY, JUST AND
RIGHT IS HE." Deuteronomy 32:4

God's work is perfect. Everything that God does is perfect.
His work is perfect; our work is wrought with flaws and
mistakes. Even the best that man can do is imperfect.

Take a sewing needle that looks so perfect and sleek. Put it under
a microscope and adjust it until you can see the intricate detail of the
needle. What will you find? It will look like a raggedy old pine
stump with broken bark.

Now, pick a rose off a bush and put one of its petals under that
microscope. You will be amazed at the miniature world of design and
delicacy because God's work is perfect. He never makes a mistake.

❦

Do you feel like a mistake today? Ask God to give you a special
anointing of His presence. And remind yourself of these things:
*I am not a mistake. I am created in His image. I am in the palm of
His loving hands and under the shelter of His wings. I am chosen
and loved by the Lord God to fulfill a special purpose.* Then believe
on those things because God's Word has said so.

Spiritual concerns and prayer requests ....

....

....

....

....

....

....

Today I will... ....

....

AUGUST 23

"FOR WHOSOEVER SHALL GIVE YOU A CUP OF WATER TO DRINK IN
MY NAME, BECAUSE YE BELONG TO CHRIST, VERILY I SAY UNTO
YOU, HE SHALL NOT LOSE HIS REWARD." Mark 9:41

Do you ever look at other Christians and say, "I wish I could pray as eloquently as him." Or, "I wish I could sing as pretty as her." Or, "I wish I could boldly share my faith like him."

My friend, you may not feel you have much talent, but I want you to know God sees your heart. He knows your desires. And He sees every little thing you do—however trivial you think it is. You may not be able to give as much as somebody else can. You may not have the intelligence of someone else. You may not have the talents of someone else.

My friend, God doesn't want your gifts. He doesn't need your gifts. He wants your love.

❦

Do you find that you compare yourself to others more than you would like? What have you learned in today's devotional that you can apply the next time you get caught up in the comparison game?

Spiritual concerns and prayer requests..
....
....
....
....
....
....

Today I will...
....

AUGUST 24

"ACCORDING AS HE HATH CHOSEN US IN HIM BEFORE THE FOUNDATION OF THE WORLD, THAT WE SHOULD BE HOLY AND WITHOUT BLAME BEFORE HIM IN LOVE." Ephesians 1:4

The church, as the bride of Christ, was in the heart and mind of God before the foundation of the world.

In the same way, Abraham sent one of his servants to find a bride for his son Isaac and she didn't even know anything about it (see Genesis 24). There she was, not dreaming two very important persons were holding a conversation about her. They were making plans for her. And in Genesis 24:14, we learn she was divinely appointed. She had already been chosen in the heart and mind of God.

I like to call this the predetermination of the bride. In the secret counsel halls of the Almighty, a conference was held. A bride was chosen. He set His affection upon us. Isn't it wonderful that we were chosen in Him before the foundation of the world?

What a glorious truth for you to share with someone today who may be feeling like they're not worth much. Ask God to lead you to that someone right now.

Spiritual concerns and prayer requests...

....

....

....

....

....

....

Today I will... ....

....

"For it pleased the Father that in Him should all fullness dwell." Colossians 1:19

Do you know why everything happens? It is to bring glory to God the Father, God the Son, and God the Holy Spirit. In fact, God's Word tells us Jesus Christ is to have preeminence in all of history. All of history is culminating in this one thing.

Do you know why the world was created? Jesus. Do you know why the Holy Spirit ministers? Jesus. Do you know why there is going to be a final judgment? Because "every tongue shall confess that Jesus Christ is Lord, to the glory of God the Father" (Philippians 2:11).

Hitler and Hemingway will confess it. Buddha and Mohammad will confess it. None of us can change that fact—all of creation will acknowledge Jesus Christ as Lord.

Next time someone asks you why something happens, tell them: "for the glory of God."

Spiritual concerns and prayer requests..
....
....
....
....
....
....

Today I will…...
....

AUGUST 26

"LEAVE THERE THY GIFT BEFORE THE ALTAR, AND GO THY WAY;
FIRST BE RECONCILED TO THY BROTHER, AND THEN COME AND
OFFER THY GIFT." Matthew 5:24

Jesus tells us to leave our offering and make things right with a
brother before we can worship. No one can be right with God
and consciously wrong with his brother.

Notice that Jesus doesn't say you need to leave your tithe and go
reconcile with a brother if you have something against him (see
Matthew 18:15-20). Here, Jesus is saying you need to get things
right with a brother who has something against you.

Before you sing, before you pray, before you teach, before you
give, before you worship, the Bible says you are *first* to be reconciled
to your brother. There is no offering on earth that can substitute for
getting right with your brother. As far as you know, is there anyone
who is harboring ill feelings toward you? Then, the Lord says,
"Leave it there and go get it right."

Before you do anything else, right now, this very minute, ask God
to show you if there is anyone with whom you need to reconcile.
Then, go and do it my friend.

Spiritual concerns and prayer requests...

....

....

....

....

....

....

Today I will... ....

....

AUGUST 27

"SHOW ME THY WAYS, O LORD; TEACH ME THY PATHS. LEAD ME IN THY TRUTH, AND TEACH ME: FOR THOU ART THE GOD OF MY SALVATION; ON THEE DO I WAIT ALL THE DAY." Psalm 25:4-5

When I obey God, I am a blessing to you. When you obey God, you are a blessing to me. You cannot obey God without your obedience spilling out in a blessing to all those around you.

The same is true in the negative. When we disobey God, we break the hearts of those around us. Perhaps you are breaking the hearts of your father, mother, wife, husband, or best friend today because you are disobeying God rather than letting the joy of Jesus be manifest in you.

Why do you obey God? For your good. For their gladness. And most of all, for His glory.

❧❦❧

Pray: *Lord, with all my heart, with all I am, I want to know You. I want our relationship to be close and my faith to grow. Cleanse me and make me new that I may be all that You want me to be.*

Spiritual concerns and prayer requests ....

....

....

....

....

....

....

Today I will… ....

....

AUGUST 28

"BUT THE LORD IS MY DEFENSE; AND MY GOD IS THE ROCK OF
MY REFUGE." Psalm 94:22

When you get ready to really live for God, you are going
to face three enemies.

You are going to face those who are in *despair*—they
are going to be howling calamity. You are going to face those with
disdain—they are going to laugh at you. And you're going to face those
with *discouragement*—they are going to say that it can't be done. And
you had better learn to silence their voices. How do you do that?

Get alone in the secret counsel halls of the Almighty and get your
eyes on God. If you listen to what those people say, you're not going
to be victorious in what God is calling you to do. I believe David
conquered Goliath because he got alone with God. I believe Joseph
survived abandonment and imprisonment because he got alone with
God.

❦

Consider those in your life who laugh at you, who tell you to give
up, and who tell you it can't be done. Now, get alone with
God, lift them up to God and ask Him to give you the strength to
love them to Jesus.

Spiritual concerns and prayer requests ....

....

....

....

....

....

....

Today I will... ....

....

AUGUST 29

"IN HIM WAS LIFE; AND THE LIFE WAS THE LIGHT OF MEN." John 1:4

I heard about a lady who was looking in her purse for her keys. She looked casually at first, then seriously, then frantically. Do you know what she discovered? *She was looking in the wrong purse!*

We don't know everything about each other, but I do know this much: you would like to have a full, meaningful, fulfilling life. Am I right? I think most people feel that way.

But, no matter how much you search, you'll not find it apart from Jesus Christ. Now, I'm not talking about life, as in breathing and heart beating. You have that. I'm talking about a rich, abundant life that Christ died to give you. Life is in Christ. Only Christ can give you life.

❦

As the hymn says, it's time to turn your eyes to Jesus and look full in His wonderful face. That's where you will find meaning and fulfillment.

Spiritual concerns and prayer requests ....

....

....

....

....

....

....

....

Today I will… ....

....

AUGUST 30

"JESUS SAITH UNTO HIM, RISE, TAKE UP THY BED, AND WALK."
John 5:8

In the Gospels, we learn about a man who languished by a pool for 38 years along with a myriad of others, hoping for someone to put him in the pool when the waters stirred so he could be healed (see John 5:1-9). He had a place in line, but someone always stepped in front of him. What was Jesus response? Step out of line, take up your bed and walk!

Suppose a man had been standing in line for Super Bowl tickets for 38 years. His buddy comes up to him and says, "I have two tickets on the 50-yard line. Come on." If he steps out of line, he puts all of his trust in this guy's word that he has two tickets on the 50-yard line.

Do you know what a lot of us do? We want to make a provision for our flesh or we want to keep our spot in line. Jesus says, "Leave it behind."

◈

What are you holding onto in your life that God wants you to give up so you can live the life He died to give you? Can't think of anything? Maybe there's not anything, but just in case, spend some time talking to God about it and ask Him to reveal any of those things to you.

Spiritual concerns and prayer requests..

....

....

....

....

....

Today I will…...

....

"THESE THINGS HAVE I SPOKEN UNTO YOU, THAT MY JOY MIGHT REMAIN IN YOU, AND THAT YOUR JOY MIGHT BE FULL." John 15:11

D o you depend upon Jesus Christ? I mean *totally* depend upon Him? Here's the way you can tell—are you resting in Him today. You see, when you are totally committed to Jesus Christ, you rest in Him. You realize it is necessary for Him to supply your every need.

Have you ever looked at a branch? It has no other source of life than the vine. If you asked that branch, "What's your secret for your healthy leaves and fruit?" then it would say, "My secret is that I'm resting in the vine." "But, what about your needs?" you ask. "I know I have needs, but that's not my responsibility. My response is to rest in the vine's ability to provide. I don't produce the fruit. I just bear it."

Are you resting in the Lord today?

T ake a walk outside or look out the window the next few days. If you can, take a close look at the trees, shrubs, and vines. Meditate on what it means to abide in Christ "that your joy might be full."

Spiritual concerns and prayer requests...

....

....

....

....

....

....

....

Today I will..

....

SEPTEMBER 1

"I PRESS TOWARD THE MARK FOR THE PRIZE OF THE HIGH CALLING OF GOD IN CHRIST JESUS." Philippians 3:14

P aul didn't want to fail. He strained with every inch, every ounce, every nerve, and every part of his body to win the prize. He had ambition. But, it was more than just ambition, it was a *holy* ambition.

He said, "I want that prize and I'm going to have it. I'm going to be like an athlete who denies himself worldly pleasures. I am going to train like an athlete. I'm going to stay in shape for the Lord Jesus. I am going to do all that is necessary that I may win."

Friend, the Bible clearly teaches we ought to be ambitious, but for the right reason. And that reason is for Jesus. May God deliver us from pint-sized ambitions and small-time aspirations!

R ead 1 Corinthians 9:24-27. Do you want to win the prize that Paul talks about? Then, what are you waiting for? Buffet your body and make it your slave. Take every thought captive. Put on the armor and go into battle.

Spiritual concerns and prayer requests...

....

....

....

....

....

....

Today I will..

....

SEPTEMBER 2

"AND LEAD US NOT INTO TEMPTATION, BUT DELIVER US FROM
EVIL: FOR THINE IS THE KINGDOM, AND THE POWER, AND THE
GLORY, FOR EVER. AMEN." Matthew 6:13

Mike Kolen, who played linebacker for the Miami
Dolphins, once told me this story. "When I graduated
from Auburn University, Coach Shug Jordan asked me
to do some scouting for him. I said, 'Sure Coach, what kind of man
do you need?'

Coach said, 'You know the guy you can knock down and he
stays there?' I said, 'Sure!' Coach said, 'We don't need him. You
know the guy you can knock down, he gets up, you knock him down
again, and he gets up?' I said, 'Yes! You want him?' 'No,' said
Coach, 'I want the guy that's knocking everybody down. That's the
guy I want.'"

I am grateful Jesus picks us up when we are knocked down. But,
wouldn't you like to do a little knocking down of the devil for a
change? You can if you will learn to pray, "Lord, lead me not into
temptation, but keep me from evil."

❧❦❧

What is your greatest temptation? Gossip? Alcohol? Drugs?
Lust? Power? Friend, whatever your struggle, don't go out
into the world today without first praying Matthew 6:9-13.

Spiritual concerns and prayer requests..

....

....

....

....

....

Today I will..

....

SEPTEMBER 3

"NEITHER YIELD YE YOUR MEMBERS AS INSTRUMENTS OF UNRIGHTEOUSNESS UNTO SIN: BUT YIELD YOURSELVES UNTO GOD, AS THOSE THAT ARE ALIVE FROM THE DEAD, AND YOUR MEMBERS AS INSTRUMENTS OF RIGHTEOUSNESS UNTO GOD." Romans 6:13

Did you know that if you let the devil be uppermost in your life today, it is because you are doing the letting? Before you were saved, you had no choice. You were a slave to sin (John 8:34). More than that, you were dead in your trespasses and sin (Ephesians 2:1-3).

Does a dead man choose to be righteous? No. But, if you are saved, God has made you alive in Christ (Ephesians 1:4-5). Now, you don't have to let sin have the upper hand in your life.

There is absolutely no power that says you must sin. When God saved you, He gave you the power to overcome sin. When Jesus becomes your Lord, you dethrone sin and enthrone Him. We need to be like the man who prayed, "Lord, help me cooperate with You, so You won't have to operate on me."

Ask God to reveal if you have been knowingly or unknowingly yielding yourself as an instrument of <u>un</u>righteousness. Ask Him to convict you and bring you to repentance. Ask His forgiveness and for His power to be an overcomer. Now, praise God for He makes all things new! (Revelation 21:5)

Spiritual concerns and prayer requests...

....

....

....

....

Today I will...

....

"I WILL PRAISE THEE, O LORD MY GOD, WITH ALL MY HEART:
AND I WILL GLORIFY THY NAME FOR EVERMORE." Psalm 86:12

What is bringing you joy today? You say, "The Lord is making me happy." How do you know it's not that nice automobile? Or your family? Or your good looks? Or your bank account? Or your popularity?

Here's how you can know: *By the process of elimination*. If God took away your health, home, and your job, and you still have joy, then you know it is Jesus. If you lose your joy when you lose any of these things, you are an idolater because that is where you are getting your joy.

I don't mean that you cannot be temporarily upset over the loss, but if the joy goes out of your life, you weren't getting your joy from the Lord. You'll never know Jesus is all you need until Jesus is all you have.

※◆◆◆※

It's time for your heart check-up. Do you truly love God with ALL your heart? Recommit your life to Him today—surrendering every bit of who you are and what you have to Him. If necessary, ask His forgiveness for committing idolatry.

Spiritual concerns and prayer requests...

....

....

....

....

....

....

Today I will…...

....

SEPTEMBER 5

"COMMIT THY WAY UNTO THE LORD; TRUST ALSO IN HIM; AND HE SHALL BRING IT TO PASS." Psalm 37:5

Many say they have committed their lives to the Lord, but have they really? The psalmist challenges us to commit our way to the Lord.

The word "commit" in this passage has the idea of rolling a burden over to the Lord. I often recall a hymn Minnie A. Steele wrote in 1908 entitled, "I Remember When My Burdens Rolled Away."

The first verse says, "I remember when my burdens rolled away; I had carried them for years, night and day. When I sought the blessed Lord, And I took Him at His word, Then at once all my burdens rolled away."

Well, she knew what she was talking about! Do you?

Read Psalm 55:22 and once again, roll over to the Lord your burdens. Surrender everything to Him.

Spiritual concerns and prayer requests...

....

....

....

....

....

Today I will...

....

SEPTEMBER 6

"HAVING A GOOD CONSCIENCE; THAT, WHEREAS THEY SPEAK EVIL OF YOU, AS OF EVILDOERS, THEY MAY BE ASHAMED THAT FALSELY ACCUSE YOUR GOOD CONVERSATION IN CHRIST." 1 Peter 3:16

Have you ever been criticized? Maybe blamed for something you didn't do? Or been unjustly slandered? You are not alone.

Jesus was the whipping boy of much criticism and slander in His day. Was He worried? No. You, too, must not worry when others speak falsely. Just give that to the Lord.

Author and pastor, Peter Lord told me one day, "When anybody says anything bad about me, I just say, 'Thank God they don't know any more.'" Jesus tells us, "When they criticize you, just roll that over onto Me. I understand and I am in charge. You just trust in Me."

❦❖❦

Lift up your hands, as a gesture of giving, to God all of those people who have criticized or judged you over the years. Ask Him to forgive them. Ask Him to give you grace and strength to love them.

Spiritual concerns and prayer requests..

....

....

....

....

....

....

Today I will…..

....

SEPTEMBER 7

"REST IN THE LORD, AND WAIT PATIENTLY FOR HIM: FRET NOT THYSELF BECAUSE OF HIM WHO PROSPERETH IN HIS WAY, BECAUSE OF THE MAN WHO BRINGETH WICKED DEVICES TO PASS." Psalm 37:7

We don't like the word "rest" do we? We're always running around pulling up our radishes by the roots to see how they're growing, and then cramming them back into the ground.

And yet Isaiah tells us, "And therefore will the LORD wait, that He may be gracious unto you, and therefore will He be exalted, that He may have mercy upon you: for the LORD is a God of judgment: blessed are all they that wait for Him" (Isaiah 30:18).

You're not going to hurry God because He is not interested in time. He's interested in timing. Lean back, watch, wait, and trust. He knows what He is doing.

⊰⊱

Thank God for the process of waiting. Thank God for hearing every one of your prayers. Thank Him for not forgetting you. Thank Him for this opportunity He has given you to grow in trusting Him. Thank Him for His sovereignty. Thank Him for knowing better than you what you need and what is best for you.

Spiritual concerns and prayer requests...

....

....

....

....

....

Today I will... ....

....

SEPTEMBER 8

"BLESSED BE THE GOD AND FATHER OF OUR LORD JESUS CHRIST, WHICH ACCORDING TO HIS ABUNDANT MERCY HATH BEGOTTEN US AGAIN UNTO A LIVELY HOPE BY THE RESURRECTION OF JESUS CHRIST FROM THE DEAD." 1 Peter 1:3

There are some people who think you can lose your salvation once you have it. I have one truth that will dispel that idea.

Whether or not you can lose your salvation depends upon how you got it. If you were saved by your good works, then you can lose your salvation by your bad works. But, God's Word is very clear on this point. Titus 3:5 says, "Not by works of righteousness which we have done, but according to His mercy He saved us, by the washing of regeneration, and renewing of the Holy Ghost."

How is someone saved? By grace. And if it is by grace, then you're kept by grace (see Ephesians 2:8-9). Salvation is not rooted in the merit of man, but in the mercy of God.

❧❦❧

Praise God for the regenerating work of His Holy Spirit, for the atoning blood of His Son, and for His calling upon your life. And thank Him for the permanence of your salvation.

Spiritual concerns and prayer requests...

....

....

....

....

....

....

Today I will…...

....

SEPTEMBER 9

"WHO ARE KEPT BY THE POWER OF GOD THROUGH FAITH UNTO SALVATION READY TO BE REVEALED IN THE LAST TIME." 1 Peter 1:5

Believers are "kept" by the power of God. This word "kept" in 1 Peter 1:5 is a military term. It literally means to be garrisoned about as soldiers around a fort.

Think of the power of God as a fortress and you are on the inside. Now, how do you feel? Pretty secure, right? So many people get the idea that we keep ourselves safe. Friend, *He* keeps us.

A father was crossing a street with his son. The son had hold of his daddy's hand when the light changed and the cars surged forward. The father grabbed his son's chubby little hand and almost lifted his son across the street to escape the oncoming traffic.

That is the way God holds us. Psalm 37:24 promises, "Though he fall, he shall not be utterly cast down: for the LORD upholdeth him with His hand."

❦

You are in God's right hand. Write that down and post it in a place where you can meditate on it throughout the day. Now, ask yourself, "Knowing this…can anything this week change that truth?"

Spiritual concerns and prayer requests ....

....

....

....

....

....

....

Today I will… ....

....

"BUT HE KNOWETH THE WAY THAT I TAKE: WHEN HE HATH TRIED ME, I SHALL COME FORTH AS GOLD." Job 23:10

In order to refine gold, a goldsmith places it over a fire until it bubbles and glows. He skims off the impurity from the top and knows when he can see his reflection, the gold is pure.

That is what the Lord is doing when you go through trials. When He can see His likeness reproduced in your life, He'll know you have become gold fit for His use and for His glory.

But, the fire is hot! Yes, but God controls it. A jeweler is no more careful with his gold than a father is with his children. He knows what He is doing. *But, what about those things He is burning out of my life?* You don't need them. If you needed them, your loving Father would make sure you kept them.

Has God taken anything out of your life recently that you thought you couldn't live without? Thank Him.

Spiritual concerns and prayer requests...

....

....

....

....

....

....

Today I will... ....

....

SEPTEMBER 11

"SO THEN FAITH COMETH BY HEARING, AND HEARING BY THE WORD OF GOD." Romans 10:17

Have you ever wondered why some people seem to have so much faith, while others have weak faith, and some have no faith at all? Is God unfair? No, God is no respecter of persons (see 2 Chronicles 19:7). He has given to every man a measure of faith (see Romans 12:3).

And so, what is faith? Let me first say what it is not. Faith is not positive thinking or optimism. It is not a feeling that you can do something. It is not a hunch or looking on the sunny side of the street.

Faith is getting a word from God and acting upon it. You see, when you get a word from God and believe that word, it is belief. But, when you act upon it, that is faith.

Faith is belief with legs on it. Today is the day that you put your foot of faith upon the promises of God and say, "That promise is mine!"

Love Worth Finding has a statement of faith—a list of beliefs to which we ascribe. This week do the same for yourself. Start each sentence with "I believe..." Some topics you will want to cover are salvation, the nature of God, faith, and God's Word.

Spiritual concerns and prayer requests..

....

....

....

....

....

....

Today I will...

....

SEPTEMBER 12

"COME NOW, AND LET US REASON TOGETHER, SAITH THE LORD: THOUGH YOUR SINS BE AS SCARLET, THEY SHALL BE AS WHITE AS SNOW; THOUGH THEY BE RED LIKE CRIMSON, THEY SHALL BE AS WOOL." Isaiah 1:18

Every rebel has a reason for his or her actions. You've probably heard a young person say, "Well, my dad drinks, so I smoke pot." Do you know what kind of reasoning that is? Brute beast reasoning, like Peter mentions in 2 Peter 2:12.

This young person doesn't think he has to obey his father. And he further reasons, "Well, he's not worthy of my obedience."

Do you know the only people who can demand perfect parents? Perfect children. The only person who can demand a perfect pastor is a perfect church member. The only person who can demand a perfect politician is a perfect citizen! There is *never* a license for rebellion.

There are ways to reason together in a church, home, and government. A spirit of rebellion will bring a nation to its knees.

❖❖❖

Read 2 Corinthians 5:21. Jesus gave His life for you. Ask yourself what you should do in response. Now, go do it!

*S*piritual concerns and prayer requests..

....

....

....

....

....

....

Today I will…..

....

SEPTEMBER 13

"FOR VERILY I SAY UNTO YOU, THAT WHOSOEVER SHALL SAY UNTO THIS MOUNTAIN, BE THOU REMOVED, AND BE THOU CAST INTO THE SEA; AND SHALL NOT DOUBT IN HIS HEART, BUT SHALL BELIEVE THAT THOSE THINGS WHICH HE SAITH SHALL COME TO PASS; HE SHALL HAVE WHATSOEVER HE SAITH." Mark 11:23

Did you ever play king of the mountain as a child? When you were on high ground, you could shove the others down, even though they were entrenched and determined to overtake you.

In Joshua 14, we read that Caleb faced a city of giants, and yet because he had wholly followed the Lord, he had the strength of the Lord and said, "give me this mountain" (Joshua 14:11-12).

All of us face giants every day—giants of doubt, fear, discouragement, financial ruin, sickness, broken relationships. Do you think that the giants that were in the Promised Land took God by surprise? God knew they were there all the time—they were part of His purpose to strengthen their faith. It's time you got a bulldog grip on the Word of God and believe what He says to be true.

What are the giants you are facing today? Ask God for the faith to conquer those giants.

Spiritual concerns and prayer requests..

....

....

....

....

....

....

Today I will…...

....

SEPTEMBER 14

"A MAN'S PRIDE SHALL BRING HIM LOW: BUT HONOR SHALL UPHOLD THE HUMBLE IN SPIRIT." Proverbs 29:23

Have you ever taught someone to drive? What was the first thing you showed him? If you're like me, even before I showed my children the ignition switch, the accelerator, or the blinker, I showed them the brakes.

Now, suppose your learner said, "I don't want to know anything about the brakes. I just want to know how to make this thing go!" You would probably reply, "Forget the accelerator. Before you can go, you've got to learn to stop."

Put this in a spiritual realm. If I asked you to submit to God and you said, "I'm not interested in submission. I want the victory!" God is not going to pour out His power upon you, until He sees in you a spirit of submission.

If you are physically able, get on your knees and bow low in reverence to God. Allow this position of humility to transform your spirit into one of complete surrender and submission to the Almighty.

Spiritual concerns and prayer requests...

....

....

....

....

....

....

Today I will...

....

SEPTEMBER 15

"But the end of all things is at hand: be ye therefore sober, and watch unto prayer." 1 Peter 4:7

G Campbell Morgan, who preached his first sermon at 13 years of age, was a great expositor of the Word of God many years ago. He said, "I never lay my head on the pillow without thinking that perhaps before I awake, the final morning may have dawned. I never begin work without thinking that He may interrupt it to begin His own."

Every night before we go to sleep, we ought to say, "Jesus may come tonight." And every day we get our tools and go to work, this may be the last day of work that we do. We are to be looking for His return.

We are also to be longing for His return. Are you praying for Jesus to return? If you love Him, you ought to be longing for His return. Do you have Him in your heart, and long to lay your eyes upon Him and walk with Him and talk with Him? "Even so, come Lord Jesus" (Revelation 22:20).

M ake today like the last day you have on earth. What will you do differently? How will you spend your time? Think about it...then go and live like Jesus may come at any minute. And you know what? He just might!

Spiritual concerns and prayer requests...

....

....

....

....

....

Today I will...

....

SEPTEMBER 16

"HATRED STIRRETH UP STRIFES: BUT LOVE COVERETH ALL SINS."
Proverbs 10:12

There are people in every fellowship who take joy in finding something bad about somebody else. When they hear something ugly, they take great delight in exposing it.

Love does not rejoice in iniquity. Love wishes it never happened. Love tries to cover it up. That doesn't mean we condone sin, we just cover it.

Let me illustrate. Noah had three sons, Ham, Shem, and Japheth. Ham came and saw his father's nakedness and was quick to tell others. Shem and Japheth covered their father to help him cover his shame—not to condone what he had done, but to cover it. Wouldn't the world be a lot better place if we had that spirit?

❦

Write down the names of (1) someone who has hurt you recently, (2) someone who appears to have a better life than you, (3) someone who has done something wrong, but no one else knows about it. Now, lift that person up in prayer for God to forgive him or her. Ask God to give you an opportunity to show this person His love.

Spiritual concerns and prayer requests..

....

....

....

....

....

....

Today I will…..

....

SEPTEMBER 17

"RETURN UNTO THY REST, O MY SOUL; FOR THE LORD HATH DEALT BOUNTIFULLY WITH THEE." Psalm 116:7

I heard of a woman who woke up her husband because she thought she heard a burglar downstairs. He went down with a flashlight and was shining it around. Sure enough, there was a burglar in their home. He said, "Hold it right there. I've got a gun on you." He dialed the phone and called the police. "And another thing," he said, "Before you go, I want my wife to come down here and meet you. She's been looking for you for 24 years."

A lot of people are that way. They are borrowing trouble by anticipating or worrying about what may happen. What you need to do is stop looking to yesterday in guilt or anticipating tomorrow with anxiety.

Simply rest in the day the Lord has given you today. How do you do that? The first time someone irritates you or something frustrating happens, take a deep breath and thank God for whatever it is. Ask and He will give you what you need to handle whatever it is in His grace, patience, and love.

Spiritual concerns and prayer requests..

....

....

....

....

....

....

Today I will…..

....

SEPTEMBER 18

"AND, BEHOLD, I COME QUICKLY; AND MY REWARD IS WITH ME,
TO GIVE EVERY MAN ACCORDING AS HIS WORK SHALL BE."
Revelation 22:12

The difference between people is not that one has more time than the other. The difference is whether they use their time wisely.

You say, "Well, I'm just killing time." To kill time, is to commit suicide by degrees. You are just killing yourself because you + time = life.

Now, that doesn't mean you are going to be busy every moment. There needs to be balance in your life—checking in with God first before you make plans and add things to your agenda.

Make sure you are doing what God wants you to do. Jesus came to the end of His life and do you know what He said? "I have glorified Thee on earth: I have finished the work that Thou gavest Me to do" (John 17:4).

✦

Do you have a clear idea of what God wants to do through you today? If not, ask Him right now. Let Him lead you by His Spirit through His Word to discover His will.

Spiritual concerns and prayer requests..

....

....

....

....

....

....

Today I will..

....

SEPTEMBER 19

"LIKEWISE, YE YOUNGER, SUBMIT YOURSELVES UNTO THE ELDER. YEA, ALL OF YOU BE SUBJECT ONE TO ANOTHER, AND BE CLOTHED WITH HUMILITY: FOR GOD RESISTETH THE PROUD, AND GIVETH GRACE TO THE HUMBLE." 1 Peter 5:5

To be "clothed" in 1 Peter 5:5 means to tie a knot or put on a servant's apron. Basically, this verse tells us to tie on the apron of a slave and be humble.

Why do you think Peter used that figure of speech? I think it was because Jesus laid aside His garments, girded Himself with a towel, and washed their feet. But "Peter saith unto Him, 'Thou shalt never wash my feet.' Jesus answered him, 'If I wash thee not, thou hast no part with Me,'" (John 13:8).

The act was symbolic of the fact that even though we are saved, we walk in a dirty world and we need to come to Jesus daily to cleanse us from our sins, restore and refresh us. Also, you can't look down on somebody when you're washing their feet.

❈

Are you coming to Jesus for daily cleansing? Is there someone you should be showing humility to? Take a look at Jesus' life and use Him as your example.

Spiritual concerns and prayer requests...

....

....

....

....

....

....

Today I will... ....

....

"I AM THE TRUE VINE, AND MY FATHER IS THE HUSBANDMAN.
EVERY BRANCH IN ME THAT BEARETH NOT FRUIT HE TAKETH
AWAY: AND EVERY BRANCH THAT BEARETH FRUIT, HE PURGETH IT,
THAT IT MAY BRING FORTH MORE FRUIT." John 15:1-2

When Solomon built his temple, he employed eighty
thousand stonecutters. They chipped and shaped those
stones in the quarry *before* bringing them to the Temple
Mount. Why? Because Solomon didn't want the sound of the
hammers and chisels heard on the Temple Mount.

In the same way, you are part of the living stones of His Temple
and God is shaping you down here in the quarry called "earth." Part
of your shaping is in the form of persecution.

So, don't look at your persecutors as enemies, but as God's
stonecutters.

Next time someone criticizes, mocks, or reviles you, offer this
prayer: "Thank You God for bringing me another stonecutter."
God is shaping you to be what you ought to be.

Spiritual concerns and prayer requests..
....
....
....
....
....
....

Today I will…..
....

SEPTEMBER 21

"WHEREFORE LET THEM THAT SUFFER ACCORDING TO THE WILL OF
GOD COMMIT THE KEEPING OF THEIR SOULS TO HIM IN WELL
DOING, AS UNTO A FAITHFUL CREATOR." 1 Peter 4:19

Here are three reactions you need to have when you
encounter suffering.

First, you are to *rejoice* (see 1 Peter 4:13) in what
God is allowing to happen.

Second, you need to *review* your life (see 1 Peter 4:17-18). *Am I
suffering because of something I have done?* If the Holy Spirit
convicts you that your suffering is a result of your sin, then you need
to repent.

Third, when you review your life and discover your suffering is for
the cause of Christ, then simply *rely* on Him (see 1 Peter 4:19). It is
not your problem. It is His problem.

In our verse in 1 Peter, we see the word "commit." That is a
banking term which means to put something with someone else for safe
deposit. He will take care of you; you can bank on it.

❦

How do you typically react when you encounter suffering? Ask
God to give you a readiness plan to prepare yourself for
suffering—what does that include? What should you do or not do?

Spiritual concerns and prayer requests...

....

....

....

....

....

....

Today I will...

....

SEPTEMBER 22

"BUT TO HIM THAT WORKETH NOT, BUT BELIEVETH ON HIM THAT JUSTIFIETH THE UNGODLY, HIS FAITH IS COUNTED FOR RIGHTEOUSNESS." Romans 4:5

Justification is God's act whereby He declares those who have trusted in Christ to be as righteous as His Son is righteous. Salvation is not based on our works.

Do you know what God sees when He looks at me? He sees Jesus Christ. You may think that's arrogant. No, it's not. It's the Bible. I am in Christ and therefore God cannot see my sins (see 1 Corinthians 1:30). He only sees the righteousness of His Son.

Justification is more than just a pardon, it is a promotion. God doesn't just forgive our sins, He makes us righteous. Only God can take someone who is guilty and give that person righteousness. It is the saving work of God. What is the basis of our justification? His grace.

❦❧

Next time you pass a mirror and someone is with you, start an evangelistic conversation by saying, "God taught me something the other day about my reflection. Whenever we look in a mirror we only see ourselves. But, when God looks at me, He sees His Son." See how they respond.

Spiritual concerns and prayer requests..

....

....

....

....

....

....

Today I will..

....

SEPTEMBER 23

"WHOM GOD HATH SET FORTH TO BE A PROPITIATION THROUGH
FAITH IN HIS BLOOD, TO DECLARE HIS RIGHTEOUSNESS FOR THE
REMISSION OF SINS THAT ARE PAST, THROUGH THE FORBEARANCE
OF GOD." Romans 3:25

Propitiation is a big word that means satisfaction. Because God
is a holy God, His anger and justice burns against sin. And
He has sworn that sin will be punished.

There must be a satisfactory payment for sin so God said, "If I
punish man for his sin, man will die and go to hell. On the other
hand, if I don't punish man for his sin, My justice will never be
satisfied."

The solution? God said Jesus would become our substitute. He
would take the sin of mankind upon Himself in agony and blood—a
righteous judgment and substitute for sin. His wrath burned out on the
cross when His only Son died as man's propitiation for sin. And this
is love (see 1 John 4:10).

❦

When was the last time you thanked God for not sending you to
hell as you deserved? Maybe it's time you did that.

Spiritual concerns and prayer requests...
....
....
....
....
....
....

Today I will..
....

SEPTEMBER 24

"WHO THEN IS A FAITHFUL AND WISE SERVANT, WHOM HIS LORD
HATH MADE RULER OVER HIS HOUSEHOLD, TO GIVE THEM MEAT IN
DUE SEASON? BLESSED IS THAT SERVANT, WHOM HIS LORD WHEN
HE COMETH SHALL FIND SO DOING." Matthew 24:45-46

It is sinful for us to ask God to prove Himself by a miracle or sign, though I guess we have all done it.

As a young boy at Stetson University having my quiet time in the prayer room, I asked God to move a chair from one side of the room to the other. I told him, "I already believe You and I don't want to insult You, but what a confirmation it would be to my heart and life if You would just do this small miracle."

Isn't that dumb? I am so glad God didn't let the devil nudge that chair across that room and get me hooked on some kind of hocus-pocus. Jesus said that asking God for a sign, like this, is evidence of an evil, adulterous heart (see Matthew 12:39).

Oh, that God would find us faithful and unashamed of what we do in His name.

※⟨⟨❊⟩⟩※

Have you ever done something like asking God to perform some supernatural act to confirm in your heart that He is listening or that He is God? Confess that as unbelief, and ask His forgiveness. Ask Him to give you faith that loves Him just because He is worthy of your allegiance!

Spiritual concerns and prayer requests...

....

....

....

....

Today I will… ....

....

SEPTEMBER 25

"I, EVEN I, AM THE LORD; AND BESIDE ME THERE IS NO
SAVIOR." Isaiah 43:11

It takes more of God's power to save a soul through the cross of
Jesus, than it does to do any other thing. God had no difficulty
creating the universe. The Bible tells us that He spoke and it
was so. But, when God wrote salvation's story, He went to great
difficulty.

Let me illustrate. What if I held a service and had the power to
straighten a cripple's legs or to bring sight to the blind? The next
service would be standing room only. Now, I certainly want God to
heal, but let me tell you something else.

What if I held a service and a little girl walked down the aisle
and professed that God had saved her? That is a greater miracle than
opening the eyes of the blind because the Son of God had to hang on
a cross in agony and blood to purchase her salvation! Jesus did not
come as a great healer or teacher, He came as a Savior.

Can you define or put it into words what happens when God saves
a person? Ask God to show you in His Word what salvation
means and then try to put it into your own words. Share it with
someone this week.

Spiritual concerns and prayer requests..

....

....

....

....

....

....

Today I will... ....

....

SEPTEMBER 26

"AND WHOSOEVER DOTH NOT BEAR HIS CROSS, AND COME AFTER ME, CANNOT BE MY DISCIPLE." Luke 14:27

The cross not only saves us, but it continues to sanctify us. Have you read in Mark 8:34b where Jesus said, "Whosoever will come after Me, let him deny himself, and take up his cross, and follow Me"?

Many people think this means that our "cross" is a sickness, an unsaved spouse, or a cruel boss. However, a cross is not something that is forced upon you over which you have no choice. A cross is something you willingly take up.

Jesus willingly laid down His life. He calls us to do the same. Your cross is when you willingly die to yourself. You do this by saying, "No," to sin and self and "Yes," to Christ.

❦

Offer this prayer of commitment to God today: *Father, forgive me for putting myself first and You second. Forgive me for not taking up my cross to follow after You. Give me Your grace to die to myself—to die to those things in my life which do not bring You glory—and draw me closer to You.*

Spiritual concerns and prayer requests ....

....

....

....

....

....

....

Today I will... ....

....

SEPTEMBER 27

"MY LITTLE CHILDREN, THESE THINGS WRITE I UNTO YOU, THAT
YE SIN NOT. AND IF ANY MAN SIN, WE HAVE AN ADVOCATE WITH
THE FATHER, JESUS CHRIST THE RIGHTEOUS." 1 John 2:1

The way to deal with your sins is for you to confess—that means
you are to begin by agreeing with God as to what He says
about your sin. You also need to confidently deal with your
sin.

Now, what do I mean by that? You have your own attorney
when you go into the judge's chambers for adjudication. According to
God's Word, you have an Advocate, which is another name for
attorney.

The devil is the prosecuting attorney who points the accusing
finger at us, and says, "Look at him!" And Jesus, the defense
attorney, stands by our side and says, "But Father, look at Me. I
shed My blood for him." Because Jesus died, our debt is paid.
Hallelujah! Though our sins are as scarlet, He will wash them white
as snow (see Isaiah 1:18)!

Read Colossians 3:5-10. Are there any sins in this list for which
you need to confess and repent? If so, do it now.

Spiritual concerns and prayer requests...

....

....

....

....

....

Today I will...

....

SEPTEMBER 28

"ALL THINGS ARE DELIVERED UNTO ME OF MY FATHER: AND NO MAN KNOWETH THE SON, BUT THE FATHER; NEITHER KNOWETH ANY MAN THE FATHER, SAVE THE SON, AND HE TO WHOMSOEVER THE SON WILL REVEAL HIM." Matthew 11:27

When God condescends Himself to make Himself known to us, the Bible calls that "revelation." The Infinite reveals Himself to the finite.

But what is the agent in this revelation? The Holy Spirit. Only the Holy Spirit knows the mind of God and searches the deep things of God. You and I cannot know God apart from the Holy Spirit revealing Him to us. Isaiah 55:9 says, "For as the heavens are higher than the earth, so are My ways higher than your ways, and My thoughts than your thoughts."

Even in the human realm, the only way you and I know anything about each other is when we reveal ourselves to one another. And the only way that man will ever know God is for God to reveal Himself. Praise God that He has chosen to do that!

How well do you know God? How well do you *want* to know God? One way you can tell is to add up the amount of time you spend getting to know Him. How does that compare with the time you spend getting to know your friends, or learning how to play a game? Where is *your* passion?

Spiritual concerns and prayer requests ....

....

....

....

....

Today I will... ....

....

SEPTEMBER 29

"BLESSED ARE THEY WHICH DO HUNGER AND THIRST AFTER
RIGHTEOUSNESS: FOR THEY SHALL BE FILLED." Matthew 5:6

When Jesus said the one who hungers and thirsts for righteousness will be blessed, He was not talking about someone who had a mere appetite. He was talking about a starving man. God made us in such a way that we couldn't exist long without food.

What is a starving man interested in? The latest football scores? The flower arrangement at the Pink Lemonade society? The number of stars in the universe? No! He's only interested in one thing—food!

In fact, I discovered that a man can exist about forty days without food, about three days without water, and only eight minutes without air.

In the spiritual realm of eternity, man cannot exist one second without Jesus Christ.

Ask God to help you narrow your focus to the glory of God and the saving of souls.

Spiritual concerns and prayer requests...

....

....

....

....

....

Today I will... ....

....

SEPTEMBER 30

"FOR WHICH CAUSE WE FAINT NOT; BUT THOUGH OUR OUTWARD MAN PERISH, YET THE INWARD MAN IS RENEWED DAY BY DAY."
2 Corinthians 4:16

So many people think they cannot do much for the Lord as they enter their twilight years. God doesn't change just because your health may take a turn, or you feel weaker. The faith that is inside of you has not weakened.

The things that God calls us to do in life do not hinge upon our physical stamina or financial strength. Do you know where one of the great strengths of a church lies? In its seniors who have walked with God for years. With their reservoir of wisdom and fortress of faith, they get hold of God and though their bodies are wearing a bit, they are as strong spiritually as they ever were because God is their strength.

Douglas MacArthur once said, "You are as young as your faith, as old as your doubt, as young as your self-confidence, as old as your fear, as young as your hope, as old as your despair." God gives unfading strength for His undiminishing promises.

Are you retired? How are you using your time for the Lord? Ask God to help you do something for His glory: volunteer at a homeless shelter, go on mission trips, sing in the choir, write letters to prisoners and orphans, teach a Bible study, or spend time in intercessory prayer for the needs are great!

Spiritual concerns and prayer requests ....
....
....
....

Today I will... ....
....

OCTOBER 1

"IT IS VAIN FOR YOU TO RISE UP EARLY, TO SIT UP LATE, TO EAT THE BREAD OF SORROWS: FOR SO HE GIVETH HIS BELOVED SLEEP." Psalm 127:2

In the book of Jonah, we learn that Jonah reached a place of physical despondency (see Jonah 4:3 and 8). He wanted God to kill him.

Have you ever reached a place of despair and thought that everything and everyone was against you and you didn't know what to do? Maybe you just needed to lie down and get some sleep. Now, that may not sound like the most spiritual thing to do, but we cannot abuse our bodies without suffering the consequences. And being a child of God does not make you immune to physical exhaustion.

Have you ever heard of burn out? Where do you think we got that phrase? There is enough time in the day to gracefully do everything God wants us to do.

Do you feel you are on the edge of burn out? Perhaps you are already there. Before you turn to toast, ask God for His wisdom to set some boundaries in your life, to learn to say no, to delegate some of your responsibilities, to ask for a day off from work, to ask for a hug, or to perhaps turn to a Christian counselor for help.

Spiritual concerns and prayer requests...

....

....

....

....

....

....

....

Today I will… ....

....

OCTOBER 2

"FIGHT THE GOOD FIGHT OF FAITH, LAY HOLD ON ETERNAL LIFE,
WHEREUNTO THOU ART ALSO CALLED, AND HAST PROFESSED A
GOOD PROFESSION BEFORE MANY WITNESSES." 1Timothy 6:12

Some of the greatest spiritual defeats you will ever have will follow some of your highest spiritual victories. Jonah, Moses, and Elijah—all these men learned this.

Why does this happen? Because we are tired and feel we can just coast a while. We think, *Didn't God bless and give us a great victory?* But, we forget that the devil is clever. He knows just when to pull the rug out from under us.

Let me give you a little advice: Although the residual effects of yesterday's blessings will bless you, you cannot coast on yesterday's blessings. God has made you so you cannot live by experiences; you have to live by Jesus Christ one day at a time.

Has God blessed you with an extraordinary victory? What are you doing today to live a life worthy of that blessing and in allegiance to the One who has blessed you?

Spiritual concerns and prayer requests..

....

....

....

....

....

Today I will…..

....

OCTOBER 3

"I HAVE FOUGHT A GOOD FIGHT, I HAVE FINISHED MY COURSE, I HAVE KEPT THE FAITH." 2 Timothy 4:7

Do you know the way to finish the course? Keep looking to Jesus. I've preached the Gospel for over 50 years and God knows I have my faults and sins. He also knows I have repented and aim to get right with Him each and every day.

Although all of us are far from perfect, I can say this same God to Whom I have poured out my heart has kept me on course. He has kept me preaching the Gospel.

Finishing the course God has planned for us is never easy. It takes discipline and hard work. It takes picking ourselves up, dusting ourselves off, and starting over.

One of these days you are going to have to look back on your life. And I hope you will be able to say that you fought as a warrior and finished as an athlete.

❦

What race are you running? The rat race or the royal race? Take some time to pray about and write down some goals that will assist you in staying on track to the glory of God. Use Isaiah 61:1-3 as a guide.

Spiritual concerns and prayer requests ....
....
....
....
....
....
....

Today I will... ....
....

OCTOBER 4

"I TELL YOU THAT HE WILL AVENGE THEM SPEEDILY.
NEVERTHELESS WHEN THE SON OF MAN COMETH, SHALL HE FIND
FAITH ON THE EARTH?" Luke 18:8

I believe with all my heart that the call needs to go out today more clearly than ever before for Christians to keep the faith.

William Booth, the founder of the Salvation Army, said, "The chief danger of the 20th Century will be religion without the Holy Ghost, Christianity without Christ, forgiveness without repentance, salvation without regeneration, politics without God, and Heaven without Hell."

Are you seeing that today? We are but one generation away from paganism. If this generation doesn't keep the faith and pass it to the next, there will be no faith.

❧❀❧

Do you see any ways where you or your church has not kept the faith? If so, what are those ways? Ask God to give you a vision and bring revival in your heart and life and then fan the flame of revival in your church.

Spiritual concerns and prayer requests ....

....

....

....

....

....

....

Today I will... ....

....

OCTOBER 5

"THEN SAID JESUS UNTO HIS DISCIPLES, IF ANY MAN WILL COME AFTER ME, LET HIM DENY HIMSELF, AND TAKE UP HIS CROSS, AND FOLLOW ME." Matthew 16:24

Very early in our marriage, Joyce and I got on our knees and made a solemn vow before God that all we had would belong to Jesus Christ. We would not really own title to anything.

Now, we might hold title as far as men were concerned, but everything we owned would belong to the Lord. If He wanted it, He could have it. If He wanted to use it, if He wanted to destroy it, if He wanted to give it away, if He wanted to give more, that was His business.

Have you done that? Have you transferred everything to Christ? It's not your fame; it's your faith. It's not your ability; it's your availability. It's not your scholarship; it's your sacrifice.

Is there anything in your life you have received that God has not given you? Ask God to search your heart and then give those things back to Him.

Spiritual concerns and prayer requests ....

....

....

....

....

....

....

Today I will... ....

....

OCTOBER 6

"BUT SEEK YE FIRST THE KINGDOM OF GOD, AND HIS RIGHTEOUSNESS; AND ALL THESE THINGS SHALL BE ADDED UNTO YOU." Matthew 6:33

Many Christians are so materialistic they never look past the physical world to the transcended Christ above. They can only see what they can rationalize with their five senses of touch, taste, smell, sight, and hearing.

When a problem arises, it blows out every candle in their souls, knocks the sun out of their sky, and they can't enjoy the daily bread of life that Jesus promises. For some reading this, you have a gigantic problem, that to the world has disaster written all over it.

If you are seeking first His righteousness, God will give you all that you need. You have God on your side—the King of kings, the Lord of lords. And don't you forget it.

Read the entire context from which Matthew 6:33 is drawn—Matthew 6:19-34. Now, write Matthew 6:33 on slips of paper. Put them in your daily path as reminders of where your treasure is.

Spiritual concerns and prayer requests ....

....

....

....

....

....

....

Today I will... ....

....

OCTOBER 7

"FOR WITH GOD NOTHING SHALL BE IMPOSSIBLE." Luke 1:37

Christian author and speaker S.D. Gordon, said, "In every man's life there is a throne. And when self is on the throne, Christ is on the cross. But when Christ is on the throne, self is on the cross."

In your own life, there is something you hold to be the highest good, that captivates your attention, and that controls your life. Your decisions are made in light of this thing.

God's plan is not that Christ have a place in your life or that He have prominence in your life. Jesus Christ deserves and even demands, preeminence in your life. That means there is no rebuttal, no refusal, and no rival.

❦

What occupies the throne in your life? Yourself? Your family? Your position? Your home? Your possessions? Your looks? Your talents? Ask God to forgive you for having anything or anyone on the throne besides Himself. Ask Him to give you strength to repent, then take it off the throne and "rethrone" Him as Lord.

Spiritual concerns and prayer requests...
....
....
....
....
....
....

Today I will...
....

OCTOBER 8

"BLESSED BE HE THAT COMETH IN THE NAME OF THE LORD: WE HAVE BLESSED YOU OUT OF THE HOUSE OF THE LORD." Psalm 118:26

Heaven is intently interested in what is happening here on earth. There is a grandstand in heaven filled with heroes of the faith. They are watching us and cheering us on.

We are the runners; they are the spectators. If the runners of that day were inspired when they ran their race, how much greater should our effort be today with these saints behind us. Do you feel inspired? We should! It's an encouragement to know we are not alone out there in the race and that we have men and women who have run the race knowing the pitfalls that are out there.

Friend, I hope you feel encouraged and inspired to run the unique race God has set for you today. Know that we are praying for you and would be honored to hear how God is fulfilling your every need along the way.

Read Hebrews 11 about the heroes of the faith—may their faith inspire you to leave your comfort zone and do great and mighty things for the glory of God. Then send us an email or letter and let us know what God has done so we might praise Him for guiding you in your race.

Spiritual concerns and prayer requests...

....

....

....

....

....

....

Today I will…..

....

OCTOBER 9

"WHEREFORE SEEING WE ALSO ARE COMPASSED ABOUT WITH SO
GREAT A CLOUD OF WITNESSES, LET US LAY ASIDE EVERY WEIGHT,
AND THE SIN WHICH DOTH SO EASILY BESET US, AND LET US RUN
WITH PATIENCE THE RACE THAT IS SET BEFORE US, LOOKING UNTO
JESUS THE AUTHOR AND FINISHER OF OUR FAITH." Hebrews 12:1-2a

There are a lot of athletes with natural ability, but what is it
that turns a mediocre athlete into a gold medal champion?
One crucial element is that the gold medal athlete is willing to
hurt more than the other.

When you can't take another step, your muscles are sore, your
body is aching—this is what it means to be running the race with
perseverance as mentioned in Hebrews 12:1. You are bearing up under
tremendous pressure. You are running to build endurance.

Today, you may be hurting because a family member, coworker,
or classmate has been unfair to you. Perhaps you were passed over for
a promotion. Building a faith that will go the distance takes patience.

>|≪≫|<

Today is the day you press through the injustices of life. Instead of
feeling like you're not being treated fairly, it's time to put your
eyes on the One who was treated MOST unfairly on a cross so that
you would be forgiven. Run, Christian, run! The victory is yet to be won.

Spiritual concerns and prayer requests..

....

....

....

....

....

....

Today I will..

....

OCTOBER 10

Have you ever tried to get a bone away from a dog? It's not too easy, unless you have something better for him. Try offering a T-bone steak and that dog will drop his bone like a bad habit.

In the same way, the writer of Hebrews tried to encourage the Jewish Christians. They had a tendency to cling to the old customs of the Old Testament—to leave the dry bones of ceremonies and feast upon the delights of the Lord Jesus Christ. It's a lesson, we all must appropriate in our lives.

It can become comfortable for us to hold to our traditions, rather than try something new. But friend, there is no one and nothing that can compare with Jesus. You may learn to love Jesus better, but you can never love anything better than Jesus.

***

Read John 20:31. What does it mean to "have life through His name"? Meditate upon Revelation 19:13-16.

Spiritual concerns and prayer requests...

....

....

....

....

....

....

Today I will…..

....

OCTOBER 11

"BE OF GOOD COURAGE, AND HE SHALL STRENGTHEN YOUR HEART, ALL YE THAT HOPE IN THE LORD." Psalm 31:24

The world wants to know what we should do about the problems of the world. What about crime? Poverty? War? Hatred? Do you know why we never solve the problems? *Because we don't see the problem.*

The sociologist says it is just a cultural lag. The psychologist calls it an emotional disturbance. The philosopher calls it irrational behavior. The Marxist calls it the human class struggle. The humanist calls it human weakness. The criminologist calls it anti-human conduct.

The Bible calls it sin. And the only answer for sin is *Jesus*, Who executes the will of God, expresses the love of God, and expounds the mind of God.

What do you think it means that Jesus is the executor of God's will? How does He express the love of God? Can you give examples from His Word where Jesus has remarked upon the mind of God?

*S*piritual concerns and prayer requests...

....

....

....

....

....

....

Today I will… ....

....

OCTOBER 12

A child delights in what he has. A youth delights in what he does. An adult delights in what he is. The more mature you are the more you will desire to be something—not just to *have* something or to *do* something, but to *be* something.

What do you desire to be today? Someone who is known for the way they dress? The deals they close? The house they live in? Or do you want others to know you have a pure heart—a heart that is utterly devoted and surrendered to God.

Matthew 5:8 says, "Blessed are the pure in heart for they shall see God." They will know the unknowable, they will do the impossible, and they will see the invisible. I want to have a heart like that. What about you?

Ask God to give you the strength to do the things which He asks you to do in 2 Timothy 2:22-24. Then, pray Psalm 51:7.

Spiritual concerns and prayer requests...

....

....

....

....

....

....

Today I will…...

....

OCTOBER 13

"HE THAT HATH CLEAN HANDS, AND A PURE HEART; WHO HATH NOT LIFTED UP HIS SOUL UNTO VANITY, NOR SWORN DECEITFULLY. HE SHALL RECEIVE THE BLESSING FROM THE LORD, AND RIGHTEOUSNESS FROM THE GOD OF HIS SALVATION." Psalm 24:4-5

James Nicholson wrote a song, which is the desire of my heart: "Lord Jesus, I long to be perfectly whole; I want Thee forever to live in my soul. Break down every idol, cast out every foe; Now wash me, and I shall be whiter than snow."

Nothing beats closer to my heart, than the yearning to be pure before my Lord. I know the sweet fellowship with Jesus that comes when my heart is clean. And nothing, no nothing surpasses that in this world.

Are you failing in your Christian life because you are not pure? If you are, you're not alone. It seems as though a sewer pipe of filth and debauchery has broken and poured out into our world. Someone has well said, "Not since Manhattan Island was sold for $24 has so much dirt been sold so cheaply as it is here in America."

❦

Humbly come before the Lord and ask Him to search your heart for any wicked ways. Then in sincerity, confess them and claim 1 John 1:9: "If we confess our sins, He is faithful and just to forgive us our sins, and to cleanse us from all unrighteousness."

Spiritual concerns and prayer requests..

....

....

....

....

....

Today I will...

....

OCTOBER 14

"FOR AS HE THINKETH IN HIS HEART, SO IS HE: EAT AND DRINK, SAITH HE TO THEE; BUT HIS HEART IS NOT WITH THEE." Proverbs 23:7

A teacher asked a little boy to finish this proverb: "Cleanliness is next to…" And he said, "Cleanliness is next to impossible." Well, friend that little boy wasn't that far wrong, was he?

It's amazing what people do to try and purify themselves—fast, pray, kneel, walk, self-flagellate, hibernate, isolate. But, sadly they discover that human efforts aren't the pathway to purity because they keep doing what Zig Ziglar calls "stinkin' thinkin'."

Before we can hope to have a life of purity, we must have a clean thought life. God works from the inside out. He knows you cannot purify the water by painting the pump.

❦

Do you struggle with stinkin' thinkin'? Then, ask yourself some of these questions before that stinkin' thinkin' gets the best of you: (1) Does this thought help me love God more and love this person more?; (2) Do I really trust God to take care of this situation?; (3) Have I called upon God to help me take this thought captive and make it obedient to Christ?

Spiritual concerns and prayer requests ....

....

....

....

....

....

....

Today I will… ....

....

OCTOBER 15

"WITH MY WHOLE HEART HAVE I SOUGHT THEE: O LET ME NOT WANDER FROM THY COMMANDMENTS." Psalm 119:10

In 1758, Robert Robinson wrote a hymn that echoes in my heart from time to time: "Prone to wander, Lord, I feel it, Prone to leave the God I love; Here's my heart, O take and seal it, Seal it for Thy courts above."

Do you ever wander from God? Then, you know how it feels and how hard it is to return. If you feel far from God today, I implore you with all that I am, to return to Him with all your heart.

Make Psalm 86:11-13 your prayer today, "Teach me Thy way, O LORD; I will walk in Thy truth: unite my heart to fear Thy name. I will praise Thee, O LORD my God, with all my heart: and I will glorify Thy name for evermore. For great is Thy mercy toward me: and Thou hast delivered my soul from the lowest hell."

Do you want a blessing? Sing from memory or search for the song "Come Thou Fount Of Every Blessing." Mean it from your heart and meditate upon its great truths.

Spiritual concerns and prayer requests ....

....

....

....

....

....

....

Today I will… ....

....

"THY WORD HAVE I HID IN MINE HEART, THAT I MIGHT NOT SIN AGAINST THEE." Psalm 119:11

The home is a nice place for the Bible. The hand is a good place, as well. But I tell you, the heart and the head are the best places to store the Bible.

Do you ever ask yourself, "Why do I always cave in when temptation comes? Why can't I be an overcomer? Where is my breakthrough?" Wouldn't you like to be a victor rather than a victim, an overcomer rather than overcome?

Well, if you would like to learn how to turn temptations into triumphs, let me ask you this question: How much time do you spend reading, meditating, and studying the Word of God?

Take this challenge this week. For each hour you spend watching television, spend that time in the Bible. For every hour you work out at the gym, spend that time in the Bible. Does that seem overwhelming? Okay, then for every hour in activities like these, spend 20 minutes in the Bible. Then, write us and tell us what a difference God makes in your life.

Spiritual concerns and prayer requests..

....

....

....

....

....

....

Today I will…...

....

OCTOBER 17

"FINALLY, BRETHREN, WHATSOEVER THINGS ARE <u>TRUE</u>, WHATSOEVER THINGS ARE <u>HONEST</u>, WHATSOEVER THINGS ARE <u>JUST</u>, WHATSOEVER THINGS ARE <u>PURE</u>, WHATSOEVER THINGS ARE <u>LOVELY</u>, WHATSOEVER THINGS ARE OF <u>GOOD REPORT</u>; IF THERE BE ANY <u>VIRTUE</u>, AND IF THERE BE ANY <u>PRAISE</u>, THINK ON THESE THINGS." Philippians 4:8

Fifteen college professors who taught human motivation were asked to write a concise statement on that subject. After hours of study, they said: "What the mind attends to, it considers. What the mind does not attend to, it dismisses. What the mind attends to continually, it believes. What the mind believes, it eventually does."

How much of the Bible have you read? More importantly, how much of it are you applying to your life? Many read the Bible like a math book rather than a love story. They get the words, but they don't get the music.

It is not enough to simply read the Word. You must ask God to teach you. Psalm 119:18 says, "Open Thou mine eyes, that I may behold wondrous things out of Thy law."

Write below the above underlined words from Philippians 4:8. Reflect on each one of them and note what God reveals as to how they apply to your life.

Spiritual concerns and prayer requests ....
....
....
....
....

Today I will... ....
....

OCTOBER 18

"THE MEEK SHALL EAT AND BE SATISFIED: THEY SHALL PRAISE THE LORD THAT SEEK HIM: YOUR HEART SHALL LIVE FOR EVER."
Psalm 22:26

Have you ever wondered why people stumble onto inappropriate websites? Perhaps you even struggle in that area. It's because they are not feeding on Jesus. They are seeking satisfaction in the evil pleasures of this world, rather than the eternal promises of eternity.

Suppose you just finished a wonderful meal and somebody knocks on your front door. You answer it and they hold out a plate full of stale crumbs saying, "Eat this." You would say, "No thank you, I don't need that. I'm already satisfied."

When you feast on the goodness of Jesus, you won't be down a dark alley eating tin cans with the devil's billy goats. "And Jesus said unto them, I am the Bread of life: he that cometh to Me shall never hunger; and he that believeth on Me shall never thirst" (John 6:35).

Next time you drive to church, notice the number of people who are not on their way to church—pray for them. Ask God to make them thirsty and hungry for Himself.

Spiritual concerns and prayer requests ....

....

....

....

....

....

....

Today I will... ....

....

OCTOBER 19

"AND WE HAVE KNOWN AND BELIEVED THE LOVE THAT GOD HATH
TO US. GOD IS LOVE; AND HE THAT DWELLETH IN LOVE DWELLETH
IN GOD, AND GOD IN HIM." 1 John 4:16

If you asked a Christian brother or sister why God made us, they
would probably say that we were made to serve God. But, don't
you believe it. If God wanted servants, He could do a lot better
than mere mortals.

When the scribes asked Jesus what was the first commandment,
He said, "The first of all the commandments is, Hear, O Israel;
The Lord our God is one Lord: And thou shalt love the Lord thy
God with all thy heart, and with all thy soul, and with all thy mind,
and with all thy strength: this is the first commandment" (Mark
12:29-30).

The first commandment is not to *do something* for God, but to
love God. He made you and me in the likeness of His image, that
He might have fellowship with us and that we would praise Him.

How would you define the word "love"? Is it a verb or a noun?
What are you doing right now to show God that you love
Him?

Spiritual concerns and prayer requests ....

....

....

....

....

....

....

Today I will... ....

....

OCTOBER 20

"SHE HATH DONE WHAT SHE COULD: SHE IS COME AFOREHAND TO ANOINT MY BODY TO THE BURYING." Mark 14:8

Mary loved Jesus so much that she gave all she had. She didn't just pour out a little perfume to anoint Him, she gave it all (see Mark 14:3-9).

She couldn't put that perfume back in the bottle. She had broken it! Maybe it was her inheritance or hope chest. She didn't hold back any for a rainy day or her retirement.

Most of us would have said, "Lord, I would like to give You a little of this perfume. It cost me a year in wages, so I can't give it all to You. But, I want You to have some of it to show You how much I love You."

❖❖❖

Does this speak to your heart as much as it does mine? Confess, "Lord, I'm not willing to break the alabaster box. Forgive me. Enable me to give my all. Here I am. Take all of me."

Spiritual concerns and prayer requests...

....

....

....

....

....

....

Today I will…..

....

OCTOBER 21

"Abstain from all appearance of evil. And the very God of peace sanctify you wholly; and I pray God your whole spirit and soul and body be preserved blameless unto the coming of our Lord Jesus Christ." 1 Thessalonians 5:22-23

God expects us to be holy. But, when most people talk about holiness, they get a little nervous. They're interested in heaven and the hereafter, but not holiness in the here and now. They're interested in health, happiness, even helpfulness, but not holiness.

I had the privilege years ago to spend a day in prayer with Dr. Billy Graham and some other men. As we were sitting around a table sharing, Billy Graham said something I shall never forget. He said, "Gentlemen, I long to be holy. I want to be a holy man. Pray for me, that I will be holy."

Can you say, "More than anything in this world, I long to be holy"? If you can't, then spend some time today asking God to turn your heart to His and give you the desire to live a holy life.

Spiritual concerns and prayer requests...

....

....

....

....

....

....

Today I will...

....

"IF ANY MAN'S WORK SHALL BE BURNED, HE SHALL SUFFER LOSS:
BUT HE HIMSELF SHALL BE SAVED; YET SO AS BY FIRE." 1 Corinthians 3:15

A thousand years from now, some of the things that you think are so important are not going to be so important—your meticulously groomed lawn, who won the Super Bowl, your date for the Senior Prom, the type of your car you drove.

Now, there's nothing wrong with these things, but I want to ask you: What is there about your life that is going to remain when the mountains have crumbled? When the stars have fallen from their sockets? Wood, hay, and stubble are going up in flames!

But, "if any man's work abide which he hath built thereupon, he shall receive a reward" (1 Corinthians 3:14). Things are going to look much different in the light of eternity.

❦

Are you an investor—not in stocks and bonds or real estate, but in the souls of men? If not, may I encourage you, more than that may I exhort you, to spend your time, your talents, and your treasures in those things that matter most to God?

Spiritual concerns and prayer requests...

....

....

....

....

....

....

Today I will… ....

....

OCTOBER 23

"WHEREFORE GIRD UP THE LOINS OF YOUR MIND, BE SOBER, AND HOPE TO THE END FOR THE GRACE THAT IS TO BE BROUGHT UNTO YOU AT THE REVELATION OF JESUS CHRIST; AS OBEDIENT CHILDREN, NOT FASHIONING YOURSELVES ACCORDING TO THE FORMER LUSTS IN YOUR IGNORANCE." 1 Peter 1:13-14

The figure of speech, "gird up your loins," is mentioned a few times in God's Word. Here's a phrase we use today to describe the same thing: roll up your sleeves. It means to get serious about what you're doing.

We need to get serious about being Christians and living for God. One aspect of that is to have a single mind. Have you ever heard the expression, *Don't put all your eggs in one basket?* I believe Peter would tell us to do that, then label that basket, "Jesus is coming back!"

We need to live with a passionate, burning focus upon His return.

What are you doing today in anticipation of the Second Coming of Jesus Christ? It could even happen today.

Spiritual concerns and prayer requests...

....

....

....

....

....

....

Today I will...

....

"TRUST IN THE LORD, AND DO GOOD; SO SHALT THOU DWELL IN THE LAND, AND VERILY THOU SHALT BE FED." Psalm 37:3

This word "trust" is an interesting word. Its root is from the word that means "to lie face down on the ground." The idea is that a person is totally helpless. He has been cast down and has nothing to stand upon.

Some would say his pins have gone out from underneath him. He has no visible means of support. That is the place where God wants to bring us—where we have no physical means of support and all we have is God.

As a matter of fact, did you know that God will sometimes knock your feet out from beneath you so you might learn to trust Him? At that point, faith is no longer an option or a luxury; it is a necessity. To the world your situation looks hopeless, but that is right where God wants to show Himself powerful in your life.

Do you feel like you are in a hopeless situation today? A coin tossed in the air will either fall heads or tails. In the same way, fear and trust are opposite sides of a coin. When you toss your situation around, you can either choose to fear what is going to happen, or you can trust that God will take care of you. Pray Psalm 145.

Spiritual concerns and prayer requests...

....

....

....

....

....

....

Today I will…...

....

OCTOBER 25

"AND ONE CRIED UNTO ANOTHER, AND SAID, HOLY, HOLY, HOLY,
IS THE LORD OF HOSTS: THE WHOLE EARTH IS FULL OF HIS
GLORY." Isaiah 6:3

Of all the reasons I can think of for living a holy life, one of the most important is for us to identify with God. He is the thrice–holy God of Israel. Holy is the Father, holy is the Son, and holy is the Spirit.

What does it mean to be identified with God's character of holiness? Have you ever heard the expression *like father, like son?* That's what it means to be identified with God. I am a Rogers. My father's name is Arden Duncan Rogers. I have become a partaker of his nature and you would expect to find his characteristics in me because in the physical realm, he has fathered me.

Because we are God's children, there ought to be His likeness in our lives and His likeness is holiness.

Worship God by singing the hymn "Holy, Holy, Holy" right now. Spend a few more minutes worshipping God by doing a search for the word "holy" or "holiness" in your Bible. And worship the Most High and Holy God.

*S*piritual concerns and prayer requests...

....

....

....

....

....

....

Today I will...

....

"FOR GOD HATH NOT GIVEN US THE SPIRIT OF FEAR; BUT OF POWER, AND OF LOVE, AND OF A SOUND MIND." 2 Timothy 1:7

If you want victory, you must expose the place of your doubts and fears. Many of us are not willing to do that.

The devil has intimidated so many of us that we hide our eyes from the Sonshine of God's Light. There is really nothing to be afraid of when it comes to the devil.

Do you know what fear is? It is False Evidence Appearing Real. You can be fooled by false evidence.

Take a bank robber with his hand in his coat pocket pretending it is a gun. His power comes from the power of deception. His power is the power of fear! Friend, victory's arrows cannot be shot through closed windows.

Is there any area of your life that you have been unwilling to open the window on? Humbly turn your face to His Light and give your fears to God.

Spiritual concerns and prayer requests ....

....

....

....

....

....

....

....

Today I will... ....

....

OCTOBER 27

"FOR HIS ANGER ENDURETH BUT A MOMENT; IN HIS FAVOR IS
LIFE: WEEPING MAY ENDURE FOR A NIGHT, BUT JOY COMETH IN
THE MORNING." Psalm 30:5

God allows us to have "blue" seasons where there is more weeping than laughing. What we must remember is that they are only for a season. That is crucial. Joy will come in the morning, just as sure as the sunrise.

If you get up tomorrow morning to see the sunrise, let me tell you what not to do. Don't try to make it hurry up. You can't do it. You can get a brass band and cheerleaders, but that sun is not going to come up one second sooner than God intends. Waiting on the Lord is like waiting on the sun to come up. You can't hurry it. You also can't stop it.

God is going to bring a sunrise to your soul. Just wait for it. And trust Him while you wait.

❧⊰❦⊱❧

Are you in a waiting game…praying days, weeks, months, even years, for something and God hasn't answered? Read Psalm 46:10-11. Be still and know that in the fullness of time, your request will be answered.

Spiritual concerns and prayer requests..

....

....

....

....

....

....

Today I will…..

....

OCTOBER 28

"WE TOOK SWEET COUNSEL TOGETHER, AND WALKED UNTO THE HOUSE OF GOD IN COMPANY." Psalm 55:14

The Church has the sweetest fellowship this side of heaven. They are brothers and sisters who are loving, encouraging, and exhorting us as we serve alongside each other to the glory of God.

But suppose God took you out of that precious fellowship. What if you became so ill you had to be hospitalized with no visitors for days on end? What if you were transferred to Siberia and there wasn't a Christian around for 250 miles?

Or, what if you decide not to smoke pot when all your friends are doing it? Or decide to abstain from premarital promiscuity? Or choose to not go drinking with your college buddies? Is God enough when your dearest friend on earth forsakes or fails you? Is He enough of a Friend that you can stand with Him alone?

❦

Get out a piece of paper and draw a circle. Write your name inside that circle. Around that circle put the names of your fellowship of friends and family. Draw a cross next to those who are Christians. Draw a star next to those who are not. Now, ask God to make you a bright and shining star to draw those people to Himself.

Spiritual concerns and prayer requests ....

....

....

....

....

....

....

Today I will… ....

....

OCTOBER 29

"AND NOW ABIDETH FAITH, HOPE, LOVE, THESE THREE; BUT THE GREATEST OF THESE IS LOVE." 1 Corinthians 13:13

A little girl was reading the Bible one day and came across a picture of angels. She asked her daddy, "What is the difference between a cherubim and a seraphim?"

Well, this daddy didn't know, but he took her to the encyclopedia and they looked for the answer. He discovered the cherubims excelled in knowledge, and the seraphims excelled in love. The little girl thought for a minute and said, "When I die, I will be a seraphim. I'd rather love God than know everything."

That's pretty good! First Corinthians 13:2 says, "And though I have the gift of prophecy, and understand all mysteries, and all knowledge; and though I have all faith, so that I could remove mountains, and have not love, I am nothing." Love excels knowledge.

Read 1 Corinthians 13. Now, write it out in your own words as a love letter to God.

Spiritual concerns and prayer requests..

....

....

....

....

....

....

Today I will...

....

"FOR THE WHICH CAUSE I ALSO SUFFER THESE THINGS:
NEVERTHELESS I AM NOT ASHAMED: FOR I KNOW WHOM I HAVE
BELIEVED, AND AM PERSUADED THAT HE IS ABLE TO KEEP THAT
WHICH I HAVE COMMITTED UNTO HIM AGAINST THAT DAY."
2 Timothy 1:12

I heard of a lady who memorized so many verses of Scripture that she quoted them back to the Lord in praise to His name. When she grew old and began to lose her memory, she could only remember one verse, "for I know whom I have believed, and am persuaded that He is able to keep that which I have committed unto Him against that day."

She would quote that verse over and over. Soon, her memory deteriorated more and all she could remember was just the phrase, "committed unto Him." It brought her much comfort.

Finally, she came to a place where all she could say was, "Him." You can distill the Bible down to that one word, "Him."

Spend the next five minutes quieting your mind, stilling your heart, and tuning all of your life to that one note of praise—Him.

Spiritual concerns and prayer requests ....

....

....

....

....

....

....

Today I will... ....

....

OCTOBER 31

"AND THAT HE WAS BURIED, AND THAT HE ROSE AGAIN THE THIRD DAY ACCORDING TO THE SCRIPTURES." 1 Corinthians 15:4

One of the grandest blessings in the entire Bible is often missed by believers. It is the burial of Jesus Christ! That's right! The burial of Jesus is a blessing to you. Because not only have you died with Him, you have been buried with Him.

When Jewish people died in Bible times, they were immediately embalmed with special oils and wrapped in linen. The body was hidden and buried in a tomb. That is what Jesus has done with your old body of sin. Not only have you been crucified with Christ, you have been buried with Christ.

Why the emphasis? So that you will not be haunted by the ghost of guilt. The devil will try to remind you what you *were*. Don't let him. Don't go prowling around in the dead bones of your old life. It is gone by the grace of God!

❖

Have the hounds of hell come after you with accusations of guilt from past sin? It's time to make them turn tail and run back to the pit. How? The Word! If you are being accused right now and know that you have confessed, repented and God has forgiven you— claim the authority God has given you and declare His Word back to them with 1 Timothy 1:12-14 and Romans 8:1.

Spiritual concerns and prayer requests *Dad's pension*
Salvation of family
Nelda's knee
Aunt Betty
Thanksgiving

Today I will... *stop + surrender myself.*
Be a servant

NOVEMBER 1

"BLESSED IS THE MAN THAT WALKETH NOT IN THE COUNSEL OF THE UNGODLY, NOR STANDETH IN THE WAY OF SINNERS, NOR SITTETH IN THE SEAT OF THE SCORNFUL. BUT HIS DELIGHT IS IN THE LAW OF THE LORD; AND IN HIS LAW DOTH HE MEDITATE DAY AND NIGHT." Psalm 1:1-2

The Beatitudes teach us the heart of the way we are to live, just like the Old Testament's Ten Commandments teach us how we are to live. Now, there is a key word in what I just said, and that word is "are."

You see, the world is more interested in the word "have." If you *have* things, then you are considered blessed by the world's interpretation of that word. The world thinks happiness comes from your ability, money, cleverness, possessions, good looks, power, or fame. But I think we both know people who have a lot and they are perfectly miserable.

Happiness does not come from what a man *has*, but from what a man *is*.

❧❈❧

Epitaphs are generally written about the character of a person. Write out what you would like your commemoration to say.

Spiritual concerns and prayer requests..

....

....

....

....

....

....

Today I will... ....

....

NOVEMBER 2

"BLESSED ARE THE POOR IN SPIRIT: FOR THEIRS IS THE KINGDOM OF HEAVEN." Matthew 5:3

What does it mean to be "poor in spirit"? To qualify as the cruise director for the Titanic? No. Jesus is talking about someone who recognizes himself as spiritually bankrupt in the sight of God. It literally means that we come to the end of our self-reliance.

You will never discover the true riches of the Christian life, until you first admit your bankrupt condition before heaven. And some of us don't want to admit that. But, let me remind you of something: God created the world out of nothing. That is His nature. He will not make anything out of you, until you become nothing.

Have you admitted you are a lost sinner in the sight of God? That you have nothing to offer Him? Friend, if you think you can get to heaven any other way, you are sorely mistaken. You don't know how holy God is and how sinful you are.

How would your neighbors, coworkers or friends describe your walk with the Lord? Would "poor in spirit" be a part of that description? Why or why not?

Spiritual concerns and prayer requests...

....

....

....

....

....

....

Today I will...

....

NOVEMBER 3

"BLESSED ARE THEY THAT MOURN: FOR THEY SHALL BE COMFORTED." Matthew 5:4

Jesus purposefully sequenced the Beatitudes because it is the way we grow in sanctification.

First, we see our bankrupt condition in Matthew 5:3, then it breaks our heart. In verse four above, the word "mourn" speaks of the strongest kind of lamentation, not just a sentimental tear.

What we need today are men and women who are broken over their sin. Proverbs 14:9 says, "Fools make a mock at sin: but among the righteous there is favor." Jesus speaks of this favor, when He says we will be comforted. The Holy Spirit is our Comforter who will strengthen us when we are broken over our sin.

Do you know where we ought to be? On our face before God in bitter tears over the barrenness of our lives, the coldness of our hearts, and the wickedness of our attitudes. And what will be the outcome? We will be comforted.

Write out the way(s) God has broken you in the past year and the healing He has brought. Use this testimony of God's grace to encourage a brother or sister, or a lost soul today.

Spiritual concerns and prayer requests...

....

....

....

....

....

....

Today I will…..

....

NOVEMBER 4

"BLESSED ARE THE MEEK: FOR THEY SHALL INHERIT THE EARTH."
Matthew 5:5

Meekness is one of the most confused adjectives in all of the Beatitudes because most people confuse meekness with weakness. Jesus said He was meek and lowly (see Matthew 11:29), but He certainly wasn't weak.

The word "meek" means "strength that is brought under control." When horse trainers "break" horses, they describe what they do as "meeked." They don't cripple the horses or take away their strength. They train them to use their strength in control.

In the same way, God doesn't come into your life to cripple you. Why would He follow the blessing with "for they shall inherit the earth"? God did not make this world for the devil's crowd. He made the world for you.

❈❈❈

For further study, here are some additional verses to read about meekness: Psalm 10:17, 22:26, 25:9, 37:11, 147:6; Proverbs 29:23; Isaiah 29:19; and 1 Corinthians 4:10-14.

Spiritual concerns and prayer requests..

....

....

....

....

....

....

Today I will… ....

....

NOVEMBER 5

"BLESSED ARE THEY WHICH DO HUNGER AND THIRST AFTER RIGHTEOUSNESS: FOR THEY SHALL BE FILLED." Matthew 5:6

Jesus tells us that when we seek after righteousness, we will be filled. Sounds like we'll be happy, don't you think? Happiness is not something we find by hungering for it, it is something we receive by serving the Lord. God doesn't want us to be happy without Christ.

God allows us to experience unhappiness in our lives in the same way we experience pain when we step on a nail. The pain tells us something is wrong. Now, for us to seek happiness without seeking righteousness would be like breaking our arm and then not taking a pain killer and getting it set.

Blessing comes when we find the Deliverer. When you hunger for Him, you will have Him. How much of God do you want today?

✦

Pull out your calendar or PDA and notice the amount of time you have spent on making yourself happy. How much time have you spent pursuing holiness? Can you do both at the same time? How?

Spiritual concerns and prayer requests..

....

....

....

....

....

....

....

Today I will…..

....

NOVEMBER 6

"BLESSED ARE THE MERCIFUL: FOR THEY SHALL OBTAIN MERCY."
Matthew 5:7

Those who have received mercy, are those who show mercy. And only those who show mercy will be those who continue to receive mercy. And this mercy isn't just sentiment or softness. It is sympathy that serves.

Jesus doesn't merely save us *from* something, He saves us *for* something. He wants to express His life through us as we serve others. I thank God for our beautiful churches, but I believe the thing that is going to touch the lives of our communities are not our buildings, but our merciful acts of kindness.

One by one, we can make a change as we go out and show the love of Christ to our neighbors. People do not care how much we know, until they know how much we care.

Does your church have a mercy ministry towards those less fortunate in your community—the elderly, homeless, sick, illiterate, or emotionally wounded? If your church does not, ask God for His direction as to what needs can best be met through you.

Spiritual concerns and prayer requests..
....
....
....
....
....
....

Today I will...
....

"FOR THOU ART MY HOPE, O LORD GOD: THOU ART MY TRUST FROM MY YOUTH." Psalm 71:5

What does the word "hope" mean in the Bible? It doesn't mean "maybe." We may use it that way in Modern English, but that's not what the word "hope" means in the Bible.

"Hope" means certainty, but not just any certainty. It is rock-ribbed assurance with anticipation based on the Word of God. When I was a little boy, my dad would take us out for a ride on Sunday afternoon. All the kids would be in the back seat getting into squabbles. If things got too heated, my dad would turn around and say, "When you boys get home, I'm going to whip you."

With my dad, I knew this was a rock-ribbed truth! Our hope, however, is glad anticipation!

⟨❖⟩

Share the hope of eternal life in Jesus Christ with someone today. Maybe there's someone at the hospital who needs a word of hope. Or perhaps it's a member of your own family!

Spiritual concerns and prayer requests...

....

....

....

....

....

....

Today I will..

....

NOVEMBER 8

"BLESSED ARE THE PEACEMAKERS: FOR THEY SHALL BE CALLED THE CHILDREN OF GOD." Matthew 5:9

Many years ago, you were really somebody if you joined the Peace Corps. But, how much peace has been established between brothers and sisters around the world as a result?

Do you know how to bring peace to earth and goodwill to all men? Introduce men, women, boys, and girls to Jesus Christ. That is the *only* way. Churches are filled every Sunday and yet where do people go during the week? Are they sharing God's salvation story with the lost? It's not your faithful attendance to church that is going to bring peace to earth.

Jesus said that His mission was not peace, but to bring death to hatred, strife, and sin through His reconciling blood. There is no other way to a holy God, but through the cross.

Are you living like a child of God and telling others about Jesus? Ask God to give you holy boldness to ask your neighbors how you can pray for them. Ask God to give you courage to ask about their lives, and while doing so to discover their needs. Then do what you can through Christ to help meet those needs to the glory of God!

Spiritual concerns and prayer requests..

....

....

....

....

....

Today I will..

....

"BLESSED ARE THEY WHICH ARE PERSECUTED FOR RIGHTEOUSNESS' SAKE: FOR THEIRS IS THE KINGDOM OF HEAVEN." Matthew 5:10

Before you can really understand what Matthew 5:10 truly means, you have to understand and be living the rest of the Beatitudes.

If you are living a life that is poor in spirit, that mourns over your sin, that lives meekly through His strength, that hungers and thirsts after righteousness, that is merciful, pure in heart, and making peace…then, you will be exceedingly glad for persecution that comes your way.

You see the world is going in the opposite direction and they are trying to push you into their mold. Yet, you are twice-born among once-born people and you are going to go against the tide. It costs to serve Jesus Christ—every day and every step. But, you are blessed! When was the last time you took some flack for Jesus? Great is your reward in heaven.

Have you felt the sting of persecution this week? Praise God! Has someone said something unkind to you for your stand for God this week? Thank the Lord! Take a stand. Speak the Truth. Read Matthew 5:13-16. Who is to be the salt of the earth? You are! Who is to be the light in the darkness? You are!

Spiritual concerns and prayer requests..

....

....

....

....

....

Today I will…..

....

NOVEMBER 10

"NEITHER GIVE PLACE TO THE DEVIL." Ephesians 4:27

Have you ever gotten into an argument with a family member on the way to church? *Don't look so pious!* Every preacher knows the devil will try to attack God's children right before and after church—on the way in the car!

There is a spiritual principle here we need to learn. It is what I call "the devil after the dove" principle. When Jesus was baptized and a dove descended, right after that He was led into the wilderness and tempted.

When God does something great, or when you get the approval of God about something, you can expect the attack of the enemy. Leonard Ravenhill said, "When God opens the windows of heaven to bless us, the devil is going to open the doors of hell to blast us."

Have you had a wonderful spiritual experience recently? Then, you better not start coasting. If the devil tempted Jesus, be sure he will tempt you, as well. Ask God to give you His strength to overcome temptation today.

Spiritual concerns and prayer requests..

....

....

....

....

....

....

Today I will... ....

....

NOVEMBER 11

"FOR WE HAVE NOT AN HIGH PRIEST WHICH CANNOT BE TOUCHED WITH THE FEELING OF OUR INFIRMITIES; BUT WAS IN ALL POINTS TEMPTED LIKE AS WE ARE, YET WITHOUT SIN." Hebrews 4:15

When some people read that Jesus "was in all points tempted like as we are, yet without sin," some eyebrows raise. You may not say anything out loud, but you think, *Was He really tempted in every way? Was He tempted to have sex? I didn't read where He was tempted to run a red light...or smoke pot.*

And yet the Bible is very clear that He was tempted in all points. And fundamentally there are only three temptations and Jesus was tempted in all three.

First John 2:16 lists them: the lust of the flesh (temptation for us to do something—our passions), the lust of the eyes (temptation for us to have something—our possessions), and the pride of life (the temptation for us to be something—our pride). If you doubt it, then reread Luke 4:1-13 about the temptation He faced in light of this explanation.

Praise God His Son was the perfect sacrifice for your sin (read Ephesians 5:2 and Isaiah 53:4-5). Praise God you have His Spirit to deliver you (read Hebrews 2:18). Praise God you have His Word to defeat Satan (read Hebrews 4:12).

Spiritual concerns and prayer requests...

....

....

....

....

....

....

....

Today I will...

....

NOVEMBER 12

"O GOD, THOU ART MY GOD; EARLY WILL I SEEK THEE: MY SOUL THIRSTETH FOR THEE, MY FLESH LONGETH FOR THEE IN A DRY AND THIRSTY LAND, WHERE NO WATER IS." Psalm 63:1

The devil tempted Jesus to turn stones into bread. I have been to Palestine and seen some stones that looked amazingly like little loaves of bread. I can just see the devil looking on the ground and knowing Jesus had been fasting for 40 days and he said, "Well, look here. Just turn this into bread!"

Now, there's nothing wrong with eating bread. In fact, Jesus taught us to pray for our daily bread. Yet, Jesus had been led into the wilderness to fast and pray and seek the face of God. The devil was trying to put the bread above the will of God, saying "Pamper your flesh." But, what he was really saying was, "Commit spiritual suicide." Jesus refused. Jesus overcame the flesh, and you can, too.

❦

Did you know every second you think negative thoughts that go against what God says, you are bowing down to Satan? That's right. Next time you start to think something that God would disapprove of, watch the second hand of a clock—you'll never get that time back, so why keep throwing it away?

Spiritual concerns and prayer requests ....
....
....
....
....
....
....

Today I will… ....
....

"WE KNOW THAT WHOSOEVER IS BORN OF GOD SINNETH NOT; BUT HE THAT IS BEGOTTEN OF GOD KEEPETH HIMSELF, AND THAT WICKED ONE TOUCHETH HIM NOT." 1 John 5:18

Do you know why the devil couldn't get to Jesus in the midst of a 40-day fast when He was starving? He was already satisfied. You see, Jesus didn't have an itch that the devil could scratch.

Temptation really comes down to this: A temptation is an inducement by the devil to satisfy a legitimate desire in an illegitimate way. That's all there is to it. Take a God-given desire and satisfy it in a God-forbidden way.

The devil says, "Hey you've got a need, and I can satisfy it." When tempted, you are given a choice. Do you get your need satisfied by the devil, or by the Lord? You see, the devil is a pervert. He has no raw material. All he can do is take what God has created and pervert it.

❦

Do you have a particular temptation which is more difficult than others to overcome? Find out the legitimate way to satisfy that desire, then you will not need the illegitimate way.

Spiritual concerns and prayer requests...

....

....

....

....

....

....

Today I will..

....

NOVEMBER 14

"THE LORD REWARDED ME ACCORDING TO MY RIGHTEOUSNESS;
ACCORDING TO THE CLEANNESS OF MY HANDS HATH HE
RECOMPENSED ME." Psalm 18:20

As the story goes, during WWII, a beautiful cathedral in Europe was destroyed by the Nazis. When the people came together to rebuild the temple, they found a statue of Christ with His hands outstretched. They repaired the statue as best they could, but they could not recover the hands.

Because they loved the statue as it was, they put a plaque underneath that reads: "He has no hands but our hands." Whether the story is true or not, remember this—*Jesus Christ is the invisible part of the Christian. The Christian is the visible part of Christ.*

He is seen in us and through us. We are the visible part of the invisible Christ. What we do in His name is representative of Him to the world.

❦

Do something today with your hands that is a testimony of Jesus Christ to a watching and lost world—rake someone's yard who can't, grocery shop for someone who is unable, baby-sit a single mother's children so she can have a night off, visit an elderly person in a nursing home or fold your hands in prayer for someone you know is going through tough times and then send them a note.

Spiritual concerns and prayer requests...

....

....

....

....

....

Today I will... ....

....

NOVEMBER 15

"Then Simon Peter answered Him, Lord, to whom shall we go? Thou hast the words of eternal life. And we believe and are sure that Thou art that Christ, the Son of the living God." John 6:68-69

Have you ever wondered why Christians were so persecuted in the days of the liberal Roman government? The Romans didn't persecute other religious people, only Christians. Why did they pick on the Christians? Because the Christians proclaimed Jesus as Lord, and not Caesar.

The Romans were a polytheistic nation—they even built the Pantheon, which was a temple for all the gods that were worshiped in ancient Rome. When they subjugated and conquered a people, they let them keep their gods—at least on one condition—that they remember that Caesar was Lord.

As the world becomes more and more syncretized and headed toward a "one world" order, men and women who say that Jesus is the only true Lord are going to be persecuted. Can you see it now? Will you stand and proclaim Jesus as Lord no matter what?

❧❖❧

Purchase a Bible this week for the sole purpose of giving it away. Then, ask God to find you that special someone to give it to.

Spiritual concerns and prayer requests..

....

....

....

....

....

....

Today I will…..

....

NOVEMBER 16

"FOR WE CANNOT BUT SPEAK THE THINGS WHICH WE HAVE SEEN AND HEARD." Acts 4:20

Somewhere in California during the gold rush of 1849, the story is told of two gold miners who struck a particularly rich vein of gold one day. They decided not to tell anyone else, so they could keep it for themselves. They went into town to get better equipment to mine the gold, but when they left scores of people followed. Their jubilation was written all over their faces.

Is what is in your heart written all over your face? Oh, how I pray each person reading this today will not hide what they have found in Jesus Christ. I want people who see you today to say, "I don't know what is going on with her, but I want what she has. I want what he has."

The gift of salvation is for you, but it is also for others to behold and desire in you.

❈❈❈

How are you going to tell someone about Jesus today? Who are you going to tell? What are you going to say? Ask God to give you the boldness and opportunity to share the greatest news someone needs to hear.

Spiritual concerns and prayer requests...
....
....
....
....
....
....

Today I will..
....

NOVEMBER 17

"STUDY TO SHOW THYSELF APPROVED UNTO GOD, A WORKMAN THAT NEEDETH NOT TO BE ASHAMED, RIGHTLY DIVIDING THE WORD OF TRUTH." 2 Timothy 2:15

When men built the Temple in the Old Testament, the Bible tells us that God gave them a spirit of wisdom. Some translators have called this the spirit of "skill" because these words are tightly linked.

Do you know what wise living is? It is living skillfully and making the most out of your life. Whatever your job—an artist, a practitioner, a cabinetmaker, an accountant, a teacher, or a mother—live your life with skill.

Are you thinking about going to vocational school or college to pursue a career? Then, don't fail to study and gain knowledge, but remember this: All our knowledge is but splendid ignorance apart from the wisdom of God.

❦

When was the last time you studied the history behind the Word of God? Go to a bookstore or your church's library, or look online and study how the translations were discovered and passed on.

Spiritual concerns and prayer requests...

....

....

....

....

....

....

Today I will... ....

....

NOVEMBER 18

"HE LAYETH UP SOUND WISDOM FOR THE RIGHTEOUS: HE IS A BUCKLER TO THEM THAT WALK UPRIGHTLY." Proverbs 2:7

In Christ, there is soundness, strength, security, and satisfaction. When you come to Him with urgency, fervency, persistency, and expectancy, you will hear from Him.

He is not going to think you are pestering Him, He is pleased when you ask Him for His wisdom. *Lord, I need to make a decision. What college do I choose? Should I marry this man or not? Is this the job You want me to have? What mechanic do I use to repair my car? Where do You want me to live? Do I rent or own?*

Annie Johnson Flint, that blessed hymn writer, wrote: "His love has no limit, His grace has no measure, His power no boundary known unto men; For out of His infinite riches in Jesus, He giveth and giveth and giveth again." Cast all your cares upon Him today, for He longs to fill you with Himself.

❈❈❈

Think about the things you considered trivial that you have **NOT** asked God about. Today, ask Him about those issues—He longs to hear all your cares.

Spiritual concerns and prayer requests ....
....
....
....
....
....
....

Today I will... ....
....

"KNOW YE NOT THAT THE UNRIGHTEOUS SHALL NOT INHERIT THE KINGDOM OF GOD? BE NOT DECEIVED: NEITHER FORNICATORS, NOR IDOLATERS, NOR ADULTERERS, NOR EFFEMINATE, NOR ABUSERS OF THEMSELVES WITH MANKIND. NOR THIEVES, NOR COVETOUS, NOR DRUNKARDS, NOR REVILERS, NOR EXTORTIONERS, SHALL INHERIT THE KINGDOM OF GOD." 1 Corinthians 6:9-10

People have the idea today that it is okay to live in immorality and that God is going to overlook their little indiscretions.

"Be not deceived; God is not mocked: for whatsoever a man soweth, that shall he also reap" (Galatians 6:7).

God doesn't miss a beat of our lives. He is the righteous judge and will judge accordingly (see Hebrews 13:4). *Well Pastor, does that mean that if I have done any of these things that I can't be saved?* No! First Corinthians 6:11 promises: "And such were some of you: but ye are washed, but ye are sanctified, but ye are justified in the name of the Lord Jesus, and by the Spirit of our God."

Hallelujah! There is no sin so awful that the blood of Christ cannot cleanse. He makes the vilest sinner clean.

Have you ever felt God could never forgive you because of a sin or sins you have committed? Then, ask Him to forgive you for elevating your sin above His blood. Satan doesn't want you to know when we come to Jesus in repentance and faith, the vilest sin can be cleansed by the blood of Jesus Christ.

Spiritual concerns and prayer requests...

....

....

....

....

Today I will…...

....

NOVEMBER 20

"For He hath made Him to be sin for us, Who knew no sin; that we might be made the righteousness of God in Him." 2 Corinthians 5:21

Have you ever laid your head on the pillow at the end of a long day and satisfyingly said, "Well, I was a good person today, so if I died tonight I will go to heaven."? If you have, you're not alone.

I would venture to say that most people believe that if you go to church, tithe your money, and do good to others, that God is going to let you into heaven. If being a religious man could get you to heaven, then why was a religious man like Paul struck down on the Road to Damascus and asked by the Lord, "Saul, Saul, why persecutest thou Me?" (Acts 9:4b).

More importantly, if we could save ourselves with our good deeds God did not need to send His only Son into the world as a sacrifice for the likes of you and me. No, it is Jesus' righteousness that saves us.

❧❦❧

Not until we admit our sin are we going to know the mercy and the forgiveness of the King. Bow before Him today and admit you are lost without Him and that your salvation is purchased by His blood alone.

Spiritual concerns and prayer requests...

....

....

....

....

....

....

Today I will… ....

....

"...WE BELIEVE AND ARE SURE THAT THOU ART THAT CHRIST, THE SON OF THE LIVING GOD." John 6:69

Jesus Christ is a fact of history. All secular historians who have any merit admit that regardless of what they believe about Him, Jesus lived! There's no way to explain that the Christian Church exists apart from the fact that Jesus Christ was here.

What did the early church preach? Not only that Jesus was here, but that He walked out of the grave. How do you explain that? Somebody said, "Well, they must have made up the story. They just said they touched Him, they said they ate with Him."

Oh? We're talking about men who died for their faith. Do you think they would willingly, knowingly die for a lie?

❦

Are you willing to die for the cause of Christ? This man who died for you—are you willing to die for Him?

Spiritual concerns and prayer requests..

....

....

....

....

....

....

Today I will...

....

NOVEMBER 22

"NOT BY WORKS OF RIGHTEOUSNESS WHICH WE HAVE DONE, BUT ACCORDING TO HIS MERCY HE SAVED US, BY THE WASHING OF REGENERATION, AND RENEWING OF THE HOLY GHOST." Titus 3:5

Paul said in Philippians 3:7-8, "But what things were gain to me, those I counted *loss* for Christ. Yea doubtless, and I count all things but *loss* for the excellency of the knowledge of Christ Jesus my Lord: for whom I have suffered the *loss* of all things, and do count them but dung, that I may win Christ." What does Paul mean by loss? He means that even good things are bad things if they become a substitute for the best thing.

Suppose you are on a plane trip. The plane is going down and you grab your knapsack instead of your parachute and jump out. Is the knapsack bad? No, it's just not the best choice to save your life.

The worst form of badness may be human goodness when that human goodness becomes a substitute for the new birth.

Think of all the terrific things you have done this week for God. How do you feel? If you are getting any glory from what you have done, read Isaiah 64:6-8. Bow before God. Surrender yourself to Him in death, that His glory—and His glory alone—may be known to the world through your life.

Spiritual concerns and prayer requests...

....

....

....

....

....

....

Today I will...

....

NOVEMBER 23

"Even as David also describeth the blessedness of the man, unto whom God imputeth righteousness without works." Romans 4:6

The same year America declared its independence from England, Augustus Toplady wrote a song declaring complete dependence upon God–"Rock of Ages."

The third verse declares: "Nothing in my hand I bring, Simply to the cross I cling; Naked, come to Thee for dress; Helpless look to Thee for grace; Foul, I to the fountain fly; Wash me, Savior, or I die."

It's hard sometimes to let go of our sins AND our righteous deeds in order to completely trust in God for our salvation. Did you know there is something about human nature that doesn't want to do this? We want to somehow help God with our good deeds. And yet "all our righteousnesses are as filthy rags" (Isaiah 64:6b). God makes us righteous.

❦

Instead of thinking you are doing God a wild favor by serving Him, meditate on what He did for you and thank Him that He "commendeth His love toward us, in that, while we were yet sinners, Christ died for us." (Romans 5:8)

Spiritual concerns and prayer requests...

....

....

....

....

....

....

Today I will... ....

....

NOVEMBER 24

"AND BE FOUND IN HIM, NOT HAVING MINE OWN
RIGHTEOUSNESS, WHICH IS OF THE LAW, BUT THAT WHICH IS
THROUGH THE FAITH OF CHRIST, THE RIGHTEOUSNESS WHICH IS
OF GOD BY FAITH." Philippians 3:9

A woman worked as a maid in the house of a mean innkeeper.
One day God saved her and she could not hide her
happiness. What used to be drudgery turned into joy.

The innkeeper was furious and began to belittle her. He hated her
for being happy. Finally, he said to her, "You say you're saved and I
can see your happiness. Can you tell me what being saved means?"
And she said, "To me, it feels as though I am standing in Jesus'
shoes, and He is standing in mine."

A theologian couldn't have said it better. Second Corinthians 5:21
says, "For He hath made Him to be sin for us, who knew no sin;
that we might be made the righteousness of God in Him."

What are you saved *from*? What are you saved *for*? If you
cannot answer these questions with certainty, read John 3:36
and 1 Thessalonians 1:10 to answer the first question. Read Isaiah
61:1-3, Matthew 28:19-20, 2 Corinthians 4:15 to answer the second
question.

Spiritual concerns and prayer requests ....

....

....

....

....

....

....

Today I will... ....

....

NOVEMBER 25

"THAT IF THOU SHALT CONFESS WITH THY MOUTH THE LORD
JESUS, AND SHALT BELIEVE IN THINE HEART THAT GOD HATH
RAISED HIM FROM THE DEAD, THOU SHALT BE SAVED." Romans 10:9

Have you ever done something so awful that you are serving
or have served time in prison? Maybe you murdered
someone, abused a child, embezzled money, or raped
someone. To many, you are a heinous criminal and the judicial system
has declared that you have no redeeming value to humanity.

Well, I'm here to tell you, God can change all that. God says,
"though your sins be as scarlet, they shall be as white as snow; though
they be red like crimson, they shall be as wool" (Isaiah 1:18b).
Every blur, every blemish, every stain that ever came upon your soul
can be cleansed by the blood of Jesus.

Jesus said, "All that the Father giveth Me shall come to Me;
and him that cometh to Me I will in no wise cast out" (John 6:37).
Jesus will save you if you ask Him.

❧❧❧

Are you certain of your salvation? If not, turn to the back of this
devotional and read the "Closing Plea" and then thank God
for saving you. If you are saved, why not share the greatest Love
worth finding–Jesus–with someone you know?

Spiritual concerns and prayer requests...

....

....

....

....

....

....

Today I will...

....

NOVEMBER 26

"DRAW NIGH TO GOD, AND HE WILL DRAW NIGH TO YOU.
CLEANSE YOUR HANDS, YE SINNERS; AND PURIFY YOUR HEARTS, YE
DOUBLE MINDED." James 4:8

Joshua had an encounter with the preincarnate Christ in the Old Testament near Jericho (see Joshua 5). His first words to Him were, "Art Thou for us, or for our adversaries?" (v. 13).

Joshua was on his guard—not wanting anyone to harm God's people. Notice the Lord's response, "Nay; but as Captain of the host of the LORD am I now come" (v. 14). Basically, He didn't come to *take sides*, He came to *take over*.

Jesus is the Captain of the host of heaven and with His drawn sword He came to give Joshua a message of victory. You will never know victory until you lay your sword at His feet, bow prostrate before His Mighty Throne, and worship Him. Before you can be a conqueror, you must be conquered.

Our prayer is that you will soon be on the sunny side of Hallelujah Avenue where Glory Road intersects!

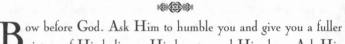

Bow before God. Ask Him to humble you and give you a fuller picture of His holiness, His beauty, and His glory. Ask Him to crucify your flesh, that His glory may be known through your life.

Spiritual concerns and prayer requests ....

....

....

....

....

....

....

Today I will… ....

....

NOVEMBER 27

"O LORD, THOU HAST SEARCHED ME, AND KNOWN ME." Psalm 139:1

God sees everything you do. God knows all about you. God loves you. It is an amazing thing that the Lord would feel this way about any of us, when we are smaller than a grain of sand compared to the universe He has created.

There is no more reason for God to be interested in us, than for the President of the United States to be interested in an ant floating on a piece of cheesecake in the middle of the Atlantic ocean. And yet, God is interested...very interested.

The sun that stays in the sky and warms the earth will ripen a bunch of bananas like it has nothing better to do. In the same way, the Almighty God runs the universe and is concerned about you as though you were His only concern.

❖❖❖

Do you have trouble realizing God is concerned with you? Just consider He sent His son to die for you. Do you think that shows just how much He cares? Praise and thank Him for His undeniable love.

Spiritual concerns and prayer requests..
....
....
....
....
....
....
....

Today I will... ....
....

NOVEMBER 28

"AND YOU, THAT WERE SOMETIME ALIENATED AND ENEMIES IN
YOUR MIND BY WICKED WORKS, YET NOW HATH HE RECONCILED
IN THE BODY OF HIS FLESH THROUGH DEATH, TO PRESENT YOU
HOLY AND UNBLAMEABLE AND UNREPROVEABLE IN HIS SIGHT."
Colossians 1:21-22

A man stretched a tightrope across Niagara Falls and pushed a
wheelbarrow across it. Next, he filled the wheelbarrow with
200 lbs. of cement and pushed it across. The onlookers were
astounded.

Then, the tightrope walker asked the crowd, "How many of you
believe I could do this with a man in the wheelbarrow?" The hands
flew into the air. He pointed to a man who had his hand up and he
said, "All right sir. You get in first."

Well, you couldn't see the man for the trail of dust he left behind.
It's not enough for you to say you believe in God. Are you willing to
act upon your belief? God is calling you to a relationship with Him.

❦

Will you answer His call if He calls you to serve Him from a
hut in the middle of Africa? What if He calls you to open
your home to the homeless? Whatever He calls you to do, He will
equip you. If you find this difficult, ask God to help you die to
yourself and live for Him.

Spiritual concerns and prayer requests...

....

....

....

....

....

Today I will..

....

NOVEMBER 29

"FOR THOU HAST BEEN A SHELTER FOR ME, AND A STRONG TOWER FROM THE ENEMY. I WILL ABIDE IN THY TABERNACLE FOR EVER: I WILL TRUST IN THE COVERT OF THY WINGS." Psalm 61:3-4

Charles Wesley wrote literally thousands of hymns and poems—from "Hark! The Herald Angels Sing" to "Christ The Lord is Risen Today." He remains one of the most prolific hymnists today.

Of the 6500 hymns written by Charles Wesley, surely none is considered finer than the one entitled "Jesus, Lover Of My Soul." Many accounts have been shared as to the inspiration behind this song, but whether any are true, indeed the song's lyrics are a poignant picture of a young man's journey into discovering the love of his life— Jesus.

The third verse of this great hymn begins, "Thou, O Christ, art all I want, more than all in Thee I find." Discover Jesus today as the lover of your life.

❧❧❧

Where is your heart today? Are you suffering from a broken relationship or the loss of a loved one? Run, don't walk, into His waiting arms of love. He wants to bind up your hurt and bring hope to your heart.

Spiritual concerns and prayer requests...

....

....

....

....

....

....

Today I will..

....

NOVEMBER 30

"WHOM GOD HATH SET FORTH TO BE A PROPITIATION THROUGH
FAITH IN HIS BLOOD, TO DECLARE HIS RIGHTEOUSNESS FOR THE
REMISSION OF SINS THAT ARE PAST, THROUGH THE FORBEARANCE
OF GOD; TO DECLARE, I SAY, AT THIS TIME HIS RIGHTEOUSNESS:
THAT HE MIGHT BE JUST, AND THE JUSTIFIER OF HIM WHICH
BELIEVETH IN JESUS." Romans 3:25-26

When I was a little boy, I thought God was like Santa
Claus with a long beard sitting up in heaven—making a
list and checking it twice, trying to find out if I was
naughty or nice.

I thought then when life was over, we would face Him and He
would pull out these massive scales and weigh our good works against
bad ones to see if we would make it into heaven.

Do you know what this thinking did? It made me fearful that at
the end of my life I would face God and He would say, "Adrian.
I'm sorry, but according to My calculations, you didn't make it."
Then, I would have to turn and ashamedly walk past family and friends.

Friend, maybe you even believe this, but let me set the record
straight—Salvation is not an attainment, it is an atonement.

❦❦❦

Read Romans 5. In your own words, write out what this passage
teaches you about God. Put this into a self-addressed, stamped
envelope and mail it to yourself next month. What better way to start
the New Year than to remember what God taught you about His
salvation.

Spiritual concerns and prayer requests ....
....
....
....
....
Today I will… ....
....

DECEMBER 1

"WHO WAS DELIVERED FOR OUR OFFENSES, AND WAS RAISED AGAIN FOR OUR JUSTIFICATION." Romans 4:25

There was a skeptic who was talking with a little girl one day. She loved the Lord Jesus with all of her heart. He was trying to shake her faith and he said, "Young lady, Christianity is not the only religion, you know. There are plenty of religions in the world. There are plenty of Christs. Which Christ do you believe in?"

She thought for a minute and said, "I believe in the One who was raised from the dead." Amen! That's the One I believe in, too! The death of Christ on the cross without His resurrection cannot save you.

If Christ died on the cross and that is all that happened, then Jesus was just one more religious leader. Do you know what the proof positive is that God accepted His payment for sin? He raised Him from the dead. If Jesus is still in the grave, your hope of heaven is not worth half a hallelujah.

Why not celebrate this week by remembering the powerful promise of His resurrection, replenishment, and restoration?

Spiritual concerns and prayer requests..

....

....

....

....

....

....

Today I will...

....

DECEMBER 2

"KNOWING THAT CHRIST BEING RAISED FROM THE DEAD DIETH NO
MORE; DEATH HATH NO MORE DOMINION OVER HIM. FOR IN
THAT HE DIED, HE DIED UNTO SIN ONCE: BUT IN THAT HE
LIVETH, HE LIVETH UNTO GOD." Romans 6:9-10

The best news this world has ever heard came from a graveside just outside Jerusalem. He is risen! On that day, life and death met in a tomb in mortal combat. Life won. Death died. Jesus died the death of debt. In that tomb, Jesus won the victory over death.

There is no more timeless truth than this: Jesus Christ was raised from the dead. That's a truth science cannot explain, history cannot repeat, and time cannot erode away. It is the truth of all truths. And the truth that proves Jesus is the Son of God.

Someone has said, "If Jesus Christ is still in that grave, nothing matters. But if He came out of the grave, nothing but that really matters."

Who are you going to tell today that Jesus is alive and has paid their sin debt? What better gift to give someone in this season of gifts. Ask God to lead you to someone and give you the boldness to share this life-changing Truth!

Spiritual concerns and prayer requests..

....

....

....

....

....

....

Today I will... ....

....

DECEMBER 3

"Blessed be the God and Father of our Lord Jesus Christ, who hath blessed us with all spiritual blessings in heavenly places in Christ." Ephesians 1:3

I was with a preacher one time and he took me to an elite section of his town where there were many palatial mansions. I said, "Oh, those are nice, but you should see my brother's place." "Oh," he said, "Has he got anything nicer than this?" I said, "Oh yes." Then, I went on to tell him a little about it.

After a brief account, I broke the suspense and said, "My brother's name is Jesus and He is rich in land and houses. In fact, He has gone to prepare a great place for both of us!"

Well friend, if you are a child in the family of God, He is preparing a place for you in glory, as well. You are a joint heir with Jesus. Now, go act like a child of the King!

❖

Meditate on this statement as you are at your desk at work, in your car or at school: "I am a child of the King. What does He want me to do in this situation?" Now, watch God's Truth change your life!

Spiritual concerns and prayer requests..
....
....
....
....
....

Today I will...
....

DECEMBER 4

"I WILL RUN THE WAY OF THY COMMANDMENTS, WHEN THOU SHALT ENLARGE MY HEART." Psalm 119:32

There is an unseen world right where you are. Did you know that in the room where you are reading this, there are cartoons, music, mysteries, and concerts going on? You just don't see them unless you have your radio or television tuned in to the right frequency.

So many people are missing out on the joys and privileges of the Christian life because they are not living a "tuned in" life to Jesus. To experience the abundant life that Jesus died to give you, all you have to do is tune in.

Christians march to a different beat. They whistle a different tune. And that is where our blessings lie—where the world cannot see.

❧❧❧

Finding God's frequency takes discipline. Ask God to help you practice the discipline of quieting your heart and listening for His voice today.

Spiritual concerns and prayer requests ....

....

....

....

....

....

....

Today I will... ....

....

DECEMBER 5

"FOR THE WAGES OF SIN IS DEATH; BUT THE GIFT OF GOD IS ETERNAL LIFE THROUGH JESUS CHRIST OUR LORD." Romans 6:23

In Christ. That is a small phrase, but it is the key that unlocks the door to the largest treasure you will ever know. You see, all that happened to Christ, happened to you.

When He was crucified, you were crucified. When He was buried, you were buried. When He arose, you arose. Christ acted for you. "But of Him are ye in Christ Jesus, who of God is made unto us wisdom, and righteousness, and sanctification, and redemption" (1 Corinthians 1:30). A man is never more secure, until he is in Christ.

Someone has asked, "What if you lose your salvation?" It can't happen to a child who is *in* Christ. Not only does He hold us, we are *in* Him. Security is not in a place called heaven, it's in a person called Jesus.

❧

Today, begin praying for God to show you five people with whom you can share today's verse. Ask Him to give you boldness.

Spiritual concerns and prayer requests...
....
....
....
....
....
....

Today I will..
....

DECEMBER 6

"ACCORDING AS HE HATH CHOSEN US IN HIM BEFORE THE FOUNDATION OF THE WORLD, THAT WE SHOULD BE HOLY AND WITHOUT BLAME BEFORE HIM IN LOVE." Ephesians 1:4

Have you really thought about the fact that God chose you before He laid the foundations of the earth? You talk about "old time religion," well friend, you can't get much older than that!

Before there were any trees, mountains, birds, and bees—God chose you to be one of His children. Charles Haddon Spurgeon said, "God certainly must have chosen me before I came into this world because He never would have chosen me afterward."

This means you and I cannot take credit for our salvation. First John 4:19 says, "We love Him, because He first loved us." Somebody asked a little boy, "Have you found the Lord?" And the little boy said, "I didn't know He was lost." How miraculous that God has chosen us, when left alone to ourselves, we would never have chosen Him.

Allow God's Word to teach you further what it means to be chosen: read Matthew 20:16, Luke 10:20; John 6:37-39; Romans 8:28-39; James 2:5; I Peter 2:9; 2 Timothy 1:9.

Spiritual concerns and prayer requests...

....

....

....

....

....

....

Today I will...

....

DECEMBER 7

"THOU HAST ALSO GIVEN ME THE SHIELD OF THY SALVATION: AND THY RIGHT HAND HATH HOLDEN ME UP, AND THY GENTLENESS HATH MADE ME GREAT." Psalm 18:35

In World War II, General Jonathan Mayhew Wainwright led a gallant but vain fight that led him to become a prisoner of war. For months, the Japanese mocked him and beat him.

Then, one day, the news arrived that the Allied Forces had won. The Japanese guards thought Wainwright hadn't heard the news, so they approached him to inflict their daily habit of abuse. Though Wainwright had grown frail and weak, he stood up straight and tall and said, "From now on, I'm giving the orders around here."

The devil doesn't want you to know the Good News that Jesus has won the victory, either. But, you must resist him and claim the power of God in your life.

Where do you think you'd be if Psalm 18:35 read, "I have saved myself. My hand has held me up. My gentleness has made me great."? Praise God that your salvation is from Him. Jesus paid it all.

Spiritual concerns and prayer requests..

....

....

....

....

....

....

Today I will..

....

DECEMBER 8

"NOR HEIGHT, NOR DEPTH, NOR ANY OTHER CREATURE, SHALL BE ABLE TO SEPARATE US FROM THE LOVE OF GOD, WHICH IS IN CHRIST JESUS OUR LORD." Romans 8:39

A historian tells us that after the Spanish Inquisition, Napoleon's soldiers uncovered a dungeon. They went down into the dungeon and found a skeleton with chains still on it. To their surprise, they looked on the wall and saw a cross. At the apex of the cross, was the word "height." At the foot of the cross, was the word "depth." And on either side of the cross were the words "breadth" and "length." To this prisoner, the cross was a picture of the dimensions of God's love. God's love is expansive and everlasting.

❧❧❧

During the frenzy of parties and shopping in December, we can easily lose the real meaning of the celebration of Christmas— "God so loved the world, that He gave His only begotten Son, that whosoever believeth in Him should not perish, but have everlasting life." (John 3:16) What are you doing today to tell others of Jesus Christ—the true meaning of the season?

Spiritual concerns and prayer requests..

....

....

....

....

....

....

Today I will…..

....

DECEMBER 9

"HEARKEN, MY BELOVED BRETHREN, HATH NOT GOD CHOSEN
THE POOR OF THIS WORLD RICH IN FAITH, AND HEIRS OF THE
KINGDOM WHICH HE HATH PROMISED TO THEM THAT LOVE
HIM?" James 2:5

Perhaps there is a decision you need to make today, but you
don't know what to do. Friend, let me tell you the way to
find what God wants for you. Take hold of the Lord with
both hands and in faith, tell Him, "Sink or swim, live or die, once
and for all, now and forever, I'm going for You, God."

John Dryden, the famous English poet, said "Reason saw not,
till faith sprung the light." Charles Haddon Spurgeon said, "Faith
goes up the stairs that love has made and looks out the window which
hope has opened."

You don't know what God can do through you until you step out
in faith.

Are you facing a decision today? Step out in faith and then write
to tell us what happens. We'd like to join you in prayer and
praise for God's provision.

Spiritual concerns and prayer requests...
....
....
....
....
....
....

Today I will...
....

DECEMBER 10

"A NEW COMMANDMENT I GIVE UNTO YOU, THAT YE LOVE ONE ANOTHER; AS I HAVE LOVED YOU, THAT YE ALSO LOVE ONE ANOTHER." John 13:34

A man and his wife were walking through a wheat field in Alberta, Canada early one evening with their young son. Being momentarily distracted, they forgot their son was with them, and then suddenly they realized he wasn't there.

They searched to no avail, and then ran back to the village to get help. Many returned with the couple to search through the night. One man said, "Let's lock arms and we'll sweep across the field." Then, across the field there was a cry, "I found him!" And everyone rushed together to the lifeless form of the little fellow who had died of exposure.

I wonder if there are people who are going to slip into a Christless eternity because we, as the body of Christ, haven't joined hands soon enough.

❖❖❖

Is your church or fellowship welcoming newcomers? Discipling believers? Ministering to the needs of others? Ask God to give you opportunities to redeem the time He has given you in selfless acts of love.

Spiritual concerns and prayer requests...

....

....

....

....

....

....

Today I will… ....

....

DECEMBER 11

"FOR WHOSOEVER SHALL BE ASHAMED OF ME AND OF MY WORDS, OF HIM SHALL THE SON OF MAN BE ASHAMED, WHEN HE SHALL COME IN HIS OWN GLORY, AND IN HIS FATHER'S, AND OF THE HOLY ANGELS." Luke 9:26

How much have you suffered because you have named the name of Jesus? Have you refused to budge on an issue that would dishonor His name?

Second Timothy 3:12 says, "All that will live godly in Christ Jesus shall suffer persecution." There's no escaping persecution for true Christians. We will be persecuted when we endeavor to live godly in Christ Jesus.

Now, on the other hand if you're not being persecuted, don't say you must be doing a wonderful job. Very frankly, you're doing a poor job. Let me ask you: *If you were arrested for being a Christian, would there be enough evidence to convict you?* Regretfully, most people would have to say no.

❦❦❦

Get out of your comfort zone today—check into a short-term missions trip; start a Bible study; witness to your neighbor; take a walk in the park and tell someone that Jesus loves them.

Spiritual concerns and prayer requests ....
....
....
....
....
....
....

Today I will... ....
....

DECEMBER 12

Are you willing to spend and be spent for the Lord today, or are there just too many other things on your agenda? Are you willing no matter what it costs to be used by the Lord, or are you more interested in your next vacation?

So many are chicken when it comes to witnessing for Jesus Christ. We cluck and duck when the subject of God or religion is raised. Many hope no one is looking when they ask God to bless their food in a public place.

We need more of the spirit of the saints who are suffering for the sake of the Gospel this very minute in prisons, in torture, in abuse—all because they profess a love for Jesus Christ. Jesus said, "Whosoever therefore shall be ashamed of Me and of My words in this adulterous and sinful generation; of him also shall the Son of Man be ashamed, when He cometh in the glory of His Father..."

Is God calling you to leave your comfort zone and tell someone that Jesus loves them and wants to save them? Will you do it, or will you be too fearful? May you bring the light of Christ to your dorm, your neighborhood, your apartment building, your baseball team—wherever God has placed you, let Him use you for His glory!

Spiritual concerns and prayer requests...

....

....

....

Today I will...

....

"BEWARE LEST ANY MAN SPOIL YOU THROUGH PHILOSOPHY AND
VAIN DECEIT, AFTER THE TRADITION OF MEN, AFTER THE
RUDIMENTS OF THE WORLD, AND NOT AFTER CHRIST." Colossians 2:8

Jesus never approved of putting the traditions of men above the
Word of God (see Mark 7:1-13). What about you? Are you
willing to change your life in order that God may use you or
had you rather hold on to your traditions?

There are three qualities, which I believe every Christian should
exhibit: *availability, expendability,* and *adaptability.* We need to be
walking with the Lord so closely that we ought to be ready to witness
at a moment's notice.

It is God's ability and your availability. It is His power and your
personality. It is His work and your witness. That's God's plan!

❦❦❦

Pretend someone is walking towards you right now with the sole
purpose of asking you how they can have a personal relationship
with God. What would you say? Get ready today to give an answer
for the hope that is within you (see 1 Peter 3:15).

Spiritual concerns and prayer requests...

....

....

....

....

....

....

Today I will... ....

....

DECEMBER 14

"BY FAITH ABRAHAM, WHEN HE WAS CALLED TO GO OUT INTO A
PLACE WHICH HE SHOULD AFTER RECEIVE FOR AN INHERITANCE,
OBEYED; AND HE WENT OUT, NOT KNOWING WHITHER HE WENT."
Hebrews 11:8

Who knows what marvelous opportunity God has waiting
for you if you were sensitive enough to listen to what the
Holy Spirit is saying to you right now.

Don't say, "Show me what You want me to do, then I'll decide
whether or not to do it." Instead, we need to say, "I'll do it—whatever
it is. You tell me. If You explain it, fine. If You don't explain it,
fine. But God, I'm going to do it."

It's just as bad to run ahead of God, as it is to run behind Him.
The Bible says Abraham went out without knowing where God was
sending him. Are you ready to travel under sealed orders?

◆◆◆

This week, think about your availability to God—are you willing to
sell your home, and go to another part of the world to share
God's plan of salvation if He called you there? Or are you willing to
go across the street? Ask God to give you a willing heart. He is the
potter; you are the clay.

Spiritual concerns and prayer requests ....
....
....
....
....
....
....

Today I will... ....
....

DECEMBER 15

"BUT WHEN THE COMFORTER IS COME, WHOM I WILL SEND UNTO YOU FROM THE FATHER, EVEN THE SPIRIT OF TRUTH, WHICH PROCEEDETH FROM THE FATHER, HE SHALL TESTIFY OF ME."
John 15:26

The Holy Spirit has one cause: to testify of Jesus Christ. He is very single-minded. He's not interested in doing ten things for God—just one.

There are some who get caught up in the Holy Spirit. They focus on what He is doing—through miracles, healings, tongues, and more. Friend, beware of those who focus on making the Holy Spirit the figurehead of their faith.

The mark that a man is filled with the Holy Spirit is that he is always talking about Jesus Christ. He can't do any more. He can do no less.

❖

Make this pledge to God today: *I surrender all that I am and have (i.e., talents, business, education, time, resources, home) for the cause of Christ. This one thing I do—sink or swim, live or die—Jesus will be glorified in my life today and every day!*

Spiritual concerns and prayer requests ....

....

....

....

....

....

....

Today I will... ....

....

DECEMBER 16

"UPHOLD ME ACCORDING UNTO THY WORD, THAT I MAY LIVE:
AND LET ME NOT BE ASHAMED OF MY HOPE." Psalm 119:116

Paul did much of his writing from a prison cell. Maybe you also feel like you are in a prison of sorts today with every door shut in your face.

Maybe you are in a prison of despair and doubt. Perhaps you just got back from the doctor and received a bad report, or you are dreading a visit this week. Maybe you're in a financial prison of debt or a domestic prison of abuse and you feel there is no way out.

Friend, I want to tell you there is a way out for you. God is still on His throne. He hears and answers every prayer. Victory over your situation is just a prayer away. The circumstances may not change, but your perspective and attitude will change as you begin to pray and praise God. You and I don't have a need God cannot meet.

Pray this prayer today: "Father, I need You. I need You to forgive me where I have failed You. I need You to change my heart and strengthen my faith so I see my prison as a palace. Change my attitude from dread to joy, from jealousy to contentment, from worry to trust. I love You. In Jesus' name. Amen."

Spiritual concerns and prayer requests...

....

....

....

....

....

....

....

Today I will...

....

"AND THE VERY GOD OF PEACE SANCTIFY YOU WHOLLY; AND I PRAY GOD YOUR WHOLE SPIRIT AND SOUL AND BODY BE PRESERVED BLAMELESS UNTO THE COMING OF OUR LORD JESUS CHRIST." 1 Thessalonians 5:23

Some people get confused about when salvation happens. Let me see if I can shed some light on this subject.

Salvation can be explained by using three verbal tenses in the English language. The moment you repent and believe upon Jesus Christ as your Lord and Savior, *you are saved*. After that, you enter a process of sanctification where *you are being saved* from the power of sin. When you get to heaven, *you will be saved* from the presence of sin.

What happens when you enter into a saving relationship with Jesus Christ? You are justified immediately in your spirit. You are sanctified progressively in your soul. And you will be glorified ultimately in your body.

Praise God, using Psalm 32:7, 41:2, 121:7-8, that the preservation of your salvation is His job and not yours.

Spiritual concerns and prayer requests...
....
....
....
....
....
....

Today I will...
....

DECEMBER 18

Postmodernism tells us there is no absolute truth. What you believe is okay. What I believe is okay, too. Whether they agree or not doesn't matter.

But, in this age of postmodern thought we must contend with this basic truth: truth stands alone. It doesn't require human interpretation. And let me add that in discussing Christian truth, there is a divine disturbance which occurs.

I don't believe we can be neutral about real truth. If Jesus is God, then we must bow down and worship. If Jesus is not God, we ought to boot Him out the door as a liar and a lunatic. You must decide. There is no neutral ground. Either you are *with* Him, or you are *against* Him.

❦

Do you find yourself taking a neutral stand in this difficult day? Pray for the hundreds of believers who are in jail around the world because they did not stand on neutral ground—they boldly proclaimed Christ knowing that doing so would cause them to be imprisoned or even killed.

Spiritual concerns and prayer requests...

....

....

....

....

....

Today I will...

....

DECEMBER 19

"Thou shalt keep therefore His statutes, and His commandments, which I command thee this day, that it may go well with thee, and with thy children after thee, and that thou mayest prolong thy days upon the earth, which the Lord thy God giveth thee, for ever."
Deuteronomy 4:40

What has happened that we cannot let children be children? May God have mercy on us who stand by while boys and girls date at the age of ten, go steady by the time they're thirteen, get married by the age of seventeen, and get divorced before they're old enough to vote.

Get back into the Word of God and stand up to the pressures of today. May God give us wisdom to help young people who are standing in tall dry grass with boxes of matches!

❦

Are you a parent or grandparent? Corral your teens into your home with love. Always keep your door open for them. Form a prayer group of parents and teens. Do whatever it takes to rescue your children before it's too late.

Spiritual concerns and prayer requests ....

....

....

....

....

....

....

Today I will... ....

....

DECEMBER 20

C hristian young people often ask if there are some specific things they can do to practice moral purity.

I tell them to first watch the crowd they hang out with— to choose their friends wisely (see Proverbs 13:20). Second, to guard what they put into their minds from books, movies, and music (see Psalm 101:3a, Proverbs 6:27). Lastly, I tell young people to control their thought life (see Proverbs 23:7a, Philippians 4:8).

The thought is the father of the deed. Someone has well said, "We cannot keep the bird from flying over our heads, but we can keep them from making a nest in our hair."

<><><>

A re you doing all you can to help your children in the three areas above? At this Christmas season, what a wonderful time to help their thought life by reflecting with them on the things of Christ instead of the world.

Spiritual concerns and prayer requests..
....
....
....
....
....
....

Today I will..

....

DECEMBER 21

"BELOVED, THINK IT NOT STRANGE CONCERNING THE FIERY TRIAL
WHICH IS TO TRY YOU, AS THOUGH SOME STRANGE THING
HAPPENED UNTO YOU: BUT REJOICE, INASMUCH AS YE ARE
PARTAKERS OF CHRIST'S SUFFERINGS; THAT, WHEN HIS GLORY
SHALL BE REVEALED, YE MAY BE GLAD ALSO WITH EXCEEDING JOY."
1 Peter 4:12-13

Andrew Murray said, "Every child of God must at one time
or another enter the school of trial." And the Scriptures
teach us we are to count it a joy when God takes us into this
school.

Just as there is no profit in the grounds being made wet by rain or
broken up by the plow, when no seed is cast into it, so are children of
God who enter into trial and have little blessing from it.

The heart may be softened for a time, but they don't know how to
obtain an abiding blessing from it. They don't regard what the Father
has in view since they are enrolled in the school of trial.

Are you in the middle of a trial? Trust that the Lord will bring
blessing as you trust in Him with all your heart.

Spiritual concerns and prayer requests..
....
....
....
....
....
....

Today I will... ....
....

DECEMBER 22

"FOR THOU, LORD, HAST MADE ME GLAD THROUGH THY WORK: I WILL TRIUMPH IN THE WORKS OF THY HANDS." Psalm 92:4

God has given the victory to every Christian—not just in the hereafter, but in the here and now. You say, "But I know some Christians who aren't living a victorious life, and I'm one of them."

Then, I hate to break it to you, but you are living beneath your privilege. God's Word admits the *possibility* of failure in our lives, but it never assumes the *necessity* of failure.

As a matter of fact, 2 Corinthians 2:14a says, "Now thanks be unto God, which always causeth us to triumph in Christ." Do you know what you need to do? You need to possess the possessions God has already given to you in Christ.

❖

Read Ephesians 1:3. What has God blessed you with? When did He bless you? Where has He blessed you? How do you reconcile that truth with the way you live?

Spiritual concerns and prayer requests..
....
....
....
....
....
....
....

Today I will…...
....

DECEMBER 23

"IN THIS WAS MANIFESTED THE LOVE OF GOD TOWARD US, BECAUSE THAT GOD SENT HIS ONLY BEGOTTEN SON INTO THE WORLD, THAT WE MIGHT LIVE THROUGH HIM." 1 John 4:9

Arnold Prater, in his book *You Can Have Joy*! wrote about an Englishman named John Deckard who had an award-winning passion for roses.

One year, John grew a rose among roses to enter in the annual Garden Show. But before he could transplant the rose, his son rushed in and exclaimed, "Daddy, look what I have for you!" And in his little hand was the prize rose.

Visitors to the Garden Show were astonished when they saw John's entry. For in the flowerpot was a photo of his son with the rose in his hands, along with an honorary blue ribbon. Sometimes your plans may go awry and sometimes your dreams may get crushed. But in their place, God sends His own Son—Jesus. And when that happens, nothing else matters but the love of His Son.

❧❧❧

What disappointment have you experienced this week? Did you choose joy or sadness? What can you learn from today's devotional thought to apply to your life the next time a disappointment happens in your life?

Spiritual concerns and prayer requests...

....

....

....

....

....

....

Today I will..

....

DECEMBER 24

"AND SAMUEL SAID, HATH THE LORD AS GREAT DELIGHT IN
BURNT OFFERINGS AND SACRIFICES, AS IN OBEYING THE VOICE OF
THE LORD? BEHOLD, TO OBEY IS BETTER THAN SACRIFICE, AND TO
HEARKEN THAN THE FAT OF RAMS." 1 Samuel 15:22

Joy and obedience are intrinsically linked together. When you
learn to obey the Lord, you will have the joy of the Lord.
It's like the hymn written by John Sammis: "Trust and
obey, for there's no other way, To be happy in Jesus, but to trust and
obey." Trust and obedience are the two hands that lay hold of the
promises of God. They are the two feet that keep you walking on the
King's highway. They are the two ears that enable you to hear the
Truth of God's Word.

Do you want to know the sweet joy and contentment that Paul
had in the depths of a Roman prison, that Corrie Ten Boom had in
the dark confines of a Nazi prison camp? Then, trust and obey.

On the eve before Christmas, think about what Mary and
Joseph did in obedience to God's call. Thank the Lord for
their trust and obedience to His divine plan.

Spiritual concerns and prayer requests ....
....
....
....
....
....
....
Today I will... ....
....

DECEMBER 25

"FOR CHRIST IS THE END OF THE LAW FOR RIGHTEOUSNESS TO EVERY ONE THAT BELIEVETH." Romans 10:4

The world thinks sin is being bad and righteousness is being good. They say, "If I am just a good person, then I will go to heaven."

God seems like a Santa Claus, making a list and checking it twice, trying to find out if we are naughty or nice. That is just not so. Righteousness lies only in Jesus Christ.

He left heaven, came to earth, lived a perfect, righteous life. Then, He suffered, bled, and died on a cross to atone for our sins. He was buried and raised to life by the power of God and has ascended into glory. His blood was applied to the mercy seat of God— *that is righteousness.*

Galatians 2:21 tells us, "If righteousness come by the law, then Christ is dead in vain." Do you know what that means? If you could be saved by being good, then Calvary was a blunder. If there was some other way for you to be saved, God would not have let His Son die upon a cross.

On this Christmas Day, how do you see God—is He your Santa Claus making sure you're naughty or nice? Is He a butler— tending to your every whim and fancy? Or is He the High and Exalted King of kings, the Almighty One, the Everlasting Father?

Spiritual concerns and prayer requests

Today I will...

DECEMBER 26

"WHEREFORE, MY BELOVED, AS YE HAVE ALWAYS OBEYED, NOT AS
IN MY PRESENCE ONLY, BUT NOW MUCH MORE IN MY ABSENCE,
WORK OUT YOUR OWN SALVATION WITH FEAR AND TREMBLING."
Philippians 2:12

Has someone ever said this to you? "While I'm gone, I want you to be on your best behavior." That is what Paul means when he gives us the directive to work out our salvation even when he is not around.

A pastor is successful when he trains his flock to love the Lord, share their faith, and minister to others when no one else is looking. It is the true test of a person's walk with God.

What happens when you are alone on a business trip and there are free movies in your motel room? How fast do you drive when you are late for a meeting and the speed limit says 35? How much money do you leave for a tip when there is no one to impress?

❦

When was the last time you did something nice for someone who could never pay you back, with whom you had nothing to gain, and who may actually use what you did against you? Maybe the day after Christmas is a great time to start (see Matthew 6:3-4).

Spiritual concerns and prayer requests ....
....
....
....
....
....
....

Today I will... ....
....

DECEMBER 27

"IF ANY MAN'S WORK ABIDE WHICH HE HATH BUILT THEREUPON,
HE SHALL RECEIVE A REWARD. IF ANY MAN'S WORK SHALL BE
BURNED, HE SHALL SUFFER LOSS: BUT HE HIMSELF SHALL BE
SAVED; YET SO AS BY FIRE." 1 Corinthians 3:14-15

I believe salvation is attained by grace through faith. That's not
Baptist rhetoric. That's Biblical doctrine (see Ephesians 2:8).
But, do you know what some people do with that? They
say, "Hot dog! I don't have to do a thing to be saved. I can just get
on the bus and coast along until we pull into the new Jerusalem." You
know, just ride along to glory.

These people don't like the idea that as Christians, we are all
going to stand before the Judgment Seat of Christ. And we are all
going to give an account for how we used our time, our resources, and
our faith. We are not saved by works, but we are rewarded by works.

R ead Romans 14:10-12. Knowing this truth how do you plan to
spend your day?

Spiritual concerns and prayer requests

Today I will...

DECEMBER 28

"I PRESS TOWARD THE MARK FOR THE PRIZE OF THE HIGH CALLING OF GOD IN CHRIST JESUS." Philippians 3:14

As we run to the finish line of this year, it makes sense that we look at how runners train themselves. They are trained to be focused on one thing—the finish line. They have one desire and they are not going to let who is lagging behind or what is going on in the stands distract them.

Paul had the same sense. He, too, believed you could not win a race by looking over your shoulder or glancing to the right or the left. You can't see what is ahead when you've got your headlight on the rear bumper.

Paul forgot his past glory, past mistakes, past grief, past everything. Paul refused to let his past keep him from reaching his goal. What are you doing in your race to claim the prize of a closer walk with God?

There are just a few more days left in the year. Take a few minutes over the next couple of days to analyze how you ran the race this year. What changes do you want to make in the coming year to better run the race?

Spiritual concerns and prayer requests...

....

....

....

....

....

....

Today I will..

....

DECEMBER 29

"My brethren, count it all joy when ye fall into divers temptations; Knowing this, that the trying of your faith worketh patience." James 1:2-3

James 1:2 is an interesting verse because it has the phrase "when" instead of "if." You see, some people think life is going to be all rose petals and sunlight. If I told you that, then I would be speaking from a closed Bible and an empty head.

If you are saved or if you are lost, life guarantees one thing—difficulty. There will be trials, oppression, and misunderstandings. And when you become a Christian, you do not become immune to these things.

Trials are a part of life, but how Christians behave in response is what causes an unbelieving world to sit up and take notice. You can tell the size of a Christian by what it takes to stop him.

Open yourself up to accountability. Ask a trusted friend or your spouse to answer these questions. How would you rate how I have responded to trials this past year on a scale of 1-10? 1 means that I'm thankful for the opportunity to learn patience and 10 means I've been resentful for every speed bump of life I've passed over. Did you learn anything new or discover anything you need to work on next year?

Spiritual concerns and prayer requests...
....
....
....
....
....

Today I will..
....

DECEMBER 30

"HE THAT LOVETH NOT KNOWETH NOT GOD; FOR GOD IS LOVE."
1 John 4:8

Wisdom is not gained by seeing the *works of God*. It is gained in knowing the *ways of God*. When the Israelites were wandering in the desert, they could only see the works of God. But, God allowed Moses to see His ways.

The Israelites were infatuated with God at first. But when troubles came, their love affair with God quickly died out. They began to murmur and complain.

However, Moses saw the wilderness from God's perspective and approached God in humility and honor. As a result, God taught him to lead His people out of darkness into light. Have you learned to see life from His point of view? Or are you still trusting in your view of life to get you through the hard times?

❦

Do you know the ways of God or just the works of God? Bow before God and ask Him to ignite a vision for His glory, a bold desire to lead the lost to Him, and an unconditional passion to love Him.

Spiritual concerns and prayer requests..
....
....
....
....
....
....

Today I will...
....

DECEMBER 31

"For the Son of man is come to seek and to save that which was lost." Luke 19:10

O n this last day of the year, has this been a year of prayer for you? Do you know what the average prayer request is about? Physical healing. *Pray for my aunt who is a Christian and she is about to die. Pray for my saved uncle who is having heart surgery.*

How many times have you heard people ask for prayer for their lost neighbor who is going to hell? We are more often interested in keeping the saints out of heaven, than we are in keeping the lost out of hell.

It is not a tragedy to die and go to heaven. It is a tragedy to die and go to hell. Friend, it's time we elevated our prayers outside of the physical realm of life into the spiritual realm.

❧❦❧

T ake a fresh look at your prayer list—where are the lost who need to be saved? What are you going to do next year to help them find their way?

Spiritual concerns and prayer requests

Today I will...

A CLOSING PLEA

My friend, have you given your life to the Lord? Do you have the assurance that if you were to die right now, you would go straight to heaven? If not, please let me tell you how you can be saved.

ADMIT YOUR SIN

First, you must understand you are a sinner. The Bible says, "For all have sinned, and come short of the glory of God" (Romans 3:23).

ABANDON SELF-EFFORT

Second, you must understand you cannot save yourself by your efforts. The Bible is very clear that it's "not by works of righteousness which we have done, but according to His mercy He saved us, by the washing of regeneration, and renewing of the Holy Ghost" (Titus 3:5).

Again, "For by grace are ye saved through faith; and that not of yourselves: it is the gift of God: Not of works, lest any man should boast" (Ephesians 2:8-9).

ACKNOWLEDGE CHRIST'S PAYMENT

Third, you must believe Jesus Christ, the Son of God, died for your sins. The Bible says, "But God commendeth His love toward us, in that, while we were yet sinners, Christ died for us" (Romans 5:8).

That means He died in your place. Your sin debt has been paid by the blood of Jesus Christ, which "cleanseth us from all sin" (1 John 1:7b).

ACCEPT HIM AS SAVIOR

Fourth, you must put your faith in Jesus Christ and Him alone for your salvation. The blood of Christ does you no good until you receive Him by faith. The Bible says, "… Believe on the Lord Jesus Christ, and thou shalt be saved …" (Acts 16:31).

Have you taken this all-important step of faith? If not, I urge you to do it right now. Why? Because Jesus is the only way to heaven!

And speaking of Jesus, the Apostle Peter said in Acts 4:12, "Neither is there salvation in any other: for there is none other name under heaven given among men, whereby we must be saved."

Jesus Himself said, "I am the Way, the Truth, and the Life: no man cometh unto the Father, but by Me" (John 14:6). It couldn't be any clearer than that.

Are you willing to offer the following prayer to God today?

O God, I'm a sinner. I'm lost, and I need to be saved. I know I can't save myself, so right now, once and for all, I trust You to save me. Come into my heart, forgive my sin, and make me Your child. I give You my life. I will live for You as You give me strength.

If you will make this your heartfelt prayer, God will hear and save you! Jesus has promised that He will not turn away anyone who comes to Him in faith (see John 6:37). He will make you a child of God if you will turn to Him (see John 1:12).

NOTES

NOTES

NOTES

NOTES

NOTES

NOTES

DR. ADRIAN ROGERS

Dr. Adrian Rogers, one of America's most respected Bible teachers, faithfully preached the Word of God for 53 years—32 of those years as senior pastor of the historic Bellevue Baptist Church near Memphis, Tennessee.

He wrote 18 books and over 50 booklets giving strength and encouragement on subjects such as marriage, prophecy, evangelism, and the Christian walk.

In 1987 he founded Love Worth Finding Ministries to communicate the glorious Gospel of Jesus Christ with millions around the world. The message of God's love continues today, and as he so aptly put it, "Truly, the sun never sets on the ministry of Love Worth Finding."

BOOKS BY ADRIAN ROGERS

ADDITIONAL RESOURCE